Blue

A HISTORY OF POSTPARTUM
DEPRESSION IN AMERICA

Rachel Louise Moran

The University of Chicago Press   Chicago and London

The University of Chicago Press, Chicago 60637
The University of Chicago Press, Ltd., London

For more information, contact the University of Chicago Press,
1427 E. 60th St., Chicago, IL 60637.
Published 2024
Printed in the United States of America

33 32 31 30 29 28 27 26 25 24   1 2 3 4 5

ISBN-13: 978-0-226-83579-2 (cloth)
ISBN-13: 978-0-226-83580-8 (e-book)
DOI: https://doi.org/10.7208/chicago/9780226835808.001.0001

Library of Congress Cataloging-in-Publication Data

Names: Moran, Rachel Louise, author.
Title: Blue : a history of postpartum depression in America /
    Rachel Louise Moran.
Other titles: History of postpartum depression in America
Description: Chicago : London ; The University of Chicago Press,
    2024. | Includes bibliographical references and index.
Identifiers: LCCN 2024005166 | ISBN 9780226835792 (cloth) |
    ISBN 9780226835808 (ebook)
Subjects: LCSH: Postpartum depression—United States—History. |
    Postpartum depression—Diagnosis—United States—History. |
    Motherhood—United States—Psychological aspects—History. |
    Mothers—Mental health—United States. | Psychiatry—United
    States—History—20th century. | Social medicine—United
    States.
Classification: LCC RG852 .M67 2024 | DDC 618.7/6—dc23/
    eng/20240227
LC record available at https://lccn.loc.gov/2024005166

♾ This paper meets the requirements of ANSI/NISO Z39.48-1992
(Permanence of Paper).

Contents

Introduction

I sat in the squeaky faux-leather chair, shifting my weight from side to side. I had seen psychiatrists off and on since I was a teenager with an eating disorder, and they did not usually make me so nervous. I appeared before this thin white-haired man, every stereotype of a psychiatrist, just a few times a year. I was not particularly unwell, in maintenance mode with some vanilla anxiety and moodiness. I would speak for about ten minutes; he would refill my prescription.

This day was different, though, and I could not sit still. Both excited and anxious, I told him I was pregnant. This meant that I wanted off the meds. My Google searches on psychopharmaceuticals during pregnancy were all over the place; I had no idea what was safe. Besides, I was going to be the perfect pregnant person. That meant no risks to the fetus, no matter how small. I would be abstaining from wine, coffee, *and* Wellbutrin while pregnant and breastfeeding.

He responded with a complete non sequitur: What kind of maternity leave do you have?

Was he even listening to me? As a historian, I flashed to generations of male psychiatrists past. To men who dismissed women's complaints as overly sensitive, maybe even hysterical.

But it was not a non sequitur after all. I told him I did not have any maternity leave. He furrowed his brow. It was best I stay on the medication, he said. The risks to the pregnancy were low, he told me, and the postpartum ahead was probably going to be very hard. I'd want to be on those drugs then.

I was surprised and frustrated. He wanted me to stay on the antidepressants not because of faulty brain wiring or the chemical imbalances all those pharmaceutical ads had told me about. Instead, he focused on this social—and political—risk factor. Would I have stopped medication with a different job, or if I lived in a country with a robust social safety net that included parental benefits? Possibly. But that's not where I was.

Neither of us believed maternity leave and subsidized daycare would magically eliminate the emotional difficulties of the postpartum period. Even in countries with much better social policy than the US, women still commonly show symptoms of postpartum depression. And yet these questions of social politics and policy are hard to underestimate. He was right; it was a hard postpartum. I did want those drugs.

I didn't decide to write this book solely because of that experience. But working on this project forced me to unpack the experience. That one psychiatrist visit brims with the tensions of the larger story. He did not use the language of postpartum depression, a language I would later learn was diagnostically quite messy. But the culture of that unspoken phrase was in the air between us, both empowering and devastating. The popular message of postpartum depression is one of exoneration for women: you are not to blame, this is hormones and synapses gone awry. It also contains a tiny voice whispering "bad mother," who knows what evil you might do? What exactly did the diagnosis mean, and how had it acquired such a complicated set of cultural and medical meanings?

I had no idea then, but my experience was the product of decades of work by activists and advocates who worked to bring the phrase "postpartum depression" into common use. The idea of a psychiatrist, especially an older man, taking the emotional risks of pregnancy and the postpartum seriously was practically unthinkable before the 1980s. The idea that he would opt for maintaining medication use in pregnancy would have been rare through the 1990s, and is something advocates still get pushback on today.

Also embedded in my experience was a much less medical story of postpartum politics. My attempt to center the pregnancy, to eliminate even the smallest risk at any cost to myself, came from cultural expectations about selfless motherhood. Here I was, a proud feminist with a PhD in women's studies, and the idea that I was of secondary importance to my fetus came without hesitation. And, as my psychiatrist helped me see, the structural problems of the American postpartum loomed large, even for a comfortable white professional woman like me: medical bills, finding childcare, parental leave policies, and distance from families and support networks.

The inseparability of the structural and the biological, the medical and the political, the exaltations and challenges of motherhood, all drew me to write this history. But the more I researched, the more I realized that this was not just a history of suffering and treatment, but one of advocacy. It is a story of groundbreaking women's health activism between the 1970s and today, and also a story of upholding the idealization of motherhood, a story of pushing against the status quo and also of pragmatically embracing the legitimizing power of medicalization and political neutrality.[1]

What Is Postpartum Depression?

Postpartum depression is a difficult illness to define. This is in part because there is not a standalone diagnosis for it in the American Psychiatric Association's *Diagnostic and Statistical Manual*. Different postpartum illnesses like depression, anxiety, and psychosis are scattered throughout the manual, rather than grouped together. Typically, postpartum depression is defined as a variety of major depressive disorder, differentiated only if a psychiatrist chooses to code it as having onset in pregnancy or the postpartum. So, without that most official of diagnostic languages, how best to understand what postpartum depression is? It has been used informally as an umbrella term for any kind of serious postpartum distress. Sometimes this has meant mild baby blues, sometimes depression, and sometimes it is used to include postpartum psychosis as well.

The phenomenon of "baby blues" was first named amid the enormous surge in births following World War II. Today, the baby blues are understood as emotional distress or fluctuations that begin a couple days postpartum and can last up to two weeks. Usually chalked up to rapidly changing hormones, this state of being is now considered very common, affecting perhaps 80 percent of new mothers. Women experiencing the baby blues in the 1950s and 1960s were often counseled to treat themselves with a new hat or some other pick-me-up.[2] Today, women are reminded about the role of hormones, and are often encouraged to prioritize rest and "self-care" as they adjust.

Between the 1970s and 1990s, psych professionals more frequently distinguished between those subclinical baby blues and a more serious, more medical postpartum depression. The 1980s was the "decade of depression" in the US, with a huge spike in general depression diagnoses and in antidepressant availability. Because of this, women with mood disturbances and emotional suffering that went beyond the baby blues were increasingly described as having postpartum depression. This could include a wide array of symptoms, from sleeplessness to panic, from hopelessness to substantial crying and irritability or rage. The baby blues remained in the popular vocabulary, but there was a new weight placed on distinguishing between cases that would benefit from medical intervention and those that did not need it. Today, experts avoid calling everything "postpartum depression," and use a more nuanced language. Advocates and clinicians are most likely to discuss PMADs (Perinatal Mood and Anxiety Disorders). PMADs include mental distress during pregnancy in addition to the postpartum and around lactation, as well as an array of disorders beyond just depression. PMADs include postpartum obsessive-compulsive disorder and postpartum anxiety, for example. But most people—and most of the people profiled in or interviewed for this book—still regularly use the language of postpartum depression that became common in the 1980s as a shorthand.

Alongside postpartum depression is postpartum psychosis, another PMAD. This is not a book about postpartum psychosis, or at least not *primarily*. I center depression and anxiety, out of an interest in how politics and social context directly influence a woman's mental and emotional wellness.[3] While psychosis might also be triggered by stressors, its causes are likely different than the more common depressions and anxieties of the postpartum. It is also much rarer. About 0.05 percent of births lead to a diagnosis of postpartum psychosis, while somewhere between 13 and 19 percent of births lead to a condition related to postpartum depression.[4]

That said, psychosis is part of this history. Many activists and advocates were driven to speak out on both depression *and* psychosis, often after their own psychosis. Women who experienced a psychosis seem more likely to have been marked by it, sticking with postpartum activism for years. And the rise of a popular understanding of postpartum depression is also inseparable from psychosis. The rare instances when postpartum psychosis has led to infanticide can draw astonishing media attention. Such cases have brought postpartum professionals and advocates into the media, making these tragedies into entering wedges for conversations about postpartum health more generally. But this also unintentionally led to a popular conflation of psychosis and depression.

Defining postpartum mental illness can be difficult because it is so inseparable from a difficult time of life. The limited official diagnostic language and the many changing names for postpartum distress and illness don't help with this. There is no agreement on how far after birth one is "postpartum," with definitions ranging from four weeks to eighteen months. Beyond that is the difficulty of determining how much distress is clinical and how much is subclinical. How depressed is okay, how depressed is too depressed? To explore the postpartum is to unpack the stresses of American parenthood (especially motherhood) between the 1950s and today.

As I found in my own difficult postpartum, being a new parent in the US is hard. It is hard in ways that I simply could not understand before I became one. Yes, you are tired and worn down and overextended. I was warned about that part. But it is almost impossible to convey the *extent* of sleep deprivation and exhaustion. Some of this is due to structural forces. But for a birthing parent, there are also massive hormonal changes and bodily changes. Physical pain for weeks at least. Watching the size of your blood clots. For a birthing parent especially, there is often guilt about the expectations of birth versus its reality, and for some people whose births are especially dangerous and different than planned, there can be birth trauma. Then there are the social stresses. Experiencing massive changes in your relationship with your partner, if you have one. For many there is limited familial and community support, leaving you both lonely and vulnerable.

For wage-earning mothers there is stress navigating working or not working, how much leave you have and how you will atone for taking that leave if you are lucky enough to have it. How to survive if you do not have leave, if your leave is unpaid, or if everyone is mad at you for taking it. There is the stress of feeding an infant, including balancing feeding needs with paid work. I had a nonstop tally of breastmilk ounces in my head while away from the baby—ten now, but maybe I can get three more if I pump in an hour? Your breasts ache and your nipples blister. Or perhaps you do not breastfeed or pump, and experience guilt and potentially shaming—as well as crazy expenses—for formula use.

Some of the difficulty of defining postpartum mood disorders comes from this long but quite incomplete list of challenges. For some the trials of new parenthood are moderate but manageable. For others they are severe and overwhelming. These stressors are some of the reasons that a newborn makes people incredibly vulnerable to mental health problems, whether new or exacerbated.[5]

The line between overwhelmed and mentally ill in the postpartum can be impossibly thin. Counting ounces of breastmilk can be a mild obsession or it can be a symptom of a postpartum obsessive-compulsive disorder. Worry occasionally that you'll drop the baby is almost universal, but for some parents it veers into intrusive thoughts, or all-consuming panic and anxiety. An exhausted, lethargic parent can simply need a long nap, but they also might be clinically depressed.

There is no easy distinction between problems with social (support systems), political (work leave and social services), and physiological (hormonal change and birth injury) origins. The causes are tangled, and the solutions just as complex. Offering a diagnosis could make one's suffering legible, but also risks confusing a person's emotional distress with problems arising from social and political issues.[6] In this way, diagnostic language risked making women's suffering seem individual and apolitical.[7] When diagnosis rates shot up in the 1980s, depression itself was characterized as a women's disease. This might have reflected a better recognition of women's pain, or it might have been an attempt to depoliticize it.[8] Some feminists asked whether it should even be called an illness, in light of its prevalence. Is that diagnosis simply an indictment of modern motherhood?

Most of the postpartum advocates in this book embrace the idea that postpartum depression is an illness, arguing that medical languages offer the best explanation of the problem, and that psychiatric recognition offers one of the most important solutions to women's suffering. Women's eager acceptance of a medicalized postpartum depression obliges us to take their self-conception seriously, while also asking how that became such a useful way of understanding their pain.[9]

Postpartum Politics

Advocates argue that postpartum depression is not just an illness, but the most common complication of pregnancy. Postpartum Support International, the largest organization of postpartum advocates in the US, began saying this in the early 1990s.[10] We understand the many other complications of pregnancy, after all. People drink a cloyingly sweet orange drink and sit around a waiting room for an hour to test for gestational diabetes. They undergo regular blood pressure checks out of a fear of preeclampsia. Ultrasounds help monitor the position of the placenta. All of this is important, but, postpartum mental health advocates argue, the possibility of mental and emotional complications needs to be taken just as seriously. Whether depression, anxiety, trauma, or psychosis, these should all fall under the rubric of "complications of pregnancy."

At the most basic level, advocates ask that people treat postpartum mental illnesses as important and "real," like other physical illnesses. When framed as the most common complication of pregnancy, these advocates seek to differentiate postpartum mental illnesses from other mental illnesses: they are serious yet situational and usually temporary, requiring surveillance, awareness, and treatment.

There is not consensus on exactly what the physiological roots of postpartum illness might be, though hormones (the postpartum drop in progesterone and estrogen) are typically at the top of the list. It might also be something about neurotransmitters, often echoing more general understandings of depression as primarily biochemical and perhaps having genetic predispositions. This emphasis on genes, and the idea that there could be some kind of postpartum depression genetic marker, has proven influential. Some research even explores links between postpartum mental illness and gut health and bacteria.

The fervor with which some advocates center mental illness in the physical body can be unnerving. The postpartum seems like a case study in why entirely biomedical explanations can never be complete. The stress of new parenthood, the loneliness, the exhaustion, the enormous life changes, these cannot be fully accounted for in a strictly chemical model. But, as someone whose own life has improved substantially with the help of psychopharmaceuticals, I also see dismissing the role of the body and physiology—whether the hormonal changes of birth or the impact that pharmacological treatments can have—as misguided.

Negotiations over how to talk about postpartum depression, over what to attribute all that pain to, over how to make sense of it, are substantial political and medical questions. And yet they rarely divide advocates. I expected the psychiatrists and psychiatric researchers I interviewed to only talk about brain chemistry, but often they talked about the importance of talk therapy and peer support.

I expected non-prescribing therapists and lay activists might complain about over-prescription, but they were mostly strong advocates of antidepressants.

Women's health is normally the stuff of endless controversy. Fights over abortion and contraception, women advocating for the right to voluntary sterilization and the end of the involuntary kind. Inter-activist tensions over breastfeeding and medicated childbirth. Clearly, something about postpartum depression is different. It has not been controversy-free, certainly, and advocates have debated whether to push for mandatory depression screenings and how much faith to put into emerging drug treatments. But advocates I interviewed were much more likely to cite the problem of popular indifference than problems of internal division or external opposition. When no one listened, no one cared, no one took it seriously, advocates took it upon themselves to do what it took to legitimize postpartum illness.

Postpartum depression advocacy has been a part of the long women's health movement, but it took a different path than much women's health activism.[11] I wanted to understand how the politics of postpartum depression are so different than those of other women's health movements, despite having many of the same 1960s and 1970s roots. What results is a story of activism in context, of advocates working amid a backdrop of American family values politics in the 1980s and 1990s, and amid their own distrust of what they imagined feminists thought of motherhood in those years.[12] It is also a story of medicalization, though hardly the nefarious story in some women's health history. It is a story of both a grassroots embrace of medical language and authority, and the simultaneous influx of women into psychology, psychiatry, and obstetrics in the 1980s. In this sense I often found I was writing not a story of postpartum depression so much as a story about women grappling with what motherhood meant in the late twentieth century, a story of supermoms and career women, a story of conservative family values and post-feminism, of adaptation and professionalization and a kind of moderate activism deeply reflective of its moment.

| 9

Women's Health Activism

I began the book thinking I needed to weigh in on this postpartum advocacy: challenging places it over-medicalized, places that it pathologized women or struggled with ambiguous definitions and symptom groupings. Places it let the biological overshadow the social. But while there are critiques to be made, obsessing over the medicalization of postpartum distress itself was superficial. Medicalization alone can be "too blunt a tool" to make sense of competing understandings of women's health activism.[13] Instead, I came to focus on why advocates simultaneously embraced and challenged medicalization, and how it reflected their navigation of American culture and politics.

Women, and some men, have fought to have postpartum depression taken more seriously since the 1960s. They have sought a variety of outcomes at different times. Sometimes the issue has been getting medical professionals to pay attention, and in other instances it has been pushing those professionals away from mother blame and psychopathology and toward a new way of thinking about postpartum depression: as common, treatable, and distinct from other mental illness. Sometimes advocates have wanted more attention to the structural inequalities that fuel postpartum depression, from medical racism to a lack of parental leave in the US. Other times they have pushed for more attention to the biological, often hormonal, roots of postpartum illnesses. Like with most health activism there is rarely a single goal, even within organizations.

It is notable that the 1960s–1970s women's health movement was a modest time for postpartum mental health activism, while postpartum advocacy thrived in the conservative 1980s. It might seem surprising or unusual, a sort of triumph for women's reproductive concerns against a backdrop of anti-abortion organizing and retrenchment. Or it might seem just the opposite, the predictable rise of a gender-specific diagnosis to pathologize and medicalize motherhood, a Reagan-era dismissal of women's distress as "hormonal."[14]

Neither explanation is satisfying or complete. The naming, and then mainstreaming, of postpartum depression in these decades is fascinating precisely because its political meaning is so hard to pin down. It belongs in the history of the women's health movement, but it does not fit into it easily. Very few of the grassroots activists who founded support organizations in the 1980s described themselves as feminists, even when they had feminist backgrounds and had been inspired by *Our Bodies, Ourselves.*

Instead, they adopted biology-heavy, politically neutral explanations of women's mental illness. Working in close partnerships with psychiatrists, they sought to legitimize and normalize postpartum depression in medicine and in popular thinking. To do this, they emphasized postpartum depression as an objective disease, not up for political debate. Its success depended on being understood as categorically different from controversial women's health issues of the same years, like abortion, birth control, and PMS.[15]

This approach was successful, but it also had limitations. When advocates emphasized their medical legitimacy and neutrality, they replicated existing power imbalances. They used media to create a palatable image of the depressed mother that was grounded in whiteness, even as Black and Latina women were statistically at greater risk of postpartum mental illness. The construction of postpartum illness in an individual, medical, and mostly politically neutral framework also limited the paths activism could take.[16] It elevated awareness raising and non-mandatory depression screenings over challenging cultural and structural problems facing mothers.

Family Values Politics

The construction of postpartum mental illness as medical, not political, emerged against a backdrop of family values America at the century's end. The number of white middle-class mothers working outside the home rose through the 1970s and 1980s. This reality led to cultural anxiety and political panic. Languages of "family values" and "culture wars" fanned the flames.[17] While motherhood has always been political, the politics of motherhood were especially volatile in these decades as women's roles became a proxy for a host of cultural grievances. Popular media and advertising co-opted elements of feminism, and encouraged women to "have it all" and become "supermoms." Conservative leaders like Phyllis Schlafly argued that mothers working outside the home were an attack on the traditional family.

At the same time, this political obsession with motherhood allowed more space for a critique of American parenting norms, including the idea that motherhood should be easy. This included the creation of parent support groups that paved the way for postpartum depression support groups. While these groups often included echoes of second-wave feminist arguments for structural change around daycare and flexible work hours, the ascending ideology of personal responsibility was inescapable.

Postpartum advocates adopted their own languages of family values, emphasizing how motherhood might feel different than the ideals women grew up with. This critique had substantial limitations. Yet bolder systemic critiques of motherhood only encouraged accusations over the breakdown of the family. Working women were put on the defensive, regularly forced to prove the soundness of their families. Postpartum advocates often wavered between the idea that women could "have it all" once they were recovered, and the idea that unreasonable expectations of motherhood were part of how women got so ill. Although they did discuss this unreasonableness of expectations, advocates nevertheless tended to center the nuclear family and the need to protect babies as justifications for paying attention to postpartum women. When they talked about mothers' wellness, it was often framed with the importance of happiness in motherhood as the goal. This vision of happiness mostly meant modest rather than revolutionary changes to motherhood.[18]

This context helps explain how framing postpartum depression as an individual and medical problem was such a pragmatic choice. Motherhood was a divisive topic, but a medical framework allowed advocates to claim neutrality and authority. Sick women needed recognition, treatment, and understanding. And, while most people seemed indifferent to the idea of postpartum illness, the argument that sickness allowed to fester might lead to bad mothering, poor bonding, and divorce highlighted the need for intervention. With help, these women could be "good mothers," usually without serious changes to the structure of American motherhood. Although some critique of the expectations of motherhood was always part of postpartum advocacy, it co-existed with the belief that treating women could strengthen American motherhood.

Navigating the Neoliberal Postpartum

At the same time as the family values discourse, American motherhood was being transformed by what we now call neoliberalism. Neoliberalism is a market-first ideology that doesn't believe in social collectives, let alone their power. It favors the individual over the group.[19] Conservatives gutted social welfare supports in the 1980s, and neoliberals took these cuts a step further in the 1990s, declaring that the state should play a greatly reduced role in individual lives. This put tremendous new stress on families as the foundational social and economic unit.[20] Shoring up the individual family became more important than ever, for while the state cut its own spending, it encouraged a standard family model and private attempts to strengthen it.[21] And it was women, of course, who were very often responsible for managing these families—and themselves—with little help.

This shift affected all kinds of disease activism in these years, especially women's disease activism.[22] Breast cancer activism embraced corporate partnerships and commercialization, while using the language of individual empowerment.[23] Individual psychotherapy exploded in the 1990s.[24] Postpartum depression activism sometimes took a similar path, and sometimes did not. It remained much less commercial than pink ribbon breast cancer advocacy, yet more professionals did become involved.[25] While pharmaceutical money came to matter more to postpartum depression research and advocacy with each decade, until recently this funding was minimal. Within the neoliberal context, activism of the 1980s onward often centered on awareness raising and the importance of both medical surveillance

| 13

and women's self-surveillance. This sometimes led to an increased focus on individual illness and healing. Overall, the professionalization of the movement risked making it more conservative, but also made it more sustainable and politically powerful.

The imprints of both conservative and neoliberal backdrops shaped postpartum advocates and their work in significant ways. That doesn't mean that they were consciously neoliberal—it was the water they swam in. Advocates who navigated this political reality had successes—even when their visions of success were themselves products of their moment.

When I asked the people I interviewed for this book how they identified their own role in this history, most struggled. Were they activists? Advocates? Simply professionals? The lines were hard to draw. "Activist" seemed too radical for most, it sounded militant and aggressive. Some psych professionals who spent decades lobbying for change considered that work an extension of their professional calling.

In the chapters that follow, I examine the history of postpartum mental illness and these advocates, activists, and professionals insisting it be taken seriously. The quest to legitimize the experience of severe postpartum distress, to identify it as an illness that merited attention and treatment, shaped decades of action. To understand this quest for legitimacy, as well as this fear of being seen as too political or divisive, we must first understand the landscape at mid-century and the dismissal of women's "baby blues."

1. Baby Blues and the Baby Boom

Joanne stood in front of the baby bath, shaking. Her hands trembled as she tried to bathe her newborn daughter. It was her first day home from the hospital, after a five-day stay that was standard in the early 1960s. She was twenty years old. Joanne had dreamed about having a baby since she was a girl. But those were dreams; she had almost no experience with actual infants. This was increasingly the norm amid 1950s and 1960s suburbanization. People spread out and lived in single-generation homes. There was less extended family and more isolation, meaning fewer baby cousins and neighbors' children you might look after. Now Joanne had the baby she desired, and the baby overwhelmed her. She had trouble breastfeeding; her family told her she was too tense. Joanne's mother-in-law took over the bath while, as a writer for a health magazine later put it, "the weeping girl was comforted by her husband and led to the couch." There, "she collapsed in a cloud of blue wrapper and negligée."

Postpartum distress wasn't invented in the 1960s, but there would not have been a specific name for Joanne's experience just twenty-five years prior. By 1967, the tail end of the postwar era, there was. The health magazine called it "the 'after-baby blues.'" They could be normal—to a point. But what did Joanne have to be blue about?

In her depressed state, Joanne questioned all the trappings of white suburban motherhood: house, family, baby, everything. Really, what *didn't* she have to feel blue about, unprepared and trapped as she was in her blue-negligéed nightmare? "You're supposed to be happy, but there's a definite feeling of loss and separation," she said. "Then begins a *most* lost feeling, a feeling of I wish it hadn't happened." Her sense of loss after her birth frightened her. She felt vastly more isolated and alone than even was the norm in the postwar era. Joanne thought about mothering that tiny infant, too, and how overwhelmed she was, and explained that "sometimes you want to reject the whole thing."[1] Today, we'd probably describe her condition not as baby blues but as postpartum depression.

Later psychiatrists would describe these postwar years as the "dark ages" of postpartum mental illness, when little research was being done. If women had severe psychiatric postpartum problems, psychoanalysis might offer Freudian explanations of their flawed personalities. Too rigid, too frigid, or perhaps a repressed lesbian. The "regressive" postpartum woman struggles with giving up her sense of "oneness" with the child, doctors quoted in the article on Joanne explained. Women with severe depressions or psychotic symptoms might be hospitalized. If women had mild to moderate symptoms, they usually suffered alone.

But even in the dark ages, people were talking about postpartum depressions and anxieties, as the publication of Joanne's story in a major magazine shows. In this postwar moment, the idea of the "baby blues" emerged in women's mass media. Writers discussed the "baby blues," the "third-day blues," and less commonly "postpartum depression" as interchangeable concepts. When an advice columnist sat down to pontificate on the baby blues, they might imagine some third-day crying, or he might picture the mother of a three-month-old who can't leave her bed.

Today the baby blues refer to mild and fleeting sadness within the first two weeks postpartum. They are subclinical, outside the purview of medicine. The phrase can be insulting and dismissive, if it's used to describe a more serious or later depression. "Oh, that's just the baby blues, nothing to worry about," someone might tell a woman whose depression *is* something to worry about. And even when people use it to describe the truly subclinical emotional roller coaster of the first couple of weeks postpartum, it is condescending, minimizing difficult physical and social changes.

In the postwar era, the term was dismissive too, but its use was complicated. We can—and must—read it as sexist and infantilizing. But we can also read it as an admission of how difficult motherhood could be. Some articles in the mass media emphasized the hormonal changes of the immediate postpartum, but many also focused on so-cial stresses: a crying baby, a huge life change, a body that looked and felt alien. In this way, the spread of "baby blues" language during the 1950s and 1960s seems like a crack in the façade of postwar mother-hood. Even as individual mothers were faulted for not properly ad-justing, often in psychoanalytic terms, there was an open admission that motherhood could be hard. Motherhood was not consistently joyful, and distress in motherhood was not always an unspoken and nameless problem.

But that crack in the façade was merely that: a crack. Mainstream discussion of baby blues sought to contain the larger implications, divorcing them from criticism of motherhood itself. If women seemed more susceptible to postpartum problems than in past generations, critics explained, perhaps it was because of too much education and improper career goals. Blues were evidence that women needed to adjust and make motherhood their primary focus. The world around them would not need to change. As one psychoanalyst explained in 1959, a woman's postpartum sadness could only let up when "she is a dependable competent mother, a complete woman."[2]

Women who couldn't do that were characterized as immature and childish, or too focused on life outside the home, or too consumerist—even in an era that otherwise lionized consumerism.[3] This patron-izing approach to postpartum distress framed the blues as fleeting, and a more serious maternal depression as self-indulgent. The con-descending tone around the baby blues told women that their depres-sion, their pain, their distress, was not legitimate.

| 17

Before the Baby Blues

Discussions of the baby blues emerged in the postwar era, but they built on a much longer history. The recorded history of postpartum mental illness is usually a history of psychosis rather than of blues or depression. There is some evidence of psychosis as far back as a Hippocratic text written around 400 BCE. In it, a postpartum woman slowly becomes irrational and then dies. There is no explanation of her cause of death; a postpartum infection seems likely. Still, postpartum advocates and psychiatrists often cite this case as the first medical evidence of postpartum mental illness.[4] Whatever it meant at the time, references to this story remain popular because they are testaments to the reality of postpartum mental illness—something postpartum professionals and advocates consistently must insist on. A 2,000-year-history of postpartum psychiatry is a powerful response to skeptics.

In the nineteenth century, a severe insanity following childbirth was called puerperal insanity, a cousin of modern postpartum psychosis. One of the most famous psychiatrists of the time, French reformer Jean-Étienne Esquirol, documented insanity in ninety-two women institutionalized in their first year postpartum. He described their outbursts, hallucinations, and nonstop talking and walking.[5] A few other British doctors published on puerperal insanity in the first half of the nineteenth century. They debated whether the cause of the insanity was anemia, or perhaps "a peculiar irritation of the uterus."

Despite this lack of agreement on what caused puerperal insanity, by mid-century textbooks included it as a well-known, if ill-defined, condition. In 1858, French psychiatrist Louis-Victor Marcé wrote a monograph on the subject. Other professionals lauded the detailed descriptions he included in the nearly four-hundred-page book, the first of its kind.[6]

While women of all classes and races seemed susceptible to puerperal insanity, the treatment they received depended a great deal on their status. In Great Britain and the US, doctors treated upper- and middle-class women in the home and low-income women in asylums.

On one end was Charlotte Perkins Gilman's famous depiction of home treatment in her short story "The Yellow Wallpaper." The protagonist's insanity worsens through her isolation and forced "rest." But puerperal insanity also reportedly caused 10 percent of women's asylum admissions in the late nineteenth-century US.[7] While treatment depended on class, being insane rather than criminal in the postpartum could depend on race and ethnicity. Black and immigrant women in the US who killed their infants faced criminal charges in notably higher numbers than white women who did the same.[8]

Puerperal insanity rose in the early nineteenth century. It was an established concept in medical literature by the end of that century. And then it all but disappeared. It is not entirely clear what caused the sharp decline of puerperal insanity. In part, motherhood itself was changing. The Victorian woman gave way to an early twentieth-century "new" woman less constrained by the pursuit of "true womanhood," an ideal that had characterized women as submissive, domestic, and weak. This did not quite translate to the new century.[9] Alongside changes in gender politics came major changes in the psychiatry profession. Nineteenth-century psychiatrists used puerperal insanity to assert their authority. In the early twentieth century, though, psychiatrists spoke of that diagnosis as outdated, unscientific, and a barrier to professional legitimacy.

German psychiatrist Emil Kraepelin made this point in 1904. He agreed postpartum women seemed more vulnerable to mental disturbances than women at other times. But that was not evidence that the postpartum *caused* those disturbances, he said. Guessing at causes was not the scientific vision he had for psychiatry. It also did not mean insanity in the postpartum was a distinct illness compared to other insanities. "Where mania appears in the puerperal state," he explained, ". . . it is like every other kind of mania."[10] Why single out mania around childbearing as something special? Over the next two decades, psychiatrists overwhelmingly aligned with Kraepelin: the diagnosis had to go.

Then came a 1926 article that seemed to seal the fate of puerperal insanity, an article that still angers postpartum advocates a hundred years later. Psychiatrists Edward A. Strecker and Franklin G. Ebaugh reiterated the call against puerperal insanity. "Old names die hard," they wrote, but it was time for psychiatry to move on. In their study of fifty women's hospitalization records, they argued that insanities were better grouped by their symptoms than their causes (including childbearing). Childbirth "can scarcely be credited with more than a precipitating influence" for these conditions, Strecker and Ebaugh wrote. Sometimes, they added, the postpartum onset of these insanities was "pure coincidence."[11]

It is easy to see why later activists would look back on this article in disgust. Claims that women with postpartum psychosis had preexisting insanities, and claims that a postpartum-specific illness "does not represent a clinical entity," challenge the legitimacy of postpartum mental illness. Even aside from those concerns, the Strecker and Ebaugh article does not hold up well today. It blames women for contributing to their own poor mental states, and the tone is patronizing. There is nothing in it to make it an especially influential text, except the influence of its authors.

Edward Strecker rose in American psychiatry in the next two decades. He served as president of the American Psychiatric Association between 1943 and 1944. Then he was a supporting member of the organization's Committee on Nomenclature and Statistics. That committee authored the first *Diagnostic and Statistical Manual of Mental Disorders* (*DSM*), the so-called bible of psychiatry.[12] Some psychiatrist-advocates assume he was personally responsible for how the *DSM* approached postpartum illness. That edition mentions puerperal insanity only once, in an appendix. The omission didn't seem coincidental.

Psychiatrist James Alexander Hamilton loathed Strecker. He believed the omission of puerperal insanity was hugely consequential and directly resulted in the dearth of research on the subject.[13] Strecker and Ebaugh "sold literally thousands of professionals and professionals-in-training" on the idea that postpartum illnesses were "merely the chronic complaints of women incompetent or unwilling to perform the 'chores of women,'" Hamilton wrote.[14] In the eyes of

Hamilton and his peers, men like Strecker and Ebaugh replaced the "brilliant work" of the nineteenth century with ignorance, dogma, and "barbaric treatment."[15] At the same time researchers like Hamilton came to romanticize the diagnosis of puerperal insanity, paying little attention to the poor treatment of women who had suffered from it.

During these "dark ages," American researchers published only a small amount on postpartum mental illness. If one kind of sexism was killing off the puerperal insanity diagnosis, though, another came from those few psychiatrists who continued to write about postpartum illness in this period. Gregory Zilboorg's psychodynamic perspective led him to conclude that women with puerperal psychoses had underlying problems: latent homosexuality, chronic masturbation, frigidity.[16] In the 1940s, psychoanalyst Helene Deutsch argued that a woman with a weak ego risked "emotional derangement" in transitioning to motherhood and losing her former self.[17] What psychiatric research there was in this area often pointed to women's underlying personality flaws. A future in which postpartum women would ally with psychiatry seemed worlds away.

Some obstetricians took a similar psychoanalytic turn, developing the subfield of psychosomatic obstetrics and gynecology. While there is a long and dark history of psychosomatic gynecology, one that includes nineteenth-century surgeries on women's reproductive organs, the mid-twentieth century ushered in a modernized version.[18] From the 1950s to the 1970s, the annual conference of the American College of Obstetricians and Gynecologists included interest group meetings, luncheons, panels, and roundtables on psychosomatic topics.[19] These obstetricians sought to make sense of some women's negative reactions to childbirth by studying their personalities, family histories, and individual neuroses. They questioned women's marriages, maturity, sexuality, and motives for having children. Like psychoanalysts, they argued that neurotic problems postpartum were not new: they were preexisting personality problems brought to the surface through the "crisis point" of childbirth.[20]

The mid-twentieth century was a moment of minimal new psychiatric research on the postpartum. Perhaps even a dark age. Yet it was also a period of increased popular attention to postpartum sadness and stress. Women's magazines and advice books of the 1940s to 1960s began to discuss both subclinical and moderate postpartum distress as something noteworthy, as the "baby blues."

The Rise of the Baby Blues

In 1943, Mrs. Dave Becker of Cincinnati wrote to the federal Children's Bureau, complaining that the Bureau's popular advice booklet, *Prenatal Care*, was silent on emotional distress. "I think that in everyone's pre-natal book that something should be said about the mental health of a pregnant mother," she wrote. "During this time a slight depression can take hold and become the beginning of the mental issue, more so at this time than most others. Plenty of young women have ruined their lives because of ignorance of the danger of depression during pregnancy." It was up to the government to address this, Mrs. Becker argued. "What could be more important than [a pregnant woman's] mental health? Warn her. Too many young lives are ruined."[21] The Bureau agreed that mothers' mental health was important, and told Mrs. Becker that they might consider some changes. They emphasized, though, that they considered depression the domain of the physician.[22]

The version of *Prenatal Care* that Mrs. Becker would have seen had only a small section on emotion, which mainly encouraged women to avoid "nervousness" during pregnancy.[23] When the booklet was fully revised in 1962, though, it included a section on women's moods during pregnancy and in the postpartum. While there was no need for the "serene" woman to read this section, the guide counseled, it could be of use to mothers who are "vaguely unhappy." Those vaguely unhappy women might learn they were suffering from "a very common reaction" called the "baby blues." This unhappiness was almost always short in duration, the booklet explained, part of an adjustment to motherhood. Any blues "should disappear as your strength returns and you begin to do things that give you a new sense of purpose and enjoyment."[24]

The idea that women would experience a new sense of purpose, and deeply enjoy these new responsibilities, undergirded the baby blues. It at once allowed that new motherhood was difficult and serious, something requiring adjustment for all but the most serene of women. But that adjustment needed to come quickly. And it needed to be an adjustment to a very narrow, white, and middle-class idea of good motherhood. Happy motherhood might not be instant, but the goal was to adapt quickly and without a fuss. If a mother had problems making that adjustment within a couple weeks, she was to blame.

Adapting to those expectations could be difficult. As large numbers of middle-class white women moved to their segregated suburbs, many prioritized children. They married younger and had more children than their parents' generation. While the number of mothers in the workforce grew, the expectation was that white women who could afford it would stay home and raise children.[25] More than that, it was an expectation of "total motherhood," in the sense that raising those children ought to be emotionally fulfilling and a labor of love, never simply a labor. To feel otherwise was to be selfish and unfeminine.[26]

The 1950s have been called a moment of "domestic containment" in the Cold War context. Suburban sprawl isolated the white middle-class family, as did the imperative to keep subversion and radicalism out. Bases and nuclear laboratories were not the only sites of militarization and escalation. Cold War anxieties influenced television and popular culture, art and music.[27] Children dug for atom bomb rings in their boxes of Kix Cereal. Suburban families built fallout shelters, afraid of both nuclear bombs and nuclear accidents. At school, kids ducked under desks in anxiety-producing drills. The nuclear family became a site for managing fallout and risk as well.

Despite the popular mythology of June Cleaver and large happy families, it was also a moment of vicious, near constant attacks on mothers. Mothers were said to be smothering yet lazy, narcissistic yet identity-less. Psychiatrists blamed overbearing mothers for their adult sons' military ineptness, attributed children's autism to cold "refrigerator mothers," and argued that overprotective "momism" wrecked masculinity.[28] Advice books accused depressed and anxious mothers of overprotectiveness, of causing sleep problems in infants, and of spoiling children.[29] Edward Strecker, the psychiatrist who had famously rejected puerperal insanity in the 1920s, now published a book called *Their Mothers' Sons*. In it, he blamed mothers for high military rejection rates, mental problems during service, and sometimes even homosexuality.[30] It was a bestseller. Americans were hungry for mother blame.

That kind of awful mother was usually imagined as white. There were different kinds of mother blame targeting Black women. Decades of social science research pathologized the Black family, especially the mother. In the 1930s and 1940s, sociologist E. Franklin Frazier blamed woman-headed households for the problems facing Black families. These ideas fermented, reinforcing discrimination in social welfare programs. Policy makers eagerly blamed poverty on Black mothers' individual choices, a handy justification for limiting relief programs.[31] Politicians described employed Black mothers as a danger to gender roles and family structures, while ignoring the wage discrimination that often forced them into the paid workforce.[32] Then in 1965, Daniel Patrick Moynihan's *The Negro Family* cast Black mothers as matriarchs who stifled Black men's opportunities and authority.[33] Social scientists and policy makers described the mid-century Black family as a "tangle of pathology," with Black women under constant scrutiny.[34]

Black women were not, in these formulations, allowed to be sad or vulnerable. White women were. Popular depictions of the baby blues in the 1950s and 1960s, like Joanne dramatically collapsing in her blue negligée, were depictions of white womanhood. Discussions of the baby blues were often condescending and infantilizing, but they were built on assumptions about the presence of a male breadwinner and other norms of middle-class suburban white life.

What Caused the Baby Blues?

The baby blues in the 1950s and 1960s encompassed everything from a mild postpartum unhappiness to a severe depression. Some psychoanalysts were happy to explain what was going on with moms who could not properly adjust. They offered a variety of explanations, but the heart of it was immaturity. White women who broke down and did not properly adjust to "the most feminine of tasks" were really "still little girls not ready to handle much more than a doll."[35] At best they will "play at motherhood" without embracing it properly.[36] These "young women may resent their lost status as the 'baby doll,'" a sociologist explained. Their "every whim was indulged" before motherhood, and now they would need to mature quickly.[37]

In one woman's 1959 memoir of her postpartum institutionalization, she describes her experience using this infantilizing language. "I . . . wanted a baby, but my hunger was like that of a child who covets another's lollipop or toy." After she had a newborn, the reality of it overwhelmed her: "It's too much. Everything is too much."[38] Critics often described this postpartum reality as a "letdown." Women's unrealistic expectations about having a baby were childlike, the truth of the situation shocking. "Like a child on the day after Christmas, the average woman can hardly help being surprised and somewhat disappointed to discover that she is still the same person," one doctor wrote.[39] The modern mother might struggle "to make the transition from a young bride into responsible motherhood" and might mourn her "loss of girlhood, of being carefree," a critic explained.[40]

In much baby blues literature, this letdown began in the hospital. By the 1950s, 95 percent of American women gave birth in hospitals. This was a staggering jump from just twenty years prior, when the majority of births had taken place at home.[41] While Americans welcomed the modernity and safety of the hospital, some ambivalence about the effects of hospital birth remained. This ambivalence came out in discussions of the baby blues. All that sterility, those helpful nurses, those medical interventions—perhaps it was making the

| 25

postpartum too easy for women. New mothers needed trial by fire if they were to adjust, a range of critics argued, and all these hospitals did was coddle the mothers. No wonder they got depressed when they left!

These critics, mostly men, complained that the overly luxurious hospital set women up for that "letdown." A 1950 obstetrics textbook described baby blues as a normal reaction for a woman who "has not been educated to the necessity of personal sacrifice and the satisfaction and enjoyment derived from parenthood." When women left the hospital, the author chided, the "glamour" of motherhood dissipates.[42] Another obstetrician described women experiencing a "letdown" when "the attention and the flowers" cease. The physically weak and exhausted new mother would then leave the hospital, and "suddenly have to face grim reality in the form of increased household chores and care of the baby."[43] Beloved advice book sage Dr. Benjamin Spock described the hospital as a space where the mother "has been waited on hand and foot." In the hospital "your every need was provided for," these writers cautioned women, but home was full of household chores alongside newborn care.[44] Women needed to adapt earlier.

The hospital was a woman's "last chance for freedom for a long time," and critics argued that this freedom caused more harm than good.[45] One obstetrics professor described how rooming-in (keeping the baby in the hospital room rather than in a nursery) reduced the baby blues. He stopped seeing women with postpartum problems when the hospital he practiced at began rooming-in in 1955, he claimed. "Before that, I saw plenty of women go home practically drenched in tears they were so frightened of having a new baby and not knowing how to care for it."[46] Making women more responsible for childcare from the start with rooming-in might help women adjust to the reality of newborn care, they argued.[47]

Emerging psychology literature on maternal attachment reinforced the idea that new mothers should start motherwork immediately, not only for their own adjustment but also to better serve their infants.[48] British psychiatrist John Bowlby's work on maternal deprivation shaped thinking about the importance of the maternal-child bond. Based in studies of children who had been separated for at least six months from their mothers, it emphasized the importance of maternal nurturing for psychological development. It was quickly assumed that any separation of a child from a mother was a developmental risk. While new mothers in the hospital supposedly enjoyed their flowers and attention, nurses cared for the babies. This meant mothers missed valuable hours, maybe even days, of attaching.[49]

This anxiety about attachment was apparent in the mainstream media as well. A *Redbook* article described the hospital nursery as a site of "violence." Given the chance, in the first hour postpartum, women might speak to their baby and give it a nickname, note how it looked like other family members, or make claims about its personality ("What a happy little girl!"). The article criticized hospital policies that did not allow for this time of attaching.[50]

In additional to rooming-in to get attachment started, hospitals also encouraged women to leave earlier to maintain it. Obstetricians boasted that in the hospital of the mid-1960s, women were "up and about" soon after birth and going home by the fourth or fifth day. A minority of doctors worried that sending women home while they were still in physical pain might actually cause blues.[51] But the majority, especially the more modern obstetricians who feared coddling, thought it was best to get new mothers out of the hospital as soon as possible. Of course, if you send women home sooner, you are less likely to *see* their blues, which might be mistaken for women not experiencing them. The solution for a social structure in which women increasingly lacked childcare experience was to minimize recovery time, intensify immediate childcare responsibilities, and make sure a new mother was not getting "spoiled" when she should be adjusting.

Some experts writing on the blues were sure that this inability to adjust had other sources, too. White middle-class women might have improper expectations—not just of how new mothering would feel, but of their lives overall. Education and jobs, in this assessment, were to blame for unhappiness.

A young woman named Anna, for instance, had an "active, artistic life" in New York City before she became pregnant in the mid-1960s. Anna worked a pink-collar job during the day and took college courses at night. Once pregnant, she and her husband moved to New Jersey. Anna felt isolated in the suburbs; she was not connecting with her new neighbors; she missed her job and school and friends. After she had the baby, she could not easily travel back to the city to see people from her old life. She found herself isolated, "with a strange, frightening small being whose demands kept her continually on the edge of exhaustion." Anna got headaches, then insomnia. Eventually, she had nightmares about stabbing her husband and the baby. Anna's postpartum distress led her to question both herself and the institution of motherhood. "Weren't mothers supposed to love their babies instinctively and always? Why didn't she? Why wasn't motherhood a joyful experience?"[52]

To the journalist writing about Anna, at least, the source of Anna's baby blues was clear. She was among those women "well educated—but for business, not motherhood." Postpartum problems, magazines and advice books claimed, were greater among women who had worked before having children than women who had not. As a *New York Times Magazine* article explained in 1960, "professionally trained women who marry and become mothers—a relatively new, significant phenomenon . . . have special problems."[53]

Dr. Spock also described these problems. When middle-class women worked before children, he said, they had "an illusion of freedom," and always had "an escape hatch in the mind's eye." A woman believed she had control over her life. Once this woman had a newborn, that sense of freedom was gone. "In motherhood, there is no quitting," he emphasized. Spock argued that motherhood is harder for American women than for women in "civilizations that are simpler than ours" because of that illusion of freedom. Spock's comparison to "simpler societies" used a common, racist trope: white Americans were so advanced and civilized, they had special problems. In those so-called "simpler" societies, Spock wrote, girls assume motherhood will be their future and they have no other "tantalizing choices." While American women might choose motherhood, from a set of limited mid-century choices (they are "not abducted into motherhood," Spock insisted), they did not always know what it meant to make such a choice.[54]

Women's magazine articles offered advice on leaving the paid workforce for motherhood. Women needed to make new friends, unrelated to their work. Friendships with non-mothers confused women's priorities, the magazines said, as they may have spent too much of their lives "caught up in a highly competitive social whirl."[55] After leaving their job, women might also feel "deprived of money," as they find their husband's income gets spent "before they can refresh their own wardrobes."[56] In this writing, women mourning lost careers came off as selfish and immature, longing for fun and new dresses rather than for external validation or intellectual stimulation. In more psychoanalytic takes they had "sex-role confusion," or a "deep-seated hostility toward the husband" that left women envying their husband's freedom while dreading their own sentence of care work.[57]

These new articulations of baby blues made plain how common women's postpartum adjustment problems could be. But they required women to adjust to a rigid and totalizing idea of motherhood rather than challenging this version of motherhood.[58] They reinforced high-intensity theories of child-rearing and questioned women's work outside the home. Descriptions of the baby blues often emphasized women's innate incompetence, superficiality, and flightiness. Occasionally discussions of the baby blues criticized the expectations on new mothers, but the bulk of baby blues writing reminded women that they should not "feel sorry for yourself," but needed to fix the problem by fixing themselves up. It was a time for white middle-class women to adjust, calm down, and go shopping.

Solutions to the Baby Blues

"If you begin to feel at all depressed," Dr. Benjamin Spock wrote, "go to a movie, or to the beauty parlor, or to get yourself a new hat or dress."[59] Spock reprinted this advice from his 1946 book verbatim

| 29

through the 1962 edition. A handful of women needed psychotherapy, he acknowledged, but most depressed new mothers just needed
retail therapy. In the postwar era, it was not unusual for Americans
with the means to seek pleasure and happiness in consumer goods.[60]
Advice-givers argued that consumerism was of special use in the
postpartum. It offered a fleeting site of pleasure when the other options, like an enjoyable career or time with friends, evaporated amid
new motherhood. It also served as a counter to isolation. Spock jokingly recounted a conversation with one mother who "actually looked
forward to a trip to the market as if it were a gay social event."[61] Magazines suggested women have husbands or a babysitter watch the baby
so they could go "on a shopping trip or [enjoy] a quiet, well-earned
respite at the beauty shop."[62]

For white suburban mothers, it was critical they not "allow your
emotions to get the best of you."[63] Some advice suggested women ask
that their husband take them to "dinner or to a show, whether you
can afford it or not."[64] "Such brief respites will more than pay for
themselves in an improved disposition," the writer justified. Retail
therapy demonstrated class bias, recommending that women hire
help around the house for cooking, cleaning, or childcare until (if)
they felt up to managing the household themselves.[65] Sanity for
middle- and upper-class mothers required the labor of low-income
women, especially women of color.

While a new dress or haircut might make a woman happier, it had
another important effect: it could make her prettier. The expectation
that women avoid any postpartum frumpiness, including the imperative that they lose weight quickly, filled literature for postwar new
mothers. In 1953, a syndicated columnist described the problems of
the postpartum body: the large and rounded "tummy," stringy hair,
"limp and flabby" breasts. The physical changes lead to mothers' depression, and "confirms in their own minds that they have paid a high
price for motherhood."[66] Similarly, Dr. Spock attributed the blues in
part to a woman's fear "that she has lost all her looks."[67]

Some women did seem to attribute their baby blues to their
changing bodies, and to fears they would "lose my looks."[68] Nurses

described postpartum women preoccupied with "the changed configuration of their bodies, their breasts, and the fit of their clothes."[69] The idea of "losing one's looks" postpartum hit on the legitimate issue that the postwar middle-class ideal required women to accept that their attractiveness was central to their value. A woman's postpartum sex appeal was not just a worry of the "narcissistic woman" who might "become hysterical at losing her appeal."[70] For women who left jobs for motherhood, their sex appeal was now an economic imperative. Their arrangements reinforced a male breadwinner model, and they had to rely on their relationship with a husband to provide for themselves and their child.

Magazines described postpartum body panic as an individual stress, but the advice to lose weight postpartum was widespread in the culture. As one doctor wrote in *Redbook*, a new mother needed rest but also needed to be put "back into her former shape—the shape, presumably, that caught her husband's eye in the first place."[71] One advice manual encouraged postpartum women to "watch weight, if you are the kind of person who puts it on easily." After all, "you don't want to look as though you are pregnant again three months after delivering the baby."[72] A doctor's column in *McCall's* connected the issues of attractiveness and depression: "You survey your abdomen. It is stretched and lumpy. You look to the future; it seems dull and dismal."[73]

For middle-class women who could not get their mood bright enough through shopping and dieting alone, another option loomed: the notorious "mother's little helpers." The 1950s and early 1960s introduction of minor tranquilizers like Miltown, Librium, and Valium changed prescribing patterns. Major tranquilizers, those primarily used in hospital settings, were too powerful to give to an outpatient still expected to do mothering work and household chores. The new minor tranquilizers offered a more practical option. Soon the drugs were everywhere. Psychiatrists disproportionally prescribed them to women.[74]

The minor tranquilizers opened a door for other outpatient prescriptions, and anti-anxiety medications and antidepressants eventually took over the psychopharmaceutical market. Some were marketed as ideal for overwhelmed mothers, but only a couple were described as postpartum specific. Ritalin's advertisements suggested an extraordinary laundry list of uses, for everything from depression to minimal brain dysfunction to managing the stress of urban life.[75] In the late 1950s, marketers described Ritalin as a postpartum mood brightener. At least one advertisement for postpartum Ritalin mentioned depression, but others did not specify what type of problem the "postpartum patient" was managing.

Another early psychopharmaceutical that claimed to treat the baby blues was Niamid. Pfizer developed Niamid as an antidepressant in the late 1950s and promoted the monoamine oxidase inhibitor as having many uses. One was as a postpartum mood brightener. Outlets published multiple profiles of a woman chemist working on the drug in 1959, presumably arranged by the manufacturer. They described chemist Joan Pepin as looking "more like a pin-up than a scientist" and weighing "a well distributed 108 pounds."[76] They highlighted how the new drug could combat "a common affliction known as the After-Baby Blues, Second or Third-Day Blues, or Post-Partum Blues."[77] Pepin clarified the drug helped postpartum women by "giving them an increased interest in their surroundings." Niamid "brightens their mood," she said, an oft-repeated line that was also part of the drug's branding (Pfizer distributed Niamid sundials to play up this idea of "brightening").

Pepin emphasized the emerging possibility of drugs for all kinds of people who are "suffering from border-line mental upsets without even realizing it." The baby blues fit this well. Another news article described Niamid as targeted to help women "to combat the useless and forlorn feeling which often follows a birth."[78] Yes, she explained, the baby blues are usually short-lived and "not too serious." But a drug like Niamid offered an easy solution, typical for the times: Consume this, brighten your mood, adjust. Pfizer withdrew the drug in 1974, after it was linked to liver disease.[79]

While advice literatures increasingly deemed it normal to feel mildly depressed, anxious, and lonely in new motherhood, they

Brighten the day

for the chronically fatigued, the chronically ill, the convales-
cent, the apathetic and depressed older patient, the postpartum patient, the oversedated, the retarded child

with **Ritalin**® hydrochloride
(methylphenidate hydrochloride CIBA)

a new *mild* antidepressant, chemically unrelated to
the amphetamines. Ritalin brightens outlook and
renews vigor—counteracts drug sedative effects—
often improves performance in the elderly. In most
cases, Ritalin does not overstimulate, has little or
no effect on appetite, blood pressure or pulse rate.

Average dosage: 10 mg. b.i.d. or t.i.d.

Supplied: TABLETS, 5 mg. (yellow), 10 mg. (light blue),
20 mg. (peach colored).

C I B A
SUMMIT, N. J.

Figure 1.1 Advertisement for Ritalin that features a woman holding a baby and
mentions the postpartum patient. It includes the language of mood "brightening"
common in these ads. From *Bulletin of the New York Academy of Medicine,* January
1958, vol. 34, no. 1, p. xx.

stressed that it was a woman's responsibility to manage her situation. Most solutions to women's blues centered on individual choices that aggressively reinforced prescribed gender roles. Literature on the blues did not seriously challenge the expectations of postwar motherhood, instead encouraging women to buy things, lose weight, and brighten their mood. Still, some women whose "blues" lingered and intensified in ways we would call postpartum depression today began to question postwar motherhood itself. "Is this all?" they asked.

The Problem That Has No Name

Betty Friedan's 1963 *The Feminine Mystique* addressed that underlying question: Is this all there is? Friedan's book critiqued the gloominess of white, middle- to upper-class suburban motherhood in the postwar era. The expectations for women had narrowed. Women's magazines that ran stories about career women in the 1930s and 1940s now mostly ran stories on housewives. The baby boom carried the message that only marriage and motherhood truly fulfilled women; that was the "feminine mystique." What Friedan called the problem without a name included postpartum depression as one manifestation of discontent. "The high incidence of cramps with menstruation, nausea and vomiting during pregnancy, depression with childbirth, and . . . distress at menopause have come to be accepted as a 'normal' part of feminine biology," Friedan explained, but these might instead be symptoms of "the big lie of the mystique."[80]

34 | Friedan based her book on surveys of women from her college alma mater. The survey included the question "Were you depressed after childbirth?" Most women responded "no," but those who responded "yes" illustrated some of the larger cultural tropes around women's work. Some were simply tired, but others described the same disconnect between their elite college training and their realities as new mothers that critics worried about. One woman described herself as "somewhat" depressed, but dismissed it as that "usual status-of-college-woman problem."[81] Her use of that language about

women's education as a cause of postpartum problems echoed Friedan's own mixed feelings about the psychoanalytic mother blame of
the era. In *The Feminine Mystique*, Friedan adopts portions of Edward
Strecker's attack on mothers as evidence that an overinvestment in
motherhood could cause problems in children.[82]

Women wrote to Friedan to share their personal experiences. They
described seeing psychiatrists and taking tranquilizers to make their
lives more bearable, only to realize that "what I thought might be
wrong with me was in fact right with me!" One mother hospitalized
after overdosing on sleeping pills described *The Feminine Mystique* as
saving her life by giving her more context to understand struggles
she had thought were just her own.[83] While not specifically focused
on the postpartum, Friedan chronicled both the subclinical unhappiness of thousands of women and the more severe depression that
manifests in some.

Joanne, the young woman whose baby blues opened this chapter, knew the struggle well. "It's not like life in the storybooks," she
confessed. Joanne had once been successful in her career, but now
she was "a trembling, incompetent mother." A psychiatrist explained
that most women who had been working will struggle some with
this transition, but some "might become hysterical."[84] The charge of
hysteria eerily echoed nineteenth-century accusations of women's individual weaknesses. The "baby blues" were an individual problem,
attributable to individual psychological failings and "sex-role confusion." Blues were evidence of women's continued immaturity and
self-absorption, not evidence of a need for structural change.

As the idea of the baby blues developed in postwar culture, so
did the belief that postwar culture could fix them. Mass media like
Redbook and *Good Housekeeping* would soothe worried white mothers
by minimizing and normalizing their stress, misery, and depression.
Amid their advertisements, they encouraged women to buy hats and
dresses, and otherwise calm themselves in small and individual ways.
Solutions often reiterated demands that women lose weight, be more
cheerful and social, and try to break up the tedium—reinforcing the

| 35

idea that the problem, like so many women's problems, was frivolous.[85] They blamed the problems of motherhood on individuals' problems with modernity, while also embracing consumer solutions.

By the late 1960s, though, challenges to this framing of the blues emerged. Feminists sought ways to respond to this dismissal of women's suffering. What would it mean to take the blues seriously? What would it mean to continue the critique Friedan began, to suggest that women's postpartum illness indicated larger social problems? In response to a postwar culture that articulated but trivialized postpartum depression, women's health feminists of the late 1960s and 1970s sought ways to both challenge the institution of motherhood and legitimize women's pain.

2. A Feminist Postpartum

Paula Doress-Worters, a young feminist in Boston, gave birth to her daughter in 1966. Soon after, she became severely depressed. "I felt terrible," she recounted, "because she was a wanted child. She was lovely. But sometimes I just couldn't get out of bed." Her baby was perfect, Doress-Worters thought, so why wasn't *she*? She had heard of "baby blues," but nothing like this. Her neighbor convinced her husband something was wrong. He called the obstetrician. Doctors came to their home. She ran from them. They sedated her. They hospitalized her for a month.

While initially involuntary, Doress-Worters's hospital experience was surprisingly free from the horror stories of 1960s institutionalization. With time, rest, and medication she soon felt normal again—which in her case meant putting up a sign in her room demanding better pay for the nurses. Still, the separation from her infant daughter was painful; it haunted her for decades. The doctor and nurses did not give a specific name like "postpartum depression" to her experience. Once Doress-Worters was discharged, she struggled to make sense of what had happened.

A few years later, her involvement with the Boston Women's Health Book Collective helped her process the experience. The collective formed in 1969, when a group of women organized a health workshop.[1] It used consciousness-raising strategies to discuss women's issues, including postpartum depression.[2] Women gathered and spoke openly and honestly about their personal experiences. The personal was political.

The discussions became the sites of awakenings and awareness. After the women discussed their health problems, they often agreed both that the problems were systemic rather than individual, and that they needed to do something about them. Collective members tried to establish a list of "good doctors," meaning those who listened to their woman patients. This proved difficult. They rechanneled their efforts into creating and sharing information about women's bodies through their own printed "course" on women's health. This was the germ of *Our Bodies, Ourselves*.

The Boston Women's Health Book Collective was just one piece of the emerging women's health movement. The larger movement called out sexism in medical research, practice, and thinking. Most doctors were men, and they treated woman patients—"the 'girls,' the 'dears,' the 'honeys'"—condescendingly.[3] The movement advanced arguments that sexism both caused women's health issues and led medical professionals to ignore them.[4] Is the quality of healthcare for women lowered by the fact that men legislate, dictate, and implement most of it? asked one feminist writer. "The answer," she explained, "is an emphatic 'Yes.'"[5]

Feminists interested in mental health and psychiatry, psychotherapy, and psychology pointed out the problems of diagnosis in a sexist system.[6] "Whereas men may turn to physical violence or alcoholism, women (who are socialized to be weak) turn to psychiatrists to seek help for their weaknesses," Belita Cowan wrote.[7] Cowan, an advocate of the new project of feminist therapy, explained that psychotherapy was not only steeped in sexism but risked naturalizing that oppression by making women's problems seem individual rather than social. As a pair of feminist therapists lamented, "We are paid to treat the insanity of our patients and not the insanity of our institutions."[8] Most therapists were not feminists, and while women used therapy more frequently than men, male therapists and psychiatrists struggled to address women's problems. One feminist group argued that "low-paying, dead-end jobs, often coupled with housekeeping and childcare responsibilities," were fundamental causes of women's psychological distress even though they were overlooked by male professionals.[9]

"We put up with an insane arrangement," radical mothers wrote in a 1972 treatise. Society isolates women with babies and offers them few resources. New motherhood might as well be solitary confinement. Yet people continue to think romantically about new motherhood, and "wonder why happiness doesn't reign supreme" for all mothers.[10] For many feminists in the early 1970s, rethinking gender roles required rethinking motherhood and the family. That first year of motherhood especially, when abrupt life changes made sexism hard to ignore, became a site for consciousness-raising.

While feminists of the era mostly agreed on the need to reimagine motherhood, there was no consensus on what that meant. In the early 1960s, Betty Friedan wrote about the moderate depression "without a name" that engulfed so many white suburban mothers. In 1969, feminists including Paula Doress-Worters wrote about postpartum mental illness in the first edition of their foundational book *Our Bodies, Ourselves*. Some people responded angrily, fearing feminists were trashing American motherhood when they should go after doctors and hospitals. As these debates played out in primarily white feminist circles, Black feminists were more likely to discuss maternal mental health without labels like "postpartum depression," as they navigated a culture already quick to pathologize the Black mother. | 39

So when women wrote about the problems of early motherhood in the late 1960s and the 1970s, they often spoke across one another. There would be no consensus on what a "postpartum depression" was. Some feminists wrote about mild depression and some about psychosis; some wrote about the first week postpartum while some focused on the first year. But they shared a rejection of the condescending "baby blues" as an adequate way of explaining postpartum adjustment problems. And they agreed that new motherhood in the US was indeed an "insane arrangement" that needed to be changed, even when they disagreed about which aspects were the worst or how to change them.

The frustrating combination of shared grievances without shared solutions was familiar in the women's health movement. Rethinking intimate issues led to disagreements. Should feminists make the medical profession listen to them, or were they better off taking matters into their own hands?[11] Was the goal to mitigate women's pain, or to overthrow the systems causing that pain? Could they make the heterosexual family fairer, or should they reject it entirely? The difficulty framing maternal mental health shared a lot with other issues of the time, from home birth to abortion to sterilization and contraceptive choice.

Consciousness-raising and feminist network building were critical to psychiatric and emotional health issues just as they were for other health issues. But mental health activism was rarely at the center of the women's health movement, except for feminists resisting the abuses of psychiatry. And even though the postpartum warranted a chapter in the iconic *Our Bodies, Ourselves*, postpartum mental illness has not earned a prominent place in women's health movement history. In part, this is because feminists cared about the postpartum but not nearly at the level they devoted to childbirth or abortion.[12] The lack of a unified feminist stance on postpartum wellness also has made it less memorable. There was no agreement over the role of hormones or the role of medical sexism, or over how to prevent or treat postpartum illness. There was no single path forward. But through their diverse articulations of postpartum problems, they laid the groundwork for later advocacy.

Postpartum Bodies, Postpartum Selves

At the 1969 women's health workshop, Paula Doress-Worters first heard other women openly discuss postpartum distress as a common psychological problem. Esther Rome, another collective member, described her mother's postpartum depression. Wendy Sanford told the story of her recent depression and the physician who had not taken it seriously. She needed to lower her expectations and focus on her roles as wife and mother, he said. He suggested she was being self-indulgent.[13] The women's issues raised ran the gamut, from a lack of openness and awareness of postpartum mental problems to a lack of support for women who admitted their postpartum distress.

This workshop was also Wendy Sanford's introduction to the phrase "postpartum depression." This was "dizzying news": her problem had a name. It was "a real phenomenon, with physical and societal causes." Now it felt like "it wasn't [her] fault."

After that initial workshop, the Boston Women's Health Book Collective set to work on a booklet. Doress-Worters and Rome co-authored a chapter on postpartum depression.[14] The group mimeographed and distributed that booklet, *Women and Their Bodies*. Then, in 1970, Free Press published a book version. In 1971, the collective revised it as *Our Bodies, Ourselves*.

The collective sought to reimagine motherhood in ways that might decrease the incidence of postpartum depression. At the same time, they demanded postpartum distress be taken more seriously by professionals and by the larger culture. They simultaneously tried to present the newest research on postpartum mental health, challenge the social context of American mothering, share individual women's postpartum stories, and demand better psychological and psychiatric research. In short, they tried to fill an enormous gap in postpartum writing and activism.

Doress-Worters and Rome constructed their chapter from stories women shared in meetings and the best library research they could manage. The mainstream books available were "just as bad as the women's magazines" with their condescending discussions of baby blues. "They just said, you know, 'Don't worry about anything.' 'Don't worry your pretty little head,'" Doress-Worters recalled. To access medical journals for more serious information, one collective member borrowed a university library card, claiming to be doing research for a doctor. Doress-Worters came to realize how important what she and Rome had done was. She had retrieved all the information she could, and was now presenting it "in a way that would be helpful to other women."[15] The medical literature was written *about* postpartum women, not *for* them. Now the collective shared—and challenged—that literature.

The chapter itself was not long, running about ten pages in the 1970 self-published edition, but it packed a punch. It grew with each edition, but remained significantly shorter than the adjacent chapter on pregnancy. "Some of the women felt like if we focused too much on postpartum that we would be making women scared," Doress-Worters recounted. "Women who were pregnant . . . that we'd be scaring them or something."

Doress-Worters and Rome questioned popular psychology on maternal attachment as a myth "perpetuated to keep us isolated and privatized in keeping with the competitive capitalist ethic." Women feel guilty about not living up to societal roles for mothers, they explained, but women often failed to "ask if their roles are realizable."[16] The chapter also translated medical literature on the postpartum for a lay audience.[17] The authors were comfortable with some physiological origins to maternal problems, as well as some psychiatric definitions of those problems as mental illnesses. But the collective was founded on political critique, and the larger leftist context of rethinking psychiatry going on was inescapable.[18] "Postpartum emotional disturbances, like most, possibly all, mental disorders, are defined by the social context in which they occur," Doress-Worters wrote.[19] The authors wove together medical and political arguments, simultaneously critiquing American motherhood and seeking ways of granting women's suffering legitimacy.

The chapter proposed several causes for postpartum depression beyond hormones, including isolation or bringing children up in poverty. "Unfortunately, our society encourages a woman to fuse her role as a person with her role as a mother," Doress-Worters and Rome wrote. Then they proposed solutions.[20] Some were at the level of social policy. They included "a list of things that the government could do that could make things better," Doress-Worters explained, including parental leave and free childcare.[21] Even with her own medicalized postpartum, including severe depression and hospitalization, in her writing and activism Doress-Worters put childcare access at the center. The women also proposed grassroots approaches, including photocopying and sharing depression screeners in feminist spaces, peer counseling, and opening a phone line that women could call in the postpartum period.[22]

In 1973, the Boston Women's Health Book Collective moved *Our Bodies, Ourselves* to Simon and Schuster. For a new edition, Doress-Worters and Rome added more personal stories from women to their chapter. In story after story, women explained how cultural expectations of motherhood either caused or exacerbated postpartum emotional problems. "A good mother should be serene and happy," not depressed like her, one woman reflected. Another recalled how she felt she "ought to know what to do as a mother instinctively."[23]

The women's stories echoed those from 1950 and 1960s baby blues articles. But here they came with critique. There were plenty of material reasons a mother might not feel happy, Doress-Worters and Rome reasoned, and why was happiness an expectation anyhow? They also analyzed a key article in the field at length.[24] The article uncritically described how well-educated and working women risked a potential emotional "conflict" when they became mothers. They listed education and careers as "risks" to a new mother's mental health. Doress-Worters and Rome took issue with that. Did education put women at risk, they asked, or was the issue that motherhood was framed to cause this conflict? It was the latter, they argued, and women "are in conflict with ourselves because our society makes it so difficult for us to pursue our own goals while providing good care for our children." Consistent with the concerns of radical therapy from the 1960s, *Our Bodies, Ourselves* complained about professionals who thought treating emotional distress just meant helping women adjust to a distressing society.[25]

The 1973 edition of *Our Bodies, Ourselves* included direct criticism of medicine, both in these challenges to psychological research and in including women's stories about their experiences with medical sexism. One woman described her inpatient experience: "my psychiatrist was kind but knew little about women or babies." Another discussed

| 43

problems she experienced when enrolled in a study meant to address hormonal causes of postpartum depression. She told members of the research team she had some concerns about the study. They told her not to worry. Although this woman was still moderately depressed and agitated, she bitterly joked that "as long as I took the pills and didn't become sick enough to be hospitalized, I was counted as a success for the hormonal experiment." Medical researchers and physicians "should be prepared to work with us as whole people," Doress-Worters and Rome wrote, and should not just focus on simple solutions, or that which is "lucrative and ego-gratifying."[26]

In their next version, in 1976, Doress-Worters and Rome echoed their earlier recommendations for phone lines, support groups, and depression screening surveys distributed by peers instead of obstetricians. They also requested "federal subsidies for the diet of *all* pregnant and postpartum women," daycare provided by all places of employment, fully paid maternity and paternity leave ("as in Sweden"), and subsidized babysitting. They also wanted a mechanism for consumer input into the US Public Health Service and federal health policies, which they argued "male physicians and their specialty societies" and their lobbyists controlled.[27] They did not oppose medical interventions, but trusted few doctors. And they did not think medical interventions could ever be enough on their own. They also never argued that good childcare would fully eliminate postpartum mental illness, but they could not imagine eliminating it without that kind of social policy intervention. As the women saw it, their expansive political agenda would decrease postpartum mental problems and provide better care for women with postpartum illness. They would also improve American motherhood more generally. As Doress-Worters said, "we just had a feeling that we could somehow improve society."

The Natural Postpartum

In 1976, the feminist magazine *Ms.* published an excerpt of the *Our Bodies, Ourselves* postpartum chapter. They titled it "Postpartum

Blues: As Natural as Childbirth." The five-page piece discussed highs and lows of new motherhood and emphasized how common postpartum emotional problems were, both clinical and subclinical ones. It summarized causes, with one paragraph on hormones and three on social causes. The excerpt included the individual postpartum solutions proposed in the book, like fathers spending more time at home, but without reference to paternity leave. It omitted all the social policy recommendations.[28]

Feminist natural birth advocates, especially those opposed to hospitals, obstetricians, and medicalized childbirth, erupted in frustration. The article took no stance on natural childbirth, though it assumed hospital birth was standard. The excerpt's title, however, "as natural as childbirth," invoked natural childbirth *and* compared it with the "blues."

Letters to *Ms.* rejected a coupling of natural birth and the blues. They took offense at the article's implication that the postpartum was "a real bummer." One writer argued the blues were not natural, since there is no way that "Mother Nature (God) intended women to suffer so."[29] Postpartum blues or depression were only "as 'natural' as episiotomies, and the use of drugs in hospital births and merely another reason to avoid the hospital experience."[30] Another reasoned that "post-partum blues may indeed be as natural as childbirth, but I doubt that giving birth under glaring lights with one's genitals shaven and exposed to a roomful of sterile-masked strangers can be called natural!"[31] A woman from Maryland described several months of severe depression after her hospital birth, and no depression following a home birth. Mothers, she explained, needed to reject hospital births and separation from the newborn and instead "let their hormones ... work for them instead of against them."[32]

Contrary to the *Ms.* article, natural birthers explained, postpartum blues and depression were as *unnatural* as could be. "If more women would breastfeed their babies ... there would be a lot less talk of postpartum depression," said one.[33] Another offered that postpartum blues were virtually nonexistent in the home birth community. She added that the "vast majority of child-bearing women on the planet cannot afford to indulge in such a luxury as to plunge into being neurotic at a time when they are so directly needed by someone else."[34]

Criticism of obstetrics and hospital birth was common in the women's health movement. *Our Bodies, Ourselves* itself included disapproval of hospital birth practices. The authors argued that modern hospitals prioritized "administrative and physical needs" and dismissed emotional needs that "get in the way of efficiency." They worried that birth, which they romanticized as a once "magnificent sharing experience," was now only "a technical event."[35] But *Our Bodies, Ourselves* pushed for reimagining hospital birth, rather than rejecting it. For other activists, a similar distrust of medicalization pushed them toward a birthing counterculture. That counterculture, especially when connected to communal projects of the era, encompassed everything from birthing centers and midwifery to home birth.[36] Natural birthers sought to wrest power from medical authorities and take control of their experience. They imagined the process as a return to the "natural."[37]

Stories of disappointing hospital births and redemptive natural births permeated natural birth culture. Women described how their hospital birth "was [a] very unhappy, negative experience," while their natural birth left them "so bubbly" and "so turned-on."[38] Natural birth advocates associated hospital birth with disempowerment, trauma, and fear. "Post-partum depression, for years attributed to women's neurotic rejection of motherhood or to hormonal change, almost never occurs in mothers who deliver their infants at home with control over the birth process," one advocate wrote.[39] Activists described natural birth as "a spiritual, potentially transformational, experience for the mother."[40] There was nothing bad about new motherhood, they explained, except the parts doctors had made bad.

This position predated the *Ms. Magazine* outrage. In Raven Lang's 1972 *Birth Book*, she argued that "hospitals through a gross oversight (as was once done with puerperal fever) may be contributing to adult neuroses through present day rituals of birth."[41] A 1974 article in the feminist magazine *Country Women* attributed "a large part of the postpartum blues syndrome" to "the shock of having been disconnected from your own labor process."[42] Famed midwife Ina May's 1975 book *Spiritual Midwifery* also emphasized the relationship between the mind and body in producing a joyful birth and postpartum outcome. Ina May and partner Stephen Gaskin wrote that in new motherhood "you get stoned on hormones," which makes you attuned and responsive to your baby. "The human baby doesn't care what's going on in the material plane so long as the mother's vibrations are cool," Gaskin explained. "But if the mother is uptight, or in an uptight situation, that can make the baby cry."[43]

If a natural birth fulfilled a mother, then postpartum depression could be the predictable outcome of a woman's less natural decisions. Natural birth advocates acknowledged the existence of postpartum distress but didn't care about raising consciousness about it the way the Boston Women's Health Book Collective did. Postpartum well-being, they imagined, was a reward of natural birth. They quoted women who, after successful unmedicated births, were *"extremely* happy," and *"terrifically* proud of myself," and "so *triumphant"* [emphasis in original].[44] But this seemed to imply that women who made other choices for the birth or postpartum were responsible for their own problems.

Natural birth advocates challenged obstetrics and championed countercultural alternatives, often suggesting that women's true liberation would come through the embrace of an essentialist, empowered motherhood. If home birth, breastfeeding, and attachment came naturally to women, then it was no surprise that women who did not opt for the natural became depressed. The implication of natural birthers' claims that postpartum depression was unnatural was that women were to blame for their own postpartum outcomes.

In time, most natural birth advocates softened these ideas, at least in published work. Elizabeth Davis's 1981 *Guide to Midwifery* described how it "is *very* common and good for the mother's tears to flow" toward the end of the first week postpartum. The 1983 *Whole Birth Catalog* reassured readers that postpartum depression was unlikely in women who had "very strong and positive" birth experiences, since "the confidence you gained will help you in the postpartum period." For mothers with unsatisfying births and post-partum depression, though, the authors counseled women that "this period *will pass*."[45] These approaches echoed the "baby blues" advice of 1950s and 1960s experts, but at least they did not directly blame women for their depressions.

In a 1987 book, Ina May Gaskin now encouraged women to have reasonable expectations for the postpartum period. May Gaskin wrote that "most new mothers will feel moody and anxious at least some of the time while their babies are very young."[46] Still, she encouraged women to not think of it as a medical condition and advocated "steps to pull yourself out of it." Women might take vitamin B, get help with childcare, exercise, and take time "to fix yourself up each day." She included the story of one woman depressed after her hospital birth, though she did not have a "true postpartum depression," reinforcing the connection between hospitals and postpartum mental illness. The book described another woman whose severe postpartum reaction included "a mythic world with visions of gods and saviors." Her treatment did not involve psychiatry, but rather a few days away from childcare and peer counseling from friends.[47]

Many feminists challenged natural birthers' idealization of birth and motherhood. "The usual earth mother roles we are cast in oppress and debase us" even when they are individually "ego-boosting," wrote one woman in the feminist zine *off our backs*.[48] Not only was natural motherhood nothing to aspire to, some feminists argued, but that kind of idealization made things worse, not better. Postpartum depression was indeed a response to a new mother's circumstances, some feminists argued. But those circumstances were not specific to how she gave birth. They were the circumstances of mothering under patriarchy.

We Sense Entrapment

Ambivalence about childbirth, childcare, and the structure of mothering permeated radical feminism of the 1970s. For women defining

themselves against their mother's generation, Freidan-esque arguments about psychologically unfulfilling middle-class motherhood
were not enough. The problems of motherhood were structural.
From the pain of childbirth to depression to infanticide, radical feminists used negative stories about motherhood as evidence of sexism in the larger society. "While we feel joy," one mother wrote, "we
sense entrapment."[49] And postpartum mental illness became one of
the best metaphors for that entrapment.

To believe motherhood was so wonderful, feminist Ti-Grace Atkinson reasoned sarcastically, we would need to believe that "the
blood curdling screams that can be heard from delivery rooms are
really cries of joy." After the birth, little improved. Using the broad
definition of postpartum mental illness still common in the 1970s,
Atkinson conflated the baby blues and postpartum psychosis. She
argued that up to "two-thirds of the women bearing children suffer post-partum blues." Then she dramatically claimed that "these
depressions are expressed in large numbers by these women killing their infants, or deserting them." Other mothers, she added, in-
ternalized their hostility until they were hospitalized with severe
depression. Postpartum depression in hospitalized women, Atkinson claimed without substantiation, was "often a euphemism for
attempted murder."[50] If being a new mom was so depressing, she
asked, if women wanted to kill their infants, then what did that say
about the institution of motherhood?

Adrienne Rich also invoked postpartum mental illness in her 1976
book *Of Woman Born*. Rich wrote about the solitary nature of sub- | 49
urban 1970s motherhood, using an extreme example to critique the
institution more broadly. Rich described Joanne Michulski, a white
suburban mother who killed her youngest two children in 1974. To
Rich, Michulski's social circumstances were as important to consider
as her psychological circumstances. Michulski was the primary care-
taker for her eight children, yet she had never wanted to be a mother.
She was often depressed, a fact well known by those around her. Despite that, her neighbors and religious community members avoided
her rather than offering help. Everyone expected her to sort herself

out. After the deaths, media stories decried the failures of local mental health services. Rich was less convinced. "But what could traditional psychiatry have done for Joanne Michulski?" she asked. It could have institutionalized her, or it could have tried to "adjust" her to motherhood. It could not have done anything to address the larger isolation and depression of motherhood itself.[51]

Atkinson and Rich both used examples of severe postpartum mental illness to make these general critiques of American motherhood. Rich especially emphasized her empathy for Michulski, admitting her own occasional maternal rage. It was all a continuum of sorts, and it was all evidence of the "violence of patriarchal motherhood." The actual issue was the taboo, the power of depression and even infanticide to upend the stereotypes of natural motherhood. Was it "psychosis," or was it a rational example of "finally erupt[ing]"? Rich argued that the public discussions of these "eruptions" were sensational and dishonest. Instead of encouraging conversations about motherhood, they installed women like Michulski as an anomalous "bad mother." The story of the "bad mother" then pressured other women to try harder to be "good mothers." Mothers needed to be "more patient and long-suffering," lest they be revealed as bad.[52]

For these writers, the point of discussing postpartum mental illness was not to medicalize it but to politicize it. If a substantial number of women experienced postpartum mental health problems—blues or rage or psychosis—consciousness-raising experience told them that personal trauma was political. In an anonymous essay titled "Fuck Motherhood," one writer asked, "how can a woman reach for the sun when she is forever reaching for a shitty diaper?"[53] Feminist writers zeroed in on the confounding problems of the postpartum, the supposed apex of maternal joy, to emphasize American hypocrisy about motherhood. Still, they did not confine the suffering of motherhood to that period. One feminist described reading about the fleeting "blues" but never about "the post partum blues you'll be feeling intermittently for the next fifteen years."[54] In another anonymous essay, a woman darkly described how "motherhood to me has meant guilt, resentment, fragmentation and mutilation."[55]

Our Bodies, Ourselves had framed postpartum mental illness as a medical and political problem. To feminist writers like Atkinson and Rich, though, it was the political part that mattered. Some radical feminists proposed collective care alternatives and increased care-giving by male partners. Some suggested middle-class childcare co-ops and babysitting trades; others suggested communes.[56] They wanted to upend the patterns of white middle-class mothering that seemed to encourage depression. "The 'devoted mother', staying at home alone with her child all day is twisted and unnatural," wrote one woman. "We need not to be isolated from each other."[57] Like in *Our Bodies, Ourselves*, these recommendations included more parental labor for fathers. In mainstream women's publications "you will only find discussions on how to bathe the baby," one feminist complained, "not who will bathe the baby."[58] Some reasoned that more equal labor would make for less postpartum distress. "Postpartum blues are cured more by help with the housework than our husband complimenting our hairdo," explained one woman.[59]

Radical feminists watched women's "bad" feelings about mother-hood "dismissed as postpartum depression" rather than taken seriously.[60] They did not picture psychiatrists saving the day, or "adjusting" women to the unreasonable expectations of motherhood. Psychiatrists were the ones institutionalizing women, or sending them home with prescriptions for "dangerous, possibly habit-forming tranquilizers."[61] Instead, they tried to flip the script. They discussed postpartum mental illness as a way of framing the problems of women's subordination.

Black Postpartum Politics

American motherhood was never a single institution. As 1970s feminists debated whether psychiatrists or society were to blame, whether to worry more about hormones or hospitals, they almost always centered white middle-class women's experiences. While individual women of color were active in women's health movement groups, most of the most prominent groups were led by white women.

Feminists of color argued that even while white women's health movement activists sometimes discussed medical racism, they did not give it enough emphasis. In one instance, Chicana labor activist Dolores Huerta keynoted a 1975 conference on women and health. The conference included panels on population control, farmworker health, racism, and imperialism. But middle-class, usually white, agenda-setting still shaped the event, and Huerta's keynote felt like it was there just to distract from how white the rest of the conference was. The Third World Women's Caucus issued a press release at the event naming their primary issues: affordable, community-controlled health services and the end of forced sterilization. This conference, they wrote, "was essentially a segregated one." The concerns of working and third-world women were represented mainly in the talks they organized themselves. The women's health movement, they wrote, "is not a legitimate movement" until it makes a meaningful commitment to all women.[62]

Black feminists of the 1970s left few records specifically addressing postpartum depression. This was not because Black women escaped maternal depression. The risk of postpartum mental problems, at least today, is linked to social marginalization, and is notably higher for Black and Mexican American women than white women because of social stressors like racism and discrimination.[63]

Inequality and discrimination in healthcare made infant and maternal mortality central to Black mothers' activism.[64] Activists eventually embraced the term "reproductive justice" to encompass this wider perspective on women's health.[65] Black women also felt social pressures to articulate a positive, warm experience with motherhood, in ways that limited Black women's use of the language of baby blues or postpartum depression. Due to structural racism, Black women were also less likely to trust medical professionals (who were still overwhelmingly white men), and more likely to fear losing their children if authorities got entangled in their business. While nearly all mothers felt social pressure, the demonization of Black mothers in politics at the time created a special burden to perform "good" motherhood.[66]

Joanna Clark, a Black opera singer, wrote in 1970 about her en-
counter with psychiatry as a new mother. In the immediate postpartum, when hospital staff criticized her breastfeeding and rejection of
circumcision, she received her "first lesson in motherhood. You are
everyone's whipping boy." Clark's problems escalated from there. She
offered a list of grievances: with city planners who did not think of
strollers when designing streets and sidewalks, with stingy welfare
benefits, with the child support court, with foster care. She rejected
white critiques of Black women like the Moynihan Report while also
calling out "brothers nattering away about how we've been lopping
off balls long enough."[67] She wouldn't abide any of the longstanding
cultural critiques of mothers in general and Black ones in particular.

Clark experienced a postpartum breakdown. She framed the issue
as being as much a reasonable response to impossible conditions as a
mental illness. She had no money, her marriage was ending, and her
soon-to-be-ex-husband could not support the children. "I refused to
go sit in the welfare office again," she wrote. "I had no intention of
going home when there was no relief in sight. The only real definitive
thing I could do under the circumstances was to nut out."[68]

Clark explained she wanted to be institutionalized so she could
sleep a couple of weeks while someone else cared for her children.
The psychiatrist at the private hospital she went to told her she could
not go there but could go to Bellevue, a public hospital with a reputation for its brutal psychiatric ward. Clark declined. He injected
her with Librium instead, which led to near-hallucinations and "a
sincere distrust in the judgement of doctors."[69] This distrust was not
unique to Clark; it was a staple of radical Black criticism of psychiatry
of the era.[70] Clark did not discuss the problems of new motherhood
in "postpartum"-specific language. She saw her mental issues as inseparable from her life circumstances, not unlike how the Boston
Women's Health Book Collective members had thought of it. For her,
the issue that women needed to organize around was not the postpartum so much as general social welfare supports for mothers.

Women of color in the women's health movement created their
own social support systems, including community women's health

clinics to serve otherwise underserved populations. Women created multiracial feminist health centers like the health elements of the Third World Women's Resource Center in Seattle.[71] Black women in Gainesville, Florida, founded a health center focused on abortion and gynecology in the early 1970s, and then an alternative birth center in 1978. Emblematic of the layered goals of Black activists' health concerns, the center included testing for sickle cell anemia alongside reproductive health services. Byllye Avery, a co-founder of the center, became a leader in the National Black Women's Health Project in the early 1980s.[72]

Avery wrote about the way the birthing center offered a happy, positive atmosphere for Black women giving birth.[73] With so few supports for Black maternal health, this positive atmosphere mattered. Avery described Black women as "empty wells; we give a lot, but we don't get much back." She linked birth inequalities and maternal mental health, though she did not explicitly discuss the postpartum. "We're asked to be strong," she wrote, but "if one more person tells me that black women are strong I'm going to scream in their face."[74]

This stereotype of the strong Black woman influenced diagnosis. Psychiatrists in the late 1960s and 1970s were more likely to diagnose Black patients with schizophrenia than depression, seeing Black patients as more "disorderly." Historically, depression has been a disease of the "civilized," and psychological research in the 1970s reinforced this point.[75] In a 1971 study on Black Southern women and postpartum depression, the male researchers lauded Black "stoicism and subtle defiance." These researchers interviewed Black and white women in the first two to three days postpartum. The white mothers were substantially more likely to rate themselves as depressed. Black postpartum women rated themselves as "happy-go-lucky, cheerful, and impulsive." The researchers concluded that Black women were less inclined toward a depression in the postpartum. Perhaps it was because of the idea of Black strength and stoicism, and perhaps it was because, they argued, the Black women in their sample were also less likely to use contraception. Noting that "the procreative function is overused in the poor," the researchers theorized that Black women might simply find motherhood "a relatively anxiety-free experience, and a source of gratification."[76] The dual conclusions—Black mothers were simultaneously stoic and "happy-go-lucky"—illustrates the range of stereotypes Black feminists were up against.

Black women's health activists argued that Black mothers' experiences were "inextricably connected" to the status of the Black family.[77] The 1965 Moynihan Report described Black families as in crisis, in part blaming Black women. Black "matriarchs" contributed to the state of low-income urban Black families, the report suggested. Black mothers were "greedy, lazy, and ignorant," and dangers to both their men and their children.[78] With social science already pathologizing Black motherhood, embracing the language of mental illness could be dangerous. While many white women also found the language of postpartum mental illness risky, white women were typically cast as "good," docile patients.[79]

Narratives of Black women's strength, adaptability, and coping were politically important in the larger context of 1960s and 1970s racism, even as they led to more stress for Black women.[80] Black women's health activism does not appear to have included much discussion of postpartum depression then, but it more broadly included efforts to address the mental health effects of the need "to transcend ordinary reality in order to survive."[81] Black researchers documented the increase in suicide rates among Black Americans over the course of the 1970s.[82] Activists discussed the importance of taking off the mask of strong Black womanhood, "a mask we wear that helps bring us closer to madness."[83]

Medicalization and Liberation

Feminists of the 1970s concerned with the postpartum had to weigh whether psychiatry was an ally or an enemy. Many radical feminists rejected the idea that male doctors could understand, let alone solve women's depression. But some feminists, like those of the Boston Women's Health Book Collective, would not let go of the possibility that a psychiatric approach to postpartum depression was beneficial.

Some feminists drew their lines pragmatically, remaining angry at both medical sexism that did not treat postpartum depression seriously *and* sexism that pathologized women's very reasonable postpartum breakdowns.[84] The way this strand of the women's health movement selectively, strategically accepted medicalization is an important predecessor to the choices of 1980s postpartum advocates.

While chemical, especially hormonal, explanations of women's emotions had long been used to pathologize postpartum women, they also offered legitimacy.[85] Descriptions of postpartum distress as "purely chemical" offered an important counter to psychoanalytic accusations of women's immaturity and frigidity.[86] Both psychoanalysis and the popular press told women in the 1960s that the baby blues were because of something within them. Feminists of the 1970s argued that postpartum distress was because of the world around them. But, some women asked, what if it was both?

In 1972, four feminists who experienced postpartum mental illness got together to write an article. Two had experienced severe depressions and two had experienced psychoses. This article, they explained, was a plea for awareness, compassion, *and* medical attention. "It is time that our needs were dealt with realistically by professionals in the field," they argued, as well as by other women.[87]

They wrote with frustration at the sheer ignorance and disinterest in the postpartum among doctors and medical researchers. So many questions remained unanswered: How widespread was postpartum depression? Who was hardest hit? Who was at greatest risk? Were the origins hormonal, and if so, how central was that piece of the puzzle? How did some women experience mild depression, and some experience such severe ones? So many unanswered questions amounted to medical neglect.[88]

The women disagreed, though, about how to handle this neglect: Should they partner with doctors or avoid them? Each of the women had received professional medical help in their depressions or psychoses, and each had criticism of that help. One woman found that her psychiatrist could do nothing for her. Another woman sought help from her obstetrician, but he dismissed her concerns. One woman who did have doctors take her illness seriously described the problems of hospitalization. They dehumanized her. They used shock and insulin treatments that damaged her memory and led to religious hallucinations. "It never dawned on me," she explained, "that I might be in for a very bad trip."[89] Despite these experiences, the women still encouraged others experiencing postpartum distress to seek a "sympathetic, supportive psychiatrist"—if they wanted one.

Even as the women argued that there was sexism in both psychiatry and obstetrics, they hoped for improved relationships. The women proposed that obstetricians hold drop-in office hours, like some pediatricians did. They emphasized that hormonal changes in the postpartum meant "there is a physical basis for doctors to deal with the topic." The interest in endocrinological changes postpartum, even among women otherwise focused on isolation and sexism as causes, suggests at least some attempt to work strategically with medical professionals. Obstetricians and gynecologists were often uncomfortable with, and almost always untrained for, women's emotional problems. "My gynecologist never talked with me about role conflict . . . in motherhood," one of the women explained, but these kinds of conversations should be as normal as the monthly urine test.[90] The four feminists did not agree on how to approach medicalization, but they united around the possibility of using medical professionals in strategic ways.

While it was important to get obstetricians, and perhaps psychiatrists, on board with postpartum health, they explained, feminist and community help was still the chief priority. They argued for postpartum consciousness-raising groups and feminist self-help, for "a forum where we can feel free to vent our feelings, whatever they may be." Such a forum, perhaps including women who were further out from their postpartum crises, "is the one thing that would have helped us all."[91] Even the women who more readily embraced medicalization wanted feminist self-help groups. One of the women explained that such a group might have kept her suicidal thoughts in check "until my doctor and I could work through the causes."[92] She did not argue that feminist self-help on its own could stop suicidal ideation, but that it might have made her situation more bearable.

In some circles, new feminist conversations about postpartum health opened up during the 1970s. Feminist therapists occasionally listed postpartum depression as an issue they could help patients through.[93] The Boston Association of Childbirth Education, for example, tested support groups for postpartum parents as a follow-up to childbirth preparation classes.[94] In Chicago and Milwaukee, a psychosis survivor and her anthropologist friend began running early postpartum self-help groups.[95] The women's health movement also inspired parent support groups that included fathers. Postpartum Education for Parents, which I discuss in depth later, began as a self-help group in 1977. Feminists in the 1970s proposed a vision of postpartum self-help, often imagined as allied with engaged and nonsexist medical professionals.

Postpartum Feminisms

In the original text of *Our Bodies, Ourselves*, Paula Doress-Worters and Esther Rome explained the problem of postpartum distress and then posed a question: What should feminists do about it? What can be done? They answered: "We, as a woman's liberation group," they wrote, can "fight those aspects of our society which make childbearing a stressful rather than a fulfilling experience." They did not fully challenge the idea that motherhood should be fulfilling, the way some radical feminists did. But they did challenge an array of social and political issues that made the postpartum hard: isolation, lack of parental leave, and the "mystique of the full-time mother." Psychiatry and counseling could help women, but not as much as women could help each other.

Doress-Worters and Rome offered one vision of the feminist postpartum. In the 1970s, though, feminists took different paths to making sense of postpartum mental health. Even as conversations crossed one another, women's health activists pushed the issue far beyond discussion of the baby blues. They brought dissatisfaction with American motherhood, with obstetrics and psychiatry, and with the dearth of resources for new mothers into a larger conversation about women's health. Feminists wrote books and led discussion and began self-help groups. The postpartum politics of 1970s feminists grounded later postpartum activism, even when that took very different forms. While postpartum mental health was not central to the women's health movement, the women's health movement was central to postpartum depression activism.

While they fashioned this path forward, the specific challenges to motherhood they made were not cohesive. Some feminists were adamant that the roots of the problem were political, and that solutions would need to come through major social change. Some embraced a more medical conception of postpartum mental illness, while others blamed mainstream medicine for the very existence of postpartum depression and advocated radical birth alternatives.

There was at least consensus that mainstream medical approaches were inadequate. Doctors did not understand or did not care, they dismissed women's distress as the blues or else called them neurotics with underlying issues. These same years, while far removed from any feminist activism, a group of psychiatrists agreed. They began a parallel conversation on maternal mental health centered on the need to medicalize it, and to distinguish it from other mental illnesses. This small, international band of psychiatrists sought to take postpartum depression out of the so-called dark ages, in ways some feminists supported and others found troubling.

3. *Psychiatric Foundations*

Dr. James Alexander Hamilton was a character. A self-described "friendly eccentric," his energy and enthusiasm made him eminently likable despite—or perhaps because of—his crusading nature.[1] "We all loved him . . . He was such a father figure," postpartum activist Jane Honikman recounted.[2] The so-called "father of postpartum depression" in the US, Hamilton helped found an international research society on postpartum mental illness.[3] He brought the society back to the US, connected activists with psychiatrists, and campaigned for American professional recognition of postpartum mental illness.

Hamilton's early biography is unremarkable. He was born in a rural part of northern Illinois in 1907.[4] His family moved to Los Angeles as a child, and his father Dwight ran a general store.[5] Hamilton earned his master's and PhD at UC Berkeley, focusing on the psychology of reading proficiency.[6] He met his future wife, Marjorie, at Berkeley as well.[7] Then he pursued his MD at Stanford, graduating just before US entry into World War II.

The war transformed Hamilton's career. Hamilton worked in the Office of Strategic Services (which preceded the CIA) as a psychiatrist. Afterward, Hamilton primarily worked as a psychiatrist in private practice and as a clinical professor of psychiatry at Stanford's School of Medicine. Hamilton became interested in postpartum mental illness in the 1950s, and in 1962 he authored the first twentieth-century monograph on postpartum mental illness, *Postpartum Psychiatric Problems*.[8] While not influential at the time, the book gained a second life in the 1980s.[9] In the book, Hamilton argued that postpartum psychosis was distinct from other psychoses, that it had unique symptoms, and that it had organic causes. Hamilton hypothesized that thyroid problems were a significant factor in serious postpartum mental illness. Postpartum psychosis was not being taken seriously enough, he argued, planting the seeds for his later activist work.

Alongside his postpartum research program, he engaged with CIA drug and radiation experiments for at least thirty years.[10] This includes the infamous MKUltra project, in which the CIA secretly tested LSD on unwitting subjects.[11] While his CIA projects appear to have been separate from his own research, the CIA funded some of that postpartum research. In 1965, a CIA-based grant awarded Hamilton funding to investigate the radioactive iodine uptake of prisoners' thyroids at the Vacaville California Prison Medical Facility. His "cover" research would be on the role of the thyroid in postpartum depression. Hamilton seems to have been much more interested in his "cover" research than his contracted research.[12] Still, he did it. Whatever those thyroid experiments entailed is also unclear; he appears to have never published those results.

Few of the psychiatrists and advocates he worked with had any awareness of his past, or had only the vague sense that he had done psychiatric work during the war. Ian Brockington, who co-founded the postpartum research society with Hamilton in 1980, was the only person who recounted Hamilton specifically revealing his association with the CIA.[13] We can speculate about the role the CIA funding and involvement played in his crusades, but not much more. I have as many questions as answers about him. He is an elusive historical character.

What is clear is Hamilton's commitment to increasing attention to postpartum mental illness carried on over decades. He described himself like "a television evangelist who gets his audience by the

Figure 3.1 Image of Dr. James Alexander Hamilton from a late 1990s magazine photoshoot. Photo by Roger Ressmeyer/Corbis/VCG via Getty Images.

sleeve and won't let go till they are also believers."[14] But he could not rouse much interest among American psychiatrists before the 1980s. He complained about the state of the field in the late 1970s. On one hand was the psychoanalytic approach, which blamed women and ignored hormones. On the other were those psychiatrists who avoided separating illnesses by causes and insisted on treating postpartum mental illness like other mental illnesses. Hamilton understood postpartum mental illness, especially postpartum psychosis, as hormonally rooted and as distinct from other mental illnesses. Frustrated, Hamilton looked abroad.

The Marcé Society

While still a small group, the research community around the post-partum in Europe, especially in the UK, was much more robust than in the US. Hamilton and psychiatrist Ian Brockington corresponded in the late 1970s over research issues around maternal bonding.[15] In 1980, Brockington hosted a conference on motherhood and mental health at the University of Manchester for psychiatrists and endocrinologists.[16] Hamilton tried to get "about 20" drug companies to fund the conference, without success. A colleague told him that to get funding they needed to found a formal organization rather than host a one-time event.[17]

After a dinner prepared by Brockington's wife during that 1980 conference, Drs. Brockington, Ralph Paffenbarger, Channi Kumar, George Winokur, Robert Kendell, and James Hamilton drank port and debated what a formal interdisciplinary and international organization for the study of maternal mental health would entail.[18] Hamilton sat on the floor and commanded the other guests to "listen to the ramblings of an old man."[19] The men agreed to name the group the Marcé Society after Louis-Victor Marcé, a nineteenth-century French psychiatrist who wrote about puerperal psychosis as a discrete disease with organic causes. The six men—they were all men—saw Marcé as a forgotten forefather, ignored for 150 years, whose conception of postpartum mental illness echoed their own.[20]

A month later, the men launched the Marcé Society formally, with Brockington as president and Kumar as vice president. It held its first official conference in London in 1982 and has held biennial conferences ever since. Birthing the first conference, Kumar joked, helped him "understand some of the psychosocial upheavals that women experience in pregnancy and childbirth."[21] Their 200-person 1982 meeting had an "uncharacteristically high proportion" of men in the audience, although a handful of women presented papers.[22] In response to concerns about the underrepresentation of women in an organization about women, the leadership sought input from women in the health professions and from laypeople. While enthusiastic about the society,

64 |

Hamilton also had some concerns. He worried it was more British than international and lacked investment in American postpartum problems. While co-founder George Winokur was also American, already a well-known researcher at this point, he did not remain heavily involved with the organization.[23] So Hamilton was the main American voice in the group its first few years.

Hamilton hosted the next meeting in San Francisco in August 1984. He appealed to American psychiatrists through a story in the *Journal of the American Medical Association*, as well as by writing personal letters encouraging research psychiatrists from around the US who had any relationship with the postpartum. He recruited Dr. Barbara Parry, a psychiatrist at the NIH. While her research on premenstrual hormones and light therapy was not postpartum specific, she had fought for a postpartum patient who wanted to keep her infant with her during treatment. George Winokur recruited his colleague at the University of Iowa, Dr. Michael O'Hara, a young psychologist who had studied the postpartum as a case study in depression. O'Hara

| 65

Figure 3.2 Photograph of activist Jane Honikman, obstetrician Dr. Jane Engeldinger, and psychologist Dr. Michael O'Hara at the 1986 Marcé Society conference at the University of Nottingham. Courtesy of Jane Honikman.

later took on leadership roles in the Marcé Society, including the presidency in the late 1990s.

For both Parry and O'Hara, this conference was invigorating and important. Parry later thanked Hamilton for the warm welcome and described becoming "very interested in that area and Dr. Hamilton and his colleagues" at the event.[24] Energy and optimism characterized the early years of Marcé. Hamilton and the other leadership encouraged researchers to imagine themselves as part of a watershed moment. Knowledge on postpartum mental health had been suppressed, ignored, forgotten. They were now going to right this wrong. Even if not all the researchers accepted Hamilton's hero narrative, the meeting was brimming with the idea that they were on to something groundbreaking.

A Decade of Depression

Some early Marcé meeting presentations were on depression, but most were on psychosis. Most members were psychiatrists or other professionals who saw women with severe mental illness. While there were some presentations on more moderate depressions and adjustment problems, the amount of interest in postpartum depression grew over the course of the 1980s. The 1980s were the decade of depression in psychiatry generally. While the term "postpartum depression" had been used sometimes before this, it was typically treated as interchangeable with the baby blues. Now, postpartum depression emerged as a separate entity. By the middle of the decade, postpartum depression would become an umbrella term for all kinds of postpartum distress.

"Adjustment problems" other than psychosis between the 1950s and 1970s were more likely to be called anxiety than depression. Most women never saw a psychiatrist, accepting the widespread definitions of baby blues as a trivial condition that would clear up on its own. Some women with anxieties and depressions in the postpartum got outpatient interventions, especially women with the means for private psychoanalytic treatment. Their distress might merit a minor tranquilizer like Miltown or Valium, or delving deeper into their psychoneuroses with an analyst.

But by the 1980s, psychiatrists increasingly agreed that distressed mothers were not just neurotic. While many still looked at women's "sexual maladjustment" or trouble "accommodating the female role," that language became dated.[25] Instead, psychiatrists shifted their attention to hormones, and then later to the brain.

In 1980, the American Psychiatric Association published a new *Diagnostic and Statistical Manual of Mental Disorders*, the *DSM-III*. This edition differed substantially from the first two. It responded to a culture shaped by criticism of psychiatry.[26] The *DSM-III* promoted an empirical, not psychodynamic, model. It focused on cataloging observable symptoms rather than addressing the unknowable causes of mental illness. It imagined symptom-based diagnosis would be more objective and replicable than what the analysts did. More measurable diagnoses, they hoped, could improve research and lead to new treatments, especially pharmacological ones.

Emphasizing the "postpartum" nature of any mental illness seemed dangerously close to making a claim about what caused an illness. The *DSM-III* therefore had no category for depression with childbirth. The *DSM-III* still discussed "psychosis with childbirth," as the *DSM-II* had, but noted that it was "to be used only when no other psychotic disorder can be diagnosed." It also included a new, chiding line: "There is no compelling evidence that post-partum psychosis is a distinct entity."[27] The book did not include language specific to a postpartum depression, and now went out of its way to undermine the postpartum psychosis diagnosis.

Hamilton had objected to previous editions, and sought to influence future revisions to treat postpartum mental illnesses more seriously. As Ian Brockington put it, Hamilton "was seized by the idea postpartum psychosis was a specific entity, with a hormonal basis."[28] Hamilton argued that the lack of a discrete diagnosis led to "many thousands of very sick women [being] very badly treated."[29] Hamilton described psychiatrists who de-emphasized the importance of the postpartum as "sociopathic" and malicious, their work "an act of female harassment."[30] Hamilton reasoned that the lack of research on and medical training in postpartum health was inseparable from the fact that there was no discrete diagnosis for postpartum psychosis or depression in the *DSM*. Hamilton became laser-focused on changing the manual.[31]

While the *DSM-III* did not acknowledge postpartum depression, the authors did substantially change the diagnosis of depression itself. After the *DSM-III*, major depressive disorder became extremely common, encompassing 40 percent of new diagnoses.[32] Before, depression had been a less common and much more severe disease, a psychotic depression that might include delusions or hallucinations. While psychiatrists still disagreed on the symptoms and causes, major depressive disorder might still mean extreme, long-lasting suicidal depression, but it also might mean fatigue and insomnia for as few as two weeks. Patients' self-reports of their mood, happiness, and adaptability grounded diagnoses.[33]

There are many reasons for this change, encompassing the influence of private health insurance, the search for professional legitimacy, and the rise of psychopharmacology.[34] Collectively, they led to more research on depression. Then fluoxetine, under the brand name Prozac, further increased investment in depression in the late 1980s. It ushered in a new class of drugs, selective serotonin reuptake inhibitors (SSRIs), which promised neuroscience as the solution to depression. The 1980s were at once an era of depression among psychiatric patients and an era of optimism about the discipline of psychiatry itself.

Depression diagnoses increased because of both diagnostic changes and the new prevalence of the language of depression in both psychiatry and popular culture.[35] As depression diagnoses increased, they did not do so evenly. Depression patients were (and still are) overwhelmingly women.[36] There are a variety of explanations why. These range from women's greater comfort with speaking to a therapist to a higher likelihood of experiencing depression-inducing events like assault, abuse, and, of course, childbirth.[37] Psychiatry reinforced this claim. Sadness, helplessness, and passivity all come off as appropriately feminine manifestations of distress. Psychiatric researchers used those same manifestations to design depression screeners. Trials and screening tools often excluded common symptoms in men, such as irritability and substance abuse. Ironically, the embrace of symptom-based diagnosis that was meant to be more objective and scientific was highly susceptible to social and cultural factors.[38] More women reported depression symptoms, and more women experienced symptoms that "counted" toward that diagnosis.

Psychiatrists explained their increased attention to women's depression as progress. The newer psychiatric approach altered mother blame in some ways, through its emphasis on biological processes beyond a woman's control. Pathology could empower, and, at least on the surface, it offered absolution from the broader attacks on motherhood. Some argued that the profession had ignored women's needs for too long, and now was the time to listen to them. For more than a decade, feminists had accused psychiatry of sexism. Now practitioners reframed themselves as allies, working alongside woman patients to help them deal with a sexist society. In their most optimistic takes, treating women for depression could even make women well enough to fight for their liberation.[39] Some critics, however, worried it would just help women more cheerfully accept inequality.

The increased diagnosis of women's depression paved the way for an increased acceptance of postpartum depression.[40] The Marcé Society grew more interested in depression, not just psychosis, over the decade. They also came to adopt the language of postpartum depression as shorthand for a variety of maternal mental illnesses, something already happening in popular culture.

While Marcé members emphasized how different they were from the psychoanalytic woman-blamers, they explained many of their goals in the family values language that permeated the 1980s. President Ian Brockington described the importance of challenging the idea that postpartum illnesses were "trivial" by producing "research on their effects on family life and the psychological development of children."[41] Marcé members argued that postpartum mental illnesses were real, and most believed they had at least partially organic

| 69

causes. These illnesses were not merely "cultural by-products of im-
personal hospital delivery in industrial society" or "antimotherhood
attitudes in some modern-day feminists."[42] Psychiatric researchers
waffled between declaring themselves the first to listen to depressed
women, while also justifying that listening with conservative talking
points on the family and feminism. It did not help that the researchers were primarily men.

Feminists Question Medicalization

In its early years, Marcé members often framed motherhood in pa-
ternalistic and prescriptive terms. Ian Brockington, for example,
acknowledged postpartum exhaustion and pain but described how
for most women feelings of "peace, fulfillment, contentment, com-
pletion and accomplishment" would carry them through.[43] "Babies
should bring happiness," a prominent woman researcher argued in
1980, "but if they do not something is wrong."[44] Another expert worried that a diagnosis like schizophrenia might suggest to a patient
that she "is a failure as a female and a mother," while he believed the
temporariness of a postpartum diagnosis would save her from that
shame.[45]

The new maternal mental health researchers at least rejected psychoanalytic explanations of postpartum illness. For some women,
this emphasis on biological psychiatry was liberatory. It made postpartum depression a legitimate problem with a name. Depressed
mothers were not alone in their suffering, and they were not to blame.
Yet these same researchers often recycled aspects of psychoanalytic
ideas and expectations.[46] This meant elevating motherhood in all the
ways 1970s feminists tried to resist—a move that was in step with the
cultural conservatism of the 1980s.

This approach suited some women who also romanticized motherhood and had limited interest in seriously changing the cultural expectations of it. They wanted to be restored to a maternal ideal. But
others questioned this premise. In the 1984 edition of *Our Bodies, Ourselves*, the Boston Women's Health Book Collective challenged what

they now saw as the psychiatric domination of the topic. Ironically, that same year, the Marcé Society lamented how little interest mainstream psychiatry showed in postpartum mental illness.

For that 1984 edition, new authors Dennie Wolf and Mary Crowe took the lead on the postpartum chapter. They challenged the role of psychiatry in defining postpartum illness, and the emphasis on biological explanations of postpartum depression. Wolf and Crowe's concern about medicalization revealed how much had changed in fifteen years. Depression needed to be understood in its social and political context, they argued. They explained how in "modern technological societies" it is normal for almost every mother to experience "periods (not just moments) of fear and depression."[47] The authors argued that women with "disabling" symptoms that do not abate should seek help from someone they trust, whether "a family practitioner, a therapist, a spiritual healer." Medical professions were useful, they argued, but had to be selected carefully. Wolf and Crowe outlined the mid-century history of postpartum mother blame and encouraged caution around any medical professional who held on to these beliefs. "What you need is practical help," they emphasized, "not psychoanalysis."[48]

While Wolf and Crowe did not doubt depression could be a medical problem, they questioned the prevalence of the diagnosis. They challenged discussions of women's depression that did not center women's political circumstances. "If you seek outside help," they wrote, "it is essential to find a counselor or therapist willing to look outside as well as within you to find the cause of your depression." Wolf and Crowe worried about prescription drugs. The new emphasis on biochemical explanations of depression was helpful for decreasing the blame on individual women, but it oversold biochemical solutions. The problem, they wrote, "is the implication that postpartum depression can be completely cured chemically with the help of mood-altering drugs. These drugs may . . . make a depressed woman feel better able to face the routines of childcare, but they do not cure depressions which are caused by nonchemical factors such as isolation, poverty or stress."[49] The approach was in line with the Boston

Women's Health Book Collective's political commitments. Sexism and inequality were inseparable from women's experience with mental illness.

Dennie Wolf was in graduate school for human development as she worked on the chapter. That fueled her skepticism about attachment theories of child-rearing and the stress they placed on mothers. Wolf described how many new mothers experience "an abrupt resorption into the heavily gendered identity of female, mommy, nurturer, caregiver, those kinds of things. And it can be a shock." Sometimes, she argued, depression can be an unconscious protest of all they are experiencing. Neither Wolf nor *Our Bodies, Ourselves* as a whole opposed psychopharmaceuticals or psychiatry, but they questioned their focus on the individual and their lack of political engagement. Wolf described the rise of the medical model of postpartum depression as treating it "as though it were native to your hormonal system or your body alone, when . . . at least a good portion of it is social and structural."

The *Our Bodies, Ourselves* approach was an outlier by the early 1980s, almost a relic of the decade and a half that preceded it. The anti-psychiatry moment of the 1960s and 1970s was on the decline, and psychological and psychiatric professionals increasingly positioned themselves as allies, empowering and supporting women. More women entered psychiatry, and the number of women in related professions like counseling and clinical social work exploded. Women joined the Marcé Society in greater numbers over the decade, and other organizations filled with woman postpartum clinicians emerged by the end of the 1980s.

As a result, psychological and psychiatric researchers in the 1980s were not oblivious to how social pressures shaped women's experiences. Even as most psychiatrists embraced biological explanations of postpartum mental illness, they acknowledged that a woman's stress, her income, her relationships were also risk factors for maternal mental illnesses, especially postpartum depression. But as medical professionals increasingly took maternal mental illness seriously,

it was more practical to try to improve an individual woman's functioning than to try to change her political and social realities.

Measuring Postpartum Depression

While *Our Bodies, Ourselves* questioned the medicalization of postpartum depression, some Marcé psychiatrists pursued even more quan-
tified and medicalized discussions. In 1983, Scottish researcher and
Marcé co-founder John L. Cox began work on a postnatal-specific
depression inventory. In 1987, he and psychologist Jeni Holden (who
had experienced postnatal depression herself) published the first
version of what became the popular Edinburgh Postnatal Depression
Scale (EPDS). (The British use post*natal* instead of post*partum*.)[50] The
American College of Obstetrics and Gynecologists recommends it for
postpartum depression screening, and encourages obstetricians to
use it at the six-week-postpartum visit.[51] The wide adoption of this
scale was an important marker for the emergence of postpartum
depression as a standalone illness in the 1980s. It defined maternal
depression as something distinct from other depressions, and also
illustrated the ways depression was becoming the focus of discussions of maternal distress.

Its creators did not actually intend it to differentiate between postpartum depression and other depressions, just to do a better job researching women during this period of heightened vulnerability to
depression.[52] There were several popular depression inventories, but
none were specific to the postpartum. The most popular of those was | 73
often unsuccessful at measuring postpartum-specific depression.[53]
It asked about sleep problems, tiredness, and interest in sex. In a
woman caring for a newborn, exhaustion or lack of interest in sex
could not be assumed to be evidence of depression.[54] Other depression scales had similar problems. Questions about enjoying life ("I
can enjoy a good book or radio or television") made little sense for
busy new mothers.[55] Researchers and practitioners wanted reliable
and more relevant scales.[56]

The Edinburgh Postnatal Depression Scale had ten questions and took five minutes.[57] None of the questions referred specifically to babies, children, partners, or other family dynamics. Instead, it asked general depression questions that had been adjusted to the postpartum context.[58] Instead of asking broadly about sleep, for instance, it asked if someone has "been so unhappy that I have difficulty sleeping." Rather than simply ask about crying, which might occur for a number of reasons postpartum, the scale clarified: "I have been so unhappy that I have been crying." The scale made a clearer conversation across researchers possible, furthering some of the same goals as the Marcé Society.

The increased body of research, and its reinforcement of the specificity of the illness, bolstered the legitimacy of postpartum depression in psychiatry, obstetrics, and eventually among the general population. It also became the subject of some controversy. Critics worried that the scale did not produce uniform results, that some women were uncomfortable discussing their feelings in an obstetrician's office—and that most obstetricians were unprepared for the discussion.[59] In 2000, Marcé Society member and nurse Dr. Cheryl Beck proposed an alternative screening tool.[60] She argued that the EPDS was missing "huge pieces of symptoms that mothers talked about . . . like loss of control, loss of self." The screening tool that she co-developed instead, the Postpartum Depression Screening Scale, was even more grounded in the idea that depression in the postpartum period was substantively different from other depression. With items like "I had trouble sleeping even when my baby was asleep" and "I felt guilty because I could not feel as much love for my baby as I should," the scale treated postpartum depression as distinct from other types of depression.

Debates over screening spilled into the twenty-first century. Later advocates would debate legislation to mandate screening, how to appropriately translate screeners, and which screening tool they would use. Mandating screening was always divisive, but the development of specific screening tools signaled how far the subfield had come, and how quickly. The ability to quantify, medicalize, and legitimize postpartum mental illness suggested the promise of professionalized postpartum psychiatry.

The Limits of a Psychiatric Revolution

The momentum of the Marcé Society and new postpartum research in the 1980s invigorated James Hamilton. His relationship with the Society, though, was not without conflict. Some issues were about diagnostic politics and priorities, and others appear to have been interpersonal. Hamilton's 1984 conference "substantially exceeded" the Marcé Society's budget for the event.[61] British leadership later made up the deficit through a series of public talks ("Soap Operas") sponsored by the laundry detergent Persil.[62] American attendance at the 1984 conference was low, so low that Hamilton described it as "rather embarrassing."[63] There was strong representation from the UK, Australia and New Zealand, and Japan. Hamilton remained active in the society but stepped down as secretary. The Marcé Society did not hold another general meeting in the US for fourteen years.

Hamilton characterized the early 1980s as a moment of disciplinary awakening—psychiatry had spent seventy-five years asleep like Rip van Winkle, he said, but now the Marcé Society could change this.[64] Hamilton alternated between these shows of optimism and frustration. The awakening was not happening quickly enough in the US, and his British colleagues' concerns and political frameworks were different. The lack of postpartum-specific diagnosis had legal and economic ramifications in the US that were not as severe in Great Britain. Infanticide laws in the UK protected women with psychosis, allowing ill women some legal protection.

The lack of a specific postpartum depression diagnostic code in the *DSM-III* continued to concern Hamilton more than his non-American colleagues. A code was necessary for health insurance payments in the US, while most Marcé leaders lived in countries that did not depend on private health insurance. Hamilton described the case of one American woman who received psychiatric treatment for postpartum suicidal ideation and other symptoms. They diagnosed her as depressed, rather than as having a *postpartum* depression. When she switched insurance companies, she was denied coverage because of her preexisting psychiatric condition of major depressive disorder. If postpartum depression was recognized as short term and separate from chronic depressions, Hamilton reasoned, that diagnosis would protect women from these peculiarities of the US insurance system.[65] This justification for changing psychiatric diagnosis did not translate to the European context.

Other interpersonal disagreements were exacerbated by distance. In a world before email and video conferencing, maintaining an international organization was difficult. The society would not even accept dues paid in US dollars until the early 1990s, and even then it was cumbersome.[66] Marcé mainly developed partnerships with British hospitals and organizations, which made the group seem less international. The fact that the society met only biennially made true collaboration between American and European doctors difficult. Ultimately, Hamilton vacillated between seeing the Marcé Society as a platform for nudging American psychiatry and lamenting the leadership's lack of concern about the problems of the American postpartum.

In the UK, Ian Brockington grew disillusioned with the society, too. In part, he saw its focus narrow onto postpartum depression and psychosis. Other issues of reproductive psychiatry he cared about, like maternal bonding and menstruation, did not fit the group's goals. He also was skeptical of their large meetings, especially in the wake of the costly California conference. Brockington was unconvinced that large gatherings advanced the field. "Back-slapping jamborees are not the way to learn," he reflected. "The study of the written word is far more effective."[67] Brockington refocused his research on bonding disorders and eventually left the Marcé Society.[68]

While poor attendance at the 1984 conference suggested a lack of excitement about postpartum illness among psychiatrists in the US, researchers did organize conference panels at the American Psychological Association, and ran a continuing education course at the 1989 conference of the American Psychiatric Association.[69] Even Hamilton, who called the United States "a hard-core bastion of indifference and ignorance," admitted there were now "a few islands of enlightenment." These islands increasingly included nonprofessionals.

Postpartum Education for Parents (PEP), a parenting support group, emerged in California in the late 1970s. By 1984, a PEP leader and James Hamilton began collaborating. Hamilton invited PEP co-founder Jane Honikman, as well as journalist Carol Dix, to speak on "community action" at the 1984 Marcé conference. From there, Hamilton's interest in women's support and self-help groups grew. US support groups and the women in them offered a new path forward for both Hamilton and postpartum politics more broadly.

4. Supermoms and Support Groups

When Jane Honikman gave birth to her son in 1972, the responsibility for another human overwhelmed her. So did breastfeeding. Like in many women's postpartum depression stories, her disappointment at giving supplemental formula bottles to the baby crushed her.[1] Honikman also felt uncertainty about her new role. In college she had been a civil rights and feminist activist. Now she was, by choice, a suburban stay-at-home mom with an unused sociology degree. While it was not unusual for a middle-class white woman to stay home in the 1970s, in feminist settings she felt self-conscious. She got embarrassed when she introduced herself to other feminists as "only a mom." So there she was: isolated, exhausted, and struggling to define herself.

Honikman's postpartum symptoms were somatic. She developed an intense stomach pain she believed was an ulcer. Eventually things improved for her, but not through psychiatry. Her recovery instead came through community. She made friends with other women with shared experience through the Santa Barbara branch of the American Association of University Women (AAUW). Sitting in the park while their children played, these women discussed mothering honestly. They shared their postpartum guilt and unhappiness. Like in so much of the feminist consciousness raising around them, it was a revelation to discover their individual problems were much bigger than them. But what could they do with this realization?

Together, the mothers founded a volunteer parents' group in 1977. They won a $500 grant from their AAUW branch, and a $300 grant from the Santa Barbara County Department of Mental Health.[2] The group discussed anxiety, stress, and emotion around early parenting. They did not discuss postpartum problems in terms of clinical depression or postpartum depression per se. They also decided they wanted progressive, involved fathers to join them. The group brought moms and dads together to learn about and support each other through early parenthood.

They named themselves Postpartum Education for Parents (PEP). While it began as a group effort, Honikman became the face of PEP. She was enthusiastic and energetic, especially about the public-facing work of writing articles. The fact that she was a stay-at-home mother allowed her more space to focus on the organization than some of the co-founders who also worked outside the home. PEP held several weekly meetings and parent education classes. They also created a volunteer-run "warm line" as a less threatening version of a hotline for stressed parents. They encouraged local pediatricians to share the number with new parents. The first year, PEP reported 550 meeting attendees. They approached 1980 with forty regular volunteers who kept the organization running.

PEP was not as radical as the women's health movement literature that had shaped its founders, but its grassroots energy and left leanings explain some of its early choices. The founders were all members of the AAUW, which was concerned with women in the workplace and life-work balance. PEP's work aligned with this. "Women were going back to work, and they were struggling," Honikman explained, "and there was so much more pressure on them, and there wasn't good quality childcare. And of course, they get depressed."[3]

PEP focused on both working and stay-at-home parents. They held daytime and evening meetings, in an attempt to be inclusive. The overall message was family-centric and middle class in outlook, but they emphasized how American society needed to change to accommodate families, and not the other way around. "Contrary to the opinion of some experts, the American family is still a thriving institution," Honikman wrote in a newsletter.[4] PEP dedicated itself to strengthening that institution, but with some tweaks. Within the nuclear family, it advocated for men's responsibilities for childcare and for openness about how hard adjusting to parenting could be.

PEP used the language of "adjusting" to parenthood rather than medicalized language. It did not see itself as primarily reaching women who were mentally ill, and it did not have resources specific to postpartum mental illness for its first ten years. PEP never intended to convey anything medical or clinical when it used the word "postpartum" in its name. Honikman joked that the founders considered naming the group "Afterbirth" but deemed it too gross.[5]

Instead, they focused on the ambiguities of new parenthood and the emotional turmoil it could bring. It is "an exciting, yet stressful time for families," they explained, which can be "isolating, confusing and overwhelming." This was a language of psychological but not psychiatric trouble, one that emphasized the importance of help but did not require that it come from a professional. In PEP's "Baby Basics" classes, for instance, they prided themselves on their volunteer-led discussion "of the feelings they had after their babies were born."[6]

Their open discussion of negative emotions in new parenthood made them unique. But emotional issues were, at least for the first ten years, discussed primarily in subclinical terms. At first, local pediatricians worried about what kind of advice warm line volunteers could offer, and if it would step on medical toes. As a result PEP emphasized that medical issues were beyond their purview. PEP elected to not endorse, or even directly name, "any specific doctor, hospital, pharmacy, or other health-related professionals or agencies."[7]

PEP groups explained how normal most parental stress was, offering reassurance rather than medicalization. They talked about sleep problems and child development. Honikman proudly recalls an early call to the warm line. An overwhelmed postpartum woman called, saying she did not think she could handle motherhood. Honikman told her about having been in the same spot, but now her children were school age; this reassured her. Maybe motherhood did get better.

Honikman wrote an article about PEP in a national parenting magazine. Women sent her over 400 letters in response. Most emphasized how much they wished they had something like PEP, and detailed instead their very limited postpartum support. The women wrote about their isolation, their lack of extended family, their stress over breastfeeding, divorce, and the difficulty of single parenting. PEP leadership emphasized their ability to help families transition through these problems, which were so often imagined as new threats to the family in that time. The existing primary responses to struggling families were all triage and crisis management, like child abuse hotlines. Instead, Honikman imagined preventative help. PEP would address the underlying "need for friendship and support" before it escalated to crisis.[8]

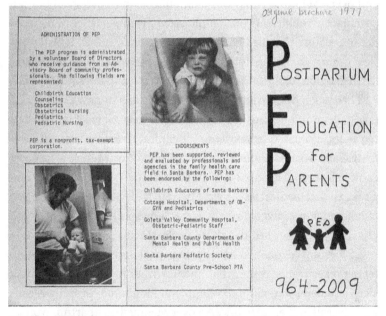

Figure 4.1 The original brochure for Postpartum Education for Parents, designed in 1977. From Jane Honikman's personal archives, Santa Barbara, California.

The PEP model of parental self-help and non-medical education held wide appeal. Women from places as diverse as Alabama, Poughkeepsie, Detroit, San Francisco, and rural Pennsylvania all wrote to PEP for help. Could Honikman tell them how to start a group, expand a group, get resources for a group? In 1979, PEP responded by self-publishing *A Guide for Establishing a Parent Support Group in Your Community*, a 100-plus-page book complete with sample fliers, warm line scripts, and guidelines for introducing postpartum adjustment issues in childbirth classes. The guide began by reiterating that the family was "still a thriving institution." PEP did not see the family as under siege the way conservative groups did but was still interested in shoring up and strengthening families.[9]

PEP was not the first parenting support and education group. There were other parent-specific warm lines and "tot lines." The breastfeeding support group La Leche League began in the 1950s and provided some postpartum camaraderie, though some women found the pressure to breastfeed did them more harm than good. Self-help and support groups exploded in popularity in the 1970s, and parent/mother's groups fit this mold. While social groups for mothers had long existed, they were often child-centric and not willing to acknowledge the challenges of mothering. They typically excluded fathers. And they often met during the day, excluding many working parents. To Honikman, the spread of more honest and more parent-centric support groups was "an actual social movement."[10] Some were grassroots and independent, like PEP, and other groups developed in partnership with hospitals or community centers.

While these groups helped countless parents, their focus on mild to moderate adjustment problems and obliviousness to severe mental health issues could frustrate and further isolate women with those problems. Some women who could barely get out of bed felt they could not share their struggles at these meetings. Severely depressed women described how attending parenting groups without a depression emphasis offered further proof of their failings. Conversations about stress or balancing work and home life were not relatable. And warm line reassurance that motherhood gets better would be at best a bandage for someone with an unrelenting postpartum depression. Honikman received a handful of letters describing severe mental illness, but these were the minority, and none of the ones she saved from this period used the phrase "postpartum depression." But for many PEP members, blunt conversations about adjustment, and camaraderie amid isolation, made the groups unique and fulfilling. "All we knew was it felt wonderful to have a safe, supportive place to meet with friends and talk about our reactions to parenthood," Honikman recalled.[11]

Family Values

Postpartum Education for Parents focused on making the family "a thriving institution." That emphasis was pointed. Amid increased numbers of white mothers working outside the home, anti-feminist backlash, and panics over sex and homosexuality, the idea of "family values" was everywhere in the 1980s. Critics invoked "family values" to shape law and policy on welfare, taxes, divorce, and even regulations on television programming.[12] Political battles over economics, welfare, and federal authority manifested in arguments centered on the intimate space of the family.

Conservative parenting advice decried divorce and the overindulgence of children, emphasizing marriage, discipline, and a family hierarchy built on obedience. They spoke at length about "family responsibility." The individual family must be responsible for itself financially, they felt, which undergirded a variety of conservative and neoliberal attacks on welfare. It also placed more pressure on parents to manage family budgets without the support of robust social services. The bar for success was impossibly high, and the consequences of failure serious. This put the importance of the emotional stability of families into sharp relief.[13]

Discussions of the need to strengthen, fix, repair, or restore the American family were relentless. Even liberals and leftists adopted the language. President Jimmy Carter discussed the "political imperative to strengthen the family," and the 1980 Democratic National Platform promised "policies which will strengthen the family."[14] The Boston Women's Health Book Collective put out a parenting-specific book titled *Ourselves and Our Children*. A history of right-wing accusations that the group and *Our Bodies, Ourselves* were "anti-family" was part of the impetus.[15]

As conservatives framed their arguments by asking Americans to "think about the children," mothers were supposed to be saving children. But mothers were also imagined to be among the threats to them.[16] Where mothers in the 1950s had been attacked as smothering, mothers in the 1980s were attacked as career-obsessed and self-absorbed. These criticisms shaped the emerging conversation about postpartum depression, leading to increased surveillance of maternal emotion and behavior. The postpartum was already a moment of especially high-intensity and high-stakes mothering where the pressure to adjust quickly was great. Now, from left, right, and everywhere in between, there was pressure on mothers not only individually but also politically. The stakes of maternal happiness were high.

The New Mother Syndrome

In the early 1980s, British journalist Carol Dix had a moderate post-partum depression. Like many of the women who became involved in postpartum work in the 1980s, Dix had a background in 1970s feminism. She wrote about *Our Bodies, Ourselves* for the *Guardian* in 1973.[17] She penned articles for the feminist magazine *Spare Rib* about the sexist social pressure on women to have children. Then something changed—perhaps something hormonal, she says—and she knew she wanted to be a mother. She moved to New York City with her American husband just before giving birth to her first child. She says she adjusted well to the first baby, in part because she could put her in a Snugli baby carrier and take her anywhere while still having an independent identity. That flexibility disappeared when she had a second child and felt much more constrained by motherhood. An unexpected trauma compounded this realization a few weeks later, when her husband was mugged and stabbed in Central Park. He recovered, but Dix became more vulnerable to postpartum stressors.

"How has my life come to this?" she wondered, echoing the cry of Betty Friedan's *The Feminine Mystique*.[18] Dix resented feeling confined in motherhood while she watched the careers of childless peers take off. Unlike most American women in the early 1980s, Dix had some language to describe her misery. She was "trapped, despondent, and consequently lethargic."[19] The British discussion of "postnatal" depression was more prominent than any equivalent American conversation; one influential newscaster publicly discussed her postnatal depression in the 1970s. Also unlike many American mothers, she had some sense that her issues were not unique to her. Nevertheless, Dix did not describe her situation as a depression or illness while she was in it. She did not seek medical treatment, and her improvement came through establishing some boundaries around motherhood, getting part-time childcare, and rebuilding her career. Having identified a silence in US conversations on new motherhood and postpartum depression, Dix figured that filling that silence could simultaneously help women and get her paid.

Going all in on her freelance writing career, Dix pitched an article on postpartum depression to several US women's magazines, which had no interest. One finally accepted it but insisted the piece "not get too heavy." Dix aimed bigger and began research on a book. She placed a questionnaire in *Working Mother* magazine—the only one open to publishing it—asking women about their postpartum experiences.[20] The questions were leading, offering respondents a language of guilt and shame to choose from: "Had you heard of PPD, or just of the three-day blues?" "Were you surprised or shocked to be so depressed?" "Do you feel guilty about having such a depression, or at your unacceptable and unexpected feelings?"[21] The questions triggered about 300 personal and emotional letters to Dix. Clearly, the subject resonated with the mostly white, professional audience of *Working Mother*.

As she researched, Dix called up professionals to provide more medical context. In 1984, she contacted Dr. James Hamilton, the "father of postpartum depression." "He is such a strong-minded person," Dix said. "For 20 years he has been battling with the American Medical Profession" over postpartum illness.[22] Hamilton's intensity convinced Dix of her book's importance and of the value of explicitly medical explanations of postpartum distress.[23] Dix adopted Hamilton's explanation of the rise and fall of the prestige of postpartum mental illness, and his blame of early twentieth-century psychiatrists for halting research into the postpartum. Hamilton's emphasis on the thyroid, especially its role in postpartum psychosis, also resonated. Dix had no experience with postpartum psychosis, but had recently had a cyst removed from her thyroid. Afterward, she had a brief bout of hallucinations and delusions about evil spirits, which helped her "understand and sympathize more with people who go through mental illness."[24] She was amenable to centering hormones in explanations of postpartum mental illness. While finishing her book, she went to San Francisco to meet Hamilton. "We spent the whole day working together and I was so pleased—he really helped pull all my ideas together," she explained.[25] Hamilton then contributed the introduction to the US edition of Dix's book.

Pocket Books published *The New Mother Syndrome* in 1985 in the US, and then released a second edition in 1988. The book came out in German, Italian, and Spanish. The US cover notably featured "a beautiful blonde mom, braided hair . . . gorgeous baby, blue eyes," although Dix's own children were biracial.[26] The white family was considered politically "neutral."

Dix begins the book by introducing "The Problem with No Name," a nod to Betty Friedan.[27] Friedan's discussion of women's neurosis and unhappiness was mostly subclinical and explicitly political. Careers, education, and rights would ease white middle-class women's dissatisfaction with motherhood. For Dix, writing two decades later, the problem was women stretched too thin balancing career and motherhood. *The New Mother Syndrome* directly discussed the

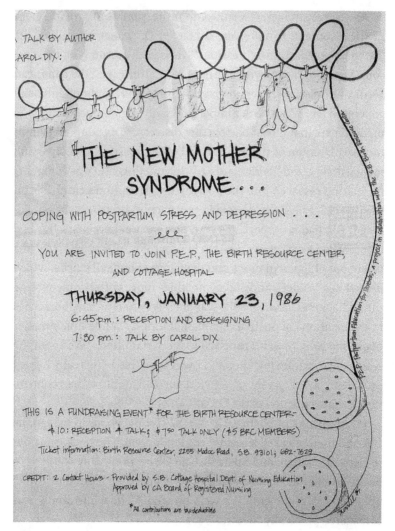

Within the image:

TALK BY AUTHOR CAROL DIX:

THE NEW MOTHER SYNDROME...

COPING WITH POSTPARTUM STRESS AND DEPRESSION...

YOU ARE INVITED TO JOIN P.E.P, THE BIRTH RESOURCE CENTER, AND COTTAGE HOSPITAL

THURSDAY, JANUARY 23, 1986

6:45 pm.: RECEPTION AND BOOKSIGNING

7:30 pm.: TALK BY CAROL DIX

THIS IS A FUNDRAISING EVENT* FOR THE BIRTH RESOURCE CENTER.

$10: RECEPTION + TALK; $7.50 TALK ONLY ($5 BRC MEMBERS)

Ticket information: Birth Resource Center, 2255 Modoc Road, S.B. 93101; 682-7529

CREDIT: 2 Contact Hours - Provided by S.B. Cottage Hospital Dept. of Nursing Education Approved by CA Board of Registered Nursing

*All contributions are tax-deductible

P.E.P. Postpartum Education for Parents, a project in collaboration with the S.B. Birth Resource Center

Figure 4.2 Flier for a 1986 Postpartum Education for Parents event featuring author Carol Dix. From Jane Honikman's personal archives, Santa Barbara, California.

pressures facing the stressed working mother, and the undervalued stay-at-home mother. Yet Dix's approach better fit the framework of self-help book than political treatise.

After explaining the structural barriers she faced in her own postpartum, Dix described her depression in psychoanalytic terms: it was an "identity crisis." Yet the solution could not be wholly individual. As Dix explained, women of the 1980s "discuss and analyze every other aspect of their lives," and when something seems off "they will push for answers."[28] Postpartum depression—PPD, as she called it—required this kind of attention. Women must demand it. Some of what Dix wrote echoed the activist language of earlier women's health feminists. But even after describing the structural problems of motherhood in the 1980s, Dix argued that the attention to the issue needed was mostly psychiatric.

After two decades of feminist disillusionment with psychiatry, the discipline had changed much by the 1980s. Biologically oriented psychiatry encouraged a new optimism. Americans grew more interested in psychiatry as brain research, psychopharmaceuticals, and MRIs all helped psychiatry seem more scientific and legitimate. New antidepressants with fewer side effects, especially the 1987 introduction of Prozac, changed the way Americans thought about depression.[29] Psychiatrists could prescribe these more precise antidepressants to patients with different degrees of severity, and media debates over the drugs normalized their use. Some feminists in the 1980s, like those of the Boston Women's Health Book Collective, worried about too eagerly embracing a "brain chemistry" model of women's mental illness. It seemed like it would overshadow the political aspects of women's unhappiness. But for many, including Dix, embracing contemporary psychiatric models seemed both pragmatic and progressive.

In *The New Mother Syndrome*, Dix rails against the most recent edition of Dr. Spock's child-rearing advice. While updated for the 1980s with a less psychoanalytic explanation of the postpartum, the Spock book offered little support for postpartum illness. It is common for women to become "blue" but it isn't serious, he explained, and most women don't get "discouraged" enough for it to be a medical depression. Dix sought to challenge this trivialization of postpartum depression, even as some feminists worried that women were being too often diagnosed with depression.

Dix countered Spock's dismissal with the work of Katharina Dalton, a British gynecologist and hormone researcher. Dalton described the frustrating neo-Freudian argument that "the woman is mentally disturbed because she has to share herself with the baby and husband." Instead, Dalton argued, "One day we will recognize that all depressions are caused by chemical disorders and imbalances." Some feminists critiqued the essentialism of this explanation. For Dalton and Dix, though, a hormonal explanation seemed both accurate and liberating. Women were not "blue" or "discouraged"; they had a biological illness.

Dix embraced this hormonal discussion of PPD, but still gave time to social and cultural factors. The problem was these factors seemed impossible to fix. Good and affordable childcare, flexible work, and maternity leave were both politically divisive and intractable. Dix tended to focus on individual solutions instead. Encouraging women to share their emotional experiences without stigma, promoting more medical research, and increasing attention and empathy from psychiatric professionals was pragmatic and offered a practical path forward.

When I interviewed her, Dix was adamant that I not overemphasize her activism. She was engaged in the endless hustle of the freelance writer. She believed what she wrote but did not see herself as making a grand statement about causes or solutions to postpartum illness. But the important role she played in connecting critical figures and raising the profile of postpartum depression is undeniable. This happenstance, the conditions driving the independent working woman (by the end of the decade she was a divorced working mother), is important to the story of 1980s women's health activism.

Despite Dix's liberal politics, she sometimes framed ill women as threats to the family. Moderate cases of postpartum depression, she wrote, "can destroy families" and "lead to divorce." They could also "set a woman's life back years."[30] In her book, Dix made dueling arguments: the pressure to be a perfect mother increased women's risk of postpartum depression *and* postpartum depression itself made women inadequate mothers. The approach reflected an uncertainty over how to frame the challenges of modern motherhood, especially for the middle- and upper-class white mother. Dix explained that women's struggle to adjust to motherhood could be painful but short-lived, or it could be a greater emotional, hormonal, and mental problem.

Dix's decision to discuss postpartum depression in the language of family spoke to the American national obsession of the era. For social conservatives, the problem of depressed new mothers seemed an obvious consequence of everything else they saw wrong with society: self-indulgence and selfishness and immaturity, a lack of respect for authority, social decay. As one conservative critic explained, women's "retreat from motherhood" was ruining families and hurting children. He claimed a woman's feelings about motherhood reflected the messages she was receiving. "If the society she lives in emphasizes the pains of motherhood and denigrates or denies its pleasures, she will approach motherhood with a negative attitude," the author argued. Unsurprisingly, he believed "women's lib" contributed to the "current retreat from motherhood" and the decline of the American family.[31]

While some conservatives railed against this supposed denigration of motherhood, it was the rise of working motherhood that really incited panic. Labor reports detailed a 44 percent growth in working mothers between the 1970s and 1980s, much of it from white married mothers. While some mothers had always worked outside the home, economic pressures of the 1970s forced more white and middle-class women to join them. While the "second shift"—the combination of unpaid mothering and paid work—rarely excited the national imagination when done by low-income women and women of color, these changing demographics made it an American preoccupation. This panic offered a clear indication of which mothers mattered to the national imagination.[32]

Discussion of the "working mother" was always political, but media often individualized the problem. Polemics on the state of the family also trickled down into stacks of glossy magazine articles and pop books. Many focused on the "supermother": a modern harried mother trying to have it all.[33] The trope, which emerged in the wake of the increased visibility of the working mother, was everywhere. And on one thing liberals and conservatives could agree—the supermother was set up for failure.

The Supermother

So what was the imagined supermother of the early 1980s up to? She was "fixing breakfast and applying mascara after four hours of sleep." She was "preparing dinner after working eight hard but successful hours."[34] She was "a working mother devoting time and energy to a career" who also still functioned as "a fifties-style mom."[35] The supermother was the family's "breadwinner, maid, cook, cuddler and family chauffeur," according to one syndicated column.[36] That column described the high numbers of these overstressed and overwhelmed women, and offered them tips in preparing for Christmas. "One lunch hour may not offer enough time to complete your Christmas shopping," the columnist admitted, "but there's always tomorrow."[37] The piece ended by noting that if stress becomes unmanageable, women should seek "professional help" after the holidays. This was the formula for an article on the supermom. It emphasized how hard it was to be a working mother, offered "helpful tips" for her to meet un-meetable expectations, and concluded that if a working mother could not adapt she might need individual psychological help.

Radical feminists hated the "supermom" concept. Calling a woman super for accepting this second shift was an insult, not a reward. Under capitalism, the only way to show mothers mattered was to pay them for the labor of mothering. But that wasn't happening. In the US, managing things like childcare and work balance was up to each individual family. The idea of the "supermom" placed the onus on individual women. These supermothers were free to "have it all" if only they accepted the ceaseless labor and judgment that came with it. Working motherhood became increasingly framed as a "choice." Its hardships were simply the burden of individual women and families, and did not merit accommodation.[38] Instead of encouraging workplace flexibility, feminists argued, US capitalism demanded that individual women navigate a lack of resources and options to emerge as a worthy "supermom." Then individual women's apparent successes would be used to prove that the impossible setup was possible, if only one could be "super" enough.

Although the archetypal supermom was white, the concept was also weaponized against Black middle-class moms. One 1984 article in *Ebony* described the stakes of the Black working mother. If she was single, her income was necessary for the family's survival, especially as welfare was being gutted. If she was part of a two-income family, her earnings might be what boosted the family into the middle class. In either case, "she is often the key to whether generations of Black children are condemned to poverty or whether they can achieve economic stability." The stable family unit was also "the nucleus for the community." This further raised the stakes of the Black working mother. Black women also navigated institutional racism and sexism at their workplaces. The myth of the supermother, the author argued, was dangerous for Black women not only because of the unreasonable expectations, but also because it undermined attempts to challenge structural problems like daycare availability, unequal pay, and racism at work by suggesting a "super" enough woman could manage.[39]

Many critiques of the supermom trope did not demand a restructuring of the American economy, though. Instead, they complained that the "supermother" was bad because it was unrealistic and harmful to women's emotional health. "We feel America has a lot of respect for motherhood, but it has almost no respect at all for its mothers," one woman explained.[40] That stress was compounded in the 1980s by all kinds of other pressures. Panics over car seat safety, daycare, sleep schedules, and child enrichment filled women's magazines.[41] Child-rearing expert T. Berry Brazelton pushed for government-funded maternity leave for working mothers but justified it by placing a huge emphasis on mother-infant bonding, and accusing working mothers of "a lack of passionate commitment" to their pregnancies.[42] Mothers were surrounded by a "hyperventilating version of attachment theory" and guilt at their failure to live up to it.[43] A mother's emotional

| 93

struggle, whether in the form of mild unhappiness or serious depression, seemed yet another risk to her child.[44]

It was nearly impossible to manage all this, especially in early motherhood. Carol Dix described the pressure on mothers told to be "superwomen, superwives, supermoms" as well as "happy people."[45] She argued that the existence of postpartum depression showed how flawed these expectations of mothering were. Ironically, the back of her book contained ads for other books the press published: *Teach Your Baby Math*, *How to Raise a Brighter Child*, and *Childwise: A Consumer Guide to Buying the Safest and Best Products for Your Children*.[46] Even when open conversations about postpartum depression challenged "super motherhood," the imperative to be super lurked a few pages away.

Not only did the pressure to "super" mother stress postpartum women, so did the fear that their postpartum depression would irreparably harm their infants. Some of the psychiatric literature argued that mothers with depression would harm the cognitive and behavioral development of infants. This could be strategic, in the sense that framing women as risky encouraged more attention to postpartum mental health. Evidence of child development problems, for instance, might be enough "to justify strenuous efforts to detect and treat maternal depression," one sympathetic psychiatrist argued.[47] But even if there was strategic value in describing unwell mothers as dangerous and children as at risk, it also fed right into the mother blame and conservative family values orientation of the moment.

Conservative Attacks on the Supermother

The trope of the supermother might have frustrated feminists, but it also upset many conservatives. To them, the "supermother" embodied a major anxiety: the declining status of the stay-at-home mother.[48] One particularly fiery letter to Dear Abby came from a woman who "had it up to [her] eyeballs with phrases like 'working mom' and 'supermom.'" Explaining that she felt attacked by the presumption she was "lazy or brain-dead" as a "less than super" mom, she then turned her attack on mothers working outside the home. She explained that the working mother likely did not have time "to read to [her children], sing songs, bake cookies, [or] go for walks," and that this working mother might not be there to witness her child's first steps, first tooth, or first words.[49]

Perhaps the most influential anti-feminist of her generation, Phyllis Schlafly decried the "supermother" as part of a larger feminist attack on motherhood. Schlafly critiqued feminist arguments about the "drudgery" of childcare and the idea that women needed careers outside the home for fulfillment. She railed against daycare, especially the idea of government-funded daycare. Ironically, even as Schlafly decried the idea of a supermother, she crafted her own image as a conservative supermom. Reporters marveled over her ability to do political writing at night, while she presented herself as spending her days baking bread, nursing babies, and managing with the "household hubbub."[50]

Schlafly's opposition to feminism rested on the idea that motherhood offered women social and political privileges, not disadvantages. Feminists, she complained, think an example of women's oppression and the patriarchy "is that we expect mothers to look after their babies."[51] Instead, Schlafly waxed poetic about motherhood. No career success, she argued, "can compare with the thrill, the satisfaction, and the fun of having and caring for babies . . . More babies multiply a woman's joy."[52] In her bestselling *The Power of the Positive Woman*, Schlafly told stories of powerful career women who regretted not having children. While daily chores could be dull, she conceded, a mother with a positive attitude could learn to make the most of them. "Most wives," she argued, "remember those years of diapers and tiny babies as the happiest of their lives."[53]

Schlafly's political arguments depended on this exalted rhetoric of motherhood. She specifically vaunted early motherhood for confirming the naturalness of the maternal role. In her account, nurturing was the "overriding psychological need of a woman," both central to women's mental well-being and necessary for the continuation of humanity. This left little recourse for women—especially conservative Christian women—when their transition to motherhood was not easy and joyful. Schlafly ordered cheerfulness in almost all circumstances, describing a positive woman as someone who "isn't always happy [but] she is always *cheerful*." She chided the dangerous, indulgent advice that women be "themselves." They can be so much better than that.[54]

The political value attributed to joyful motherhood in conservative Christianity of the era did not ban discussion of blues or depression, but it did require that it not challenge motherhood (especially stay-at-home motherhood) itself. As one Christian writer explained, "I do not have to be 'Super Mom' in other people's eyes. God . . . does not expect more of me or my child than what He planned. He also does not expect less of me or my child!"[55] Conservatives assured women they were valuable as stay-at-home mothers and expected them to transcend any emotional challenges through faith and with grace.

The required happiness of early motherhood was also used to buttress arguments against abortion. Opposition to abortion regularly bled into battles over motherhood and womanhood at the time. The abortion issue raised the stakes of mothers' contentment. As anti-abortion activists at Crisis Pregnancy Centers insisted abortion caused mental illness or a "post-abortion syndrome," it became more important to talk about the ways pregnancy and new motherhood brought about mental wellness. Abortion, it was said, could make a woman go insane with guilt and sadness. The claim was that her womanhood and mental health would be destroyed by this rejection of her natural maternal role. The "aborted woman" could be depressed or even psychotic, drug addicted and promiscuous, abusive and unlovable—all resulting from this supposedly unnatural decision.[56] When anti-abortion activists embraced this line of thinking, they came to describe abortion as a threat to women's maternal nature.

Abortion was only one such imagined threat to motherhood, alongside others like feminism, divorce, and women's paid work. The Christian *New Mothers' Guide* described the 1980s as a time when

96 |

motherhood is "undergoing constant scrutiny." Many women, the guide explained, have gone to "great extremes" to make "an image of mothering that appeals to their needs" while rejecting the idea of the traditional stay-at-home mother.[57] This perceived threat to traditional motherhood shaped other conversations about parenting. The evangelical childcare guide *On Becoming Babywise* alleged that a "proliferation of teenage pregnancies and broken families" owed to the "democratic parenting" of the 1970s and 1980s.[58] This elevation of the traditional family and motherhood could serve as a boost for women who felt threatened in the age of the "supermom." It also placed even more weight on motherhood. The expectations could be crushing.

Many Christian parenting guides ignored the possibility of mental distress postpartum, but a few entered the conversation. One 1986 guide stood out for arguing that "baby blues can hit Christian mothers even harder than the rest of the populace." This was because, besides the usual problems of new motherhood, there was "the guilty notion that you wouldn't be feeling this way if you were really trusting the Lord." The author reassured women it was not about their faith, but a combination of hormones and fatigue. She recommended time and prayer, reminding yourself that "with God's help, I will emerge from this victorious."[59] Echoing period anti-abortion language, she described women who initially worried they couldn't handle the responsibility of a child, but eventually found their prayers answered as their confidence grew.[60]

Likewise, one guide described the "tears and anger" of early motherhood and encouraged women to "pray for strength for yourself and other new mothers to make it through the blues." Like many secular books of the 1980s, they offered the vague advice that if a depression unexpectedly persisted "in a severe form for a very long time," a woman should consider finding a "professional."[61] This brief warning implied that women with problems more serious than "blues" must indeed be abnormal. Their inability to assimilate into this version of intensive motherhood only reinforced how well most new mothers would adjust.

We Need a Support System

In 1985, a mother offered another argument against the "supermom," from neither an explicitly conservative *nor* an explicitly feminist perspective. Eileen Larlee framed the problem not only as one of unreasonable expectations, but as one critically rooted in loneliness and isolation. "The supermom flying around with her cape is by herself. That can be dangerous," Larlee argued. Instead of focusing on independence, mothers "should be striving for . . . interdependence. We need a support system, family and friends."[62] While Betty Friedan wrote in the 1960s about how stay-at-home motherhood isolated women, now mothers articulated their own loneliness. "Gone are the days when mothers met with their neighbors over the back fence or in each other's kitchens," one nostalgic journalist wrote.[63] She added, though, that some women were creating their own ways around the problem through new mothers' groups.

The four women who founded Postpartum Education for Parents (PEP) in Santa Barbara were addressing these issues of isolation and loneliness, especially in the early postpartum. One of them, Judy Mrstik, described the difficulty of having her baby "2,000 miles from family and 3,000 miles from friends." She worried constantly about the cries of her colicky son, but she and her husband did not know whom to turn to. "Without the special support of close family and friends," she explained, the "TOTAL responsibility for this new life weighed heavily upon us." They did not know what they were doing wrong, as they listened to the baby cry. Only when she met other parent friends did Mrstik stop feeling so alone.[64]

PEP was cautious in this volatile moment of family politics. With its grant funding and broad mission statement, the founders did not believe they were representing any one kind of mothering. They supported working mothers with specialized support groups, but also held daytime meetups for stay-at-home mothers. Again and again, they reiterated the importance of helping parents find the confidence to parent their own way, rather than getting overwhelmed by advice books and experts.[65] PEP promised its phones were answered by "nonjudgemental listeners" who "do not teach or preach."[66] Its parent support groups and warm line were meant to encourage open conversation, which they attempted to do in both English and Spanish. Critically, "We are not giving advice on medical matters, but providing a sympathetic ear for everyday frustrations," PEP emphasized.[67]

The group told the story of one warm line caller, a woman with a ten-day-old baby. "I need somebody here with me," the moderately depressed woman explained. "I just can't get through another day by myself." The woman was local, so a PEP volunteer spent most of the next day with her, and afterward remained in phone contact with the woman. In a few days, she had weathered the worst of it and was doing better.

PEP focused on mild to moderate postpartum distress, and its volunteers rarely used the language of depression. They would deal with the loneliness and sadness and confusion about parenting, the pressures facing the "supermom," and would quickly refer anything more serious to a medical professional. But some women argued that embracing medicalization was not the same as arguing medical problems should only be dealt with individually. Instead, they said, these serious and doctor-managed postpartum problems also needed peer support groups.

5. A Different Kind of Women's Health Movement

In December 1983, Nancy Berchtold gave birth. It was a long birth; the New Jersey teacher pushed for two and a half excruciating hours. After delivering her daughter, Berchtold began hemorrhaging. For hours, no one at the hospital noticed the extent of her blood loss. While she was eventually treated, they did not give her a transfusion because of fears of hepatitis in the blood supply. Berchtold was weak and anemic when she, her husband, and their newborn drove home.

Things got bad quickly. Berchtold explained that overnight she had "turned into Supermom." This was not the "supermom" debated in the magazines of the 1980s, though. This was an extended manic episode. She was up all night nursing, cleaning, cooking, and decorating the Christmas tree. She could not stop to sleep and couldn't slow her racing thoughts. Every airplane she heard overhead might be about to drop a nuclear bomb. She called friends to ask strange questions: How do I find the missing puzzle piece? She had no appetite. Her husband and mother worried, but they also did not know how to think about the situation. Was it just a "baby blues" phase that would pass, or was it more serious? When her husband returned to work, her situation worsened. Her husband ultimately called the obstetrician, who directed her to the hospital. They admitted her for psychosis.[1]

Berchtold's hospitalization was a blur. The hospital did not allow her to see her daughter. While Berchtold was confident that she had not harmed her daughter, the lack of visitation convinced her that her daughter was dead. Antipsychotic medication helped her, and when discharged she went to stay with her parents for extra support and supervision. After her recovery from psychosis, Berchtold became depressed. "I remember waking up at one point . . . there would be a bird chirping and the sun would be rising and I'd be like ugh, I didn't want the day to come." She credits psychiatric intervention, antidepressants, and daily visits from her mother-in-law for helping her through both illnesses. Berchtold describes those illnesses as postpartum psychosis and a clinical depression that was similar to postpartum depression.

Berchtold subsequently sought other kinds of support and community. She had the benefit of a supportive family but didn't know any other women who had been through what she had. She knew how rare postpartum psychosis was—estimated at one in a thousand births—and believed no one could fully understand. Still, she believed she could find other new mothers who wanted to talk about their (non-psychotic) struggles. When her daughter was five or six months old, she drove to Princeton, New Jersey, to attend a moms' group at the Family Resource Center. Berchtold never shared her full experience with the group; she believed the psychosis would horrify them. Still, the meetings were "like heaven on earth" to her. Discussing topics like returning to work and mixed emotions about breast-feeding invigorated her. Berchtold made one friend in the group who privately admitted her own severe postpartum depression. After a bit, Berchtold had an idea: a new mothers' group specifically for women like them to talk openly about postpartum mental illness.

Women like Berchtold developed support groups for postpartum mental illness in the 1980s, and the networks of these groups made up a social movement by the end of the decade.[2] The most prominent ones in the US were Nancy Berchtold's Depression After Delivery (DAD) and Jane Honikman's second organization, Postpartum Support International (PSI). After Berchtold founded DAD, other women

Figure 5.1 Photograph of postpartum activists Jane Honikman and Nancy Berchtold. Courtesy of Nancy Berchtold.

launched chapters around the country. Honikman began PSI to organize postpartum professionals and support groups, built on her experience with Postpartum Education for Parents. DAD existed independently for over twenty years, while PSI still exists today, with volunteers in every state, online and in-person support groups, and a toll-free helpline.

It is difficult to overstate the role these two groups played in establishing the contemporary landscape of postpartum depression in the US. As we've seen, in the 1980s motherhood was aggressively political.[3] But these postpartum mental health groups sought to create a less polarizing political space. Although the women's health movement and 1970s feminism were substantial influences on DAD and PSI, postpartum activists of the 1980s saw their project differently; they tended not to question motherhood, psychiatry, and obstetrics. DAD and PSI aimed to include stay-at-home and working mothers and carefully danced around judging either. They almost never took a partisan political stance. Instead, postpartum activists centered on raising awareness about postpartum depression. They adopted the

consumer orientation that was slowly taking over other mental illness activism, whose reformist efforts fit well with the middle-class,
private insurance orientation of those at the helm of the movement.[4]
They married grassroots resources and support group settings with
psychiatric alliances and approaches. This was a serious women's
health movement, but one with a distinctively 1980s politics.

Depression after Delivery

The mothers' support group Nancy Berchtold attended was not for
women with mental illness. So she set out to create a group that was.
Berchtold read everything she could find about postpartum mental
illness. She saw estimates that one out of ten women experienced
some kind of postpartum depression. After that, she eyed the women
in her new mothers' group differently, wondering who else was
struggling with something beyond diaper selection.

In her research, she found out about the Pacific Post Partum Support Society, founded in Vancouver, British Columbia, in 1971, the
oldest group of this sort in North America.[5] As a product of the 1970s,
it had a less medicalized and more openly feminist orientation than
later groups.[6] Berchtold spoke with Penny Handford, a key figure in
the group, who encouraged her to start her own group. Berchtold
placed a free ad on the community page of the *Trenton Times*: "Support
group forming. Mothers who are experiencing anxiety or depression
after the birth of the baby please call Nancy." And women called. The
immediate interest amazed Berchtold. They were not women with
minor anxieties or "baby blues," either. Berchtold thought she would
never meet someone else who "was hospitalized and put in restraints
and drugged with these drugs that made you into a zombie." But now
she was getting calls from women who had hospitalizations, women
who also had life-changing postpartums.

The women first met at one of their houses and later used a room
at the YWCA. They named the group Depression After Delivery, or
DAD. They chose the name hastily and did not realize how confusing the acronym would be, or how important an entity they were

creating. Their first YWCA meeting was in 1985, when Berchtold's daughter was about eighteen months old. She was long past her psychotic episode, and her depression was mostly in remission. But she still had a lot to process and found that helping other women seemed to help her. "Slowly it dawned on me that I was not the only one out there to have gone through such a devastating experience and that other women too needed to find sympathetic ears to talk to."[7]

In some news profiles, writers argued that Berchtold was "fueled by the anger she felt at . . . medical hierarchy."[8] There was a degree of that, to be sure. But the real motivation was the evergreen motivation of any support group: this desire to help other women, and through that to help herself. As one DAD member described it, peer support was a revelation: "What a relief to talk to someone who had gone through it! And, to know it will go away!"[9] Jeanne Watson Driscoll, another early member, describes the meetings as "a place of warmth and concern." Berchtold's purpose, Driscoll explained, "was really taking care of the women—consciousness raising, getting people to talk about it, not being afraid to come out of the closet and discuss it." Berchtold's own account of her activism frequently frames it in that language of gendered care work. The emphasis on emotion, care, and uncompensated labor as motivation was not unique to Berchtold. Many women in the PPD support movement described "a culture of caring," sometimes framed as a distinctively female culture of caring, as part of what distinguished the movement.[10]

As she expanded DAD, people often told Berchtold about what a difference the organization had made for them and their families. That became "another reason to just keep going and going." Even as the organization grew, Berchtold kept her day job as a teacher. "I was never paid as director," she explained. "I was never paid as president. Never. I just wouldn't have done that." In the early years, a mix of adrenaline and that care-driven passion fueled Berchtold and DAD. The group organically expanded to not only include a support group but also take on advocacy work. They offered meetings and made information about postpartum mental health available to anyone who requested it. They scrounged up funds for photocopies and stamps. Berchtold's mother-in-law was an accountant who helped them track donations and expenditures. Volunteers stuffed envelopes. Berchtold described it as "grassroots" and then corrected herself. "There's a better word than grassroots. It's just like this community," she explained. These women "survived this and were just so intent on helping others and making sure that women survived this, that babies survived this, that families survived this. It was just that kind of passion."

Unlike their Vancouver predecessors, DAD leadership never understood being grassroots or passionate as at odds with a medical model of postpartum depression. Even before the first meeting, Berchtold sought a medical advisor. Many of the early members were "severely impaired women" processing serious postpartum problems, and Berchtold wanted to be sure she was okay from a legal perspective.[11] She met Dr. Ricardo Fernandez through a friend of her husband, but he said he knew very little about postpartum mental illness. There had only been one paragraph on the subject in his main psychiatry textbook, he explained. The fact that he admitted his ignorance, and his willingness to learn, pleased Berchtold. Fernandez became an expert at the same time he began advising DAD. Postpartum depression also became one of his private practice specialties.

Berchtold and Fernandez were "a team" for ten years. Journalists loved to quote Fernandez, who often spoke in colorful language. Fernandez described Berchtold as "a dynamo of a lady" and "a pit bull who won't stop charging until it gets what it wants."[12] Berchtold insists she was "passionate but not vicious!" Even more important than the color commentary in these media appearances was Fernandez's medical degree and medical explanations. They complemented Berchtold's message of care. As a male psychiatrist—even one freshly self-taught on postpartum disorders—he offered authority and, critically, legitimacy to DAD.

In the earliest years, Fernandez's arguments used psychoanalytically tinged language. He advised families to "keep an eye out" for depression in women with previous psychiatric illness or "who have poor relationships with their mothers."[13] For postpartum activists,

too much emphasis on a woman's psychiatric history seemed to di-
minish the idea that postpartum illness was a distinct disease, rather
than a variation of a "regular" depression. The focus on a woman's
relationship with her mother sounded sexist and dismissive. Later
Fernandez centered "chemical imbalance" and hormones in public
conversations, an approach more clearly aligned with late 1980s postpartum activism.[14] Hormonal language was more in line with contemporary research on postpartum, and with the direction of psychiatry as a discipline.

While DAD's broader legitimacy came from its enmeshment with
psychiatry, its core energy came from Berchtold and a growing army
of volunteers. Berchtold received a $7,500 development grant from
the New Jersey Self-Help Clearinghouse. She also connected with
Carol Dix. Dix incorporated Berchtold's story into the second edition of *The New Mother Syndrome*. Then, amid public interest in an
infanticide case, Dix, Berchtold, and psychiatrist Barbara Parry appeared on the talk show *Donahue*. Within seven months, representatives from DAD (mostly Berchtold) appeared on nine television
shows and two radio shows.

The media appearances fueled DAD expansion. After seeing
Berchtold and Dix on *Donahue* in 1985, an Ohio woman, with Berchtold's help and blessing, founded Depression After Delivery Ohio.
At first, that chapter began with more direct medical support; they
based their work in a local hospital and a nurse led its meetings. One
1987 newspaper profile of the branch illustrates how tense navigating these relationships could be. While the journalist emphasized
research showing "a true biochemical base for the problems," she
also quoted an obstetrician at the hospital who attributed most depressions to "guilt feelings" after mothers' negative thoughts.[15] The
chapter and its supporting hospital eventually split, and DAD Ohio
moved to the local YWCA.[16]

DAD Ohio was just the beginning. In the same year, women
founded a chapter in southern New Jersey. By the spring of 1987 there
was a northern New Jersey chapter, a Seattle chapter, a Pittsburgh
chapter, and a Los Angeles chapter. By 1989, there were fifty-two

DAD chapters nationwide. While all coordinated with DAD national in New Jersey, each also had its own goals and approach to postpartum. Most chapters drew on hormonal explanations of postpartum illness, and framed these explanations as critical to helping women feel better about their postpartum experience. In an interview about the Utah chapter, Berchtold explained how "women were reassured that their depression results not from some weakness of will or from their inadequacies as a mother, but from the hormonal changes that come with childbirth." To Berchtold, the hormonal explanation was liberating. Women should not feel guilty or weak, and they are not responsible for their depression. Still, Berchtold explained, "We're getting resistance from the women's movement because we say it's hormonal."[17] Most postpartum activists embraced a hormonal or related biological cause as the primary explanation of postpartum illness by the late 1980s, but this embrace was not uncomplicated.

Postpartum Support International

Dr. James Hamilton connected with Nancy Berchtold in 1987. "I wish that I had thought of organizations like yours 25 years ago," he wrote her.[18] She found Hamilton charming, funny, and "down to earth." He always seemed genuinely grateful to postpartum activists for the work they were doing, even as he downplayed his own role in it. He also told Berchtold there was another group she needed to know about, Jane Honikman's Postpartum Education for Parents (PEP). Berchtold was already aware of PEP through both Peggy Hartford in Vancouver and Carol Dix, but she had not reached out to Honikman yet. PEP was postpartum specific but not mental illness specific. Berchtold worried it was another "finding the best diapers" organization. But it was clear the women needed to talk. Hamilton told her that that summer in Santa Barbara Honikman was bringing together as many postpartum groups as they could find.[19] Berchtold agreed to attend. That meeting launched Postpartum Support International.

Carol Dix had introduced Hamilton and Honikman back in late 1983. Hamilton felt stifled in his attempts to raise the profile of postpartum mental illness, and believed consumer voices could help. He enthusiastically took on the activist, encouraging her to speak at his 1984 Marcé Conference. After, Honikman shifted her energy from so-called normal parental adjustment issues to postpartum depression. Dix sensationally recounts that Honikman's introduction to post-partum depression was "as though someone had lifted a veil from her eyes." She remembers Honikman declaring "'This is the missing link!'"[20] While it was probably not so cinematic a moment, before it Honikman had no medical language for the desperate postpartum warm-line phone calls she had been fielding for years. Now she had that language and all the clarity it promised.

Honikman returned from the 1984 meeting with a mission.[21] She brought the language of postpartum depression to Postpartum Ed-ucation for Parents, and to her new job at the Santa Barbara Birth Resource Center. In 1985, she ran a community survey of how Santa Barbara medical professionals were encountering postpartum stress and depression. What did they see, how did they treat it, whom did they refer women to? She defined "postpartum stress" in the survey, a reminder of the ways postpartum activists shaped the terms of this conversation. "Postpartum stress and depression is an emotional re-action with aggravating symptoms following childbirth" that could include "insomnia, heavy crying (commonly known as the 'baby blues'), moderate to high anxiety, changes in marriage . . . or loss of interest in sex." The results showed that many clinicians saw women with this kind of postpartum stress. It also showed that most clini-cians didn't know where to refer them: there was no clear network of Santa Barbara psychiatrists or counselors or peer support.[22]

Jane Honikman and Carol Dix agreed on the need for a coalition-style group that would help fill this gap, not simply in Santa Barbara but nationally—or maybe even internationally. The women shared in the desire to make postpartum depression better known, though their motivations were different. Dix wanted to write another parent sup-port book, and if it could tie in with a new, international postpartum depression organization that would be all the better. She suggested Honikman found "PEP International"—Dix would "be plugging [it] through the book" while Honikman could focus on building the organizational network.[23] Later she suggested they name a new group after her earlier book: New Mother Syndrome.[24]

Honikman saw an organization as the next step for her growing work on postpartum depression. She started a specialized support group within PEP called "The Emotional You." It focused on non-medical (but certainly pro-psychiatry) support for women with moderate to severe depression.[25] In 1987, Honikman co-authored a pamphlet on postpartum mental health also called "The Emotional You." PEP encouraged her efforts but never prioritized postpartum depression. While Honikman remained involved with the group, she transitioned most of her energy into postpartum mental health.

Once Hamilton realized how useful lay activists were to his goals, he found ways to nudge those goals closer to his own. Even in Hamilton's first conversations with Jane Honikman, he worked to convince her that the two were on the same page. Hamilton admitted his work was on rare, extreme cases of psychosis that affected only one out of a thousand women. But he also explained that British research suggested about one in ten women had postpartum problems "closer to the 'normal' disability." PEP surely worked with some of these women even if they were undiagnosed. Hamilton suggested Honikman think of it all as a continuum, which offered a way of helping her slot her activism into this more pathologized framework for postpartum distress.[26]

With encouragement from Hamilton, Honikman planned the 1987 meeting of postpartum depression groups from across the country. The gathering, held in Santa Barbara in June at the Birth Resource Center, included PEP, DAD, and the Pacific Post Partum Support Society in Vancouver.[27] The San Diego group Parents Adjusting to Parenting, co-led by psychologist Susan Hickman and postpartum psychosis survivor Susan Host, attended.[28] Other attendees included lawyers, psychiatrists, pediatricians, psychologists, nurses, social workers, and counselors.[29]

Honikman wanted to make something like the Marcé Society but for "the nonprofessional world."[30] By this point she had seen the limits of Marcé for non-psychiatrists. Honikman was told her talk at Marcé's 1986 conference would be better suited to the hors d'oeuvres hour than the main program. Carol Dix described how the Marcé newsletter's review of her book was "still grudging with their praise," supporting a larger belief that the society was not very interested in nonprofessionals.[31] So Honikman would build something that would revolve around the interests of laywomen and self-help networks, not the needs of psychiatric professionals. But drawing that line was not simple, and Honikman wanted to engage clinicians at the same time she organized lay postpartum activists.

MDs gave all the meeting keynotes. James Hamilton and British researcher Dr. Deborah Sharp spoke, as did a local OB-GYN and a pediatrician. It was Hamilton's "encouragement and support of women's self-help groups [that] brings us together this evening," Honikman explained to the audience. Hamilton gave an exceptionally technical talk on endocrinological research, perhaps better suited to Marcé. His peculiar decision to address the medical professionals rather than lay activists also meant discussing the "patient" as if she were separate from all the women in the audience. The patient doesn't need to know the controversy over causes and does not expect a complete explanation of the illness, he explained. Merely "the identification with a reasonable physiological phenomenon has enormous psychotherapeutic value."[32] For Hamilton, women needed to be told postpartum illness was real, and more than that they needed to know it was physiological. This was critical to their healing. This approach elevated the biomedical model, of course. More interesting was the assumption that audience members were advocates, activists, or were themselves clinicians, that they existed apart from the everyday patient.

Nevertheless, Hamilton's talk seems to have gone over fine with the mixed crowd. Dr. Deborah Sharp's keynote was more controversial, a preview of tensions between support groups. Sharp presented research on general practitioners screening women for moderate postpartum depression. She rattled off a list of risk factors, including whether a woman's husband was out of work, whether a woman had

| 111

financial problems, whether she had a history of emotional problems, and whether her marriage was harmonious. Audience members interrupted to ask her to clarify. Sharp's emphasis on social risk factors was at odds with Hamilton's focus on hormonal change. "I feel we have a real serious problem," said the first woman commenting during the Q&A. The list of predictors in Sharp's slides "have nothing to do with this illness but are indicators of what I would classify as an 'adjustment disorder.'" They "have absolutely nothing to do with a person being at risk" for serious depression or psychosis, she argued.[33] Sharp responded that psychosis was serious but rare, while these moderate depressions were common and needed attention. "It isn't usually the sort . . . that requires a psychiatrist's intervention . . . I'd say [a psychiatrist is needed for] 3 per cent, but you've got another 10 or 15 per cent who don't want to talk with their husbands, who don't want to have sex, who feel bloody miserable . . . they've got a depressive illness." Honikman spoke up to explain the problem she saw: "the language we have is not common . . . when researchers and people get together we're not talking the same language."[34]

These issues of language and etiology both hindered coalition building. Sharp's talk opened a conversation about the real tension in the room: Did these women concerned with moderate postpartum depression really have the same goals as the women there to discuss postpartum psychosis? When Honikman began the meeting, she vaguely referred to audience members as "touched by postpartum experience, directly or indirectly."[35] At the same time, the researchers and clinicians she recruited to speak favored a more medical model, where the "experience" was mental illness.

Honikman's effort to cast a broad net annoyed women like Nancy Berchtold, who remembered hiding her bout with psychosis in that first new moms' group she attended. Activists with similar experiences brought this up throughout the conference: with severe postpartum depression, "you can't figure out how to dress in a normal way." The groups with other mothers who seem to be holding it together make you feel terrible. What kind of coalition could these groups build? The mix of severe depression and psychosis with moderate, even subclinical, depression and anxiety had trade-offs that were made clear throughout the meeting. Psychosis was much more dramatic; it could feed media attention and put the stakes of post-partum illness in stark relief. It was unquestionably a medical issue and required an alliance with psychiatry and other professionals. It had biological causes. Including less severe depression and mood disorders promised a much larger base of suffering women, though. These conditions seemed to have some biological causes too, but also plenty of social and psychological ones. The discussion of postpar-tum ailments often bled together, feeding a medicalized definition of even moderate postpartum depression.

This disagreement fueled conflict between Honikman and Berch-told. "They're both very strong women but very different women," an advocate who worked with both explained.[36] Berchtold recalled that "there was always a tension between PSI and DAD." While Berchtold spoke openly about her psychosis, Honikman did not offer an equiv-alent origin story. She seemed to have "only" had a mild to moderate depression that did not require any psychiatric intervention. With-out it, Berchtold and other women with histories like hers distrusted Honikman's motives and her leadership role. What was driving her to do this work for over a decade?

A few years later Honikman began sharing her full postpartum story: she and her eventual husband secretly had a baby in college. She gave birth while studying in Denmark, placed the baby for adop-tion there, and returned home to California. The secret weighed on her and her family for decades and was fundamental to her life's work. The fact that Honikman needed to confess this to finally earn the trust of the other activists spoke to a larger issue: What counted as postpartum mental illness and who got to decide? Whose voices mattered?

The 1987 conference led to the creation of a new organization, which attendees dubbed the International Postpartum Social Sup-port Network. James Hamilton privately vetoed the clunky name. He favored a cleaner title, perhaps featuring "PPD." He observed that "there was a need for a generic term . . . to relate all of the groups

| 113

to a common cause."[37] Honikman conceded: "YES WE WILL CHANGE THE NAME!"[38] They renamed the organization Postpartum Support International, or PSI. Honikman kept depression out of the name, making its appeal as broad as possible. Including "support" in the title nodded to the centrality of support groups but was vaguer and more medicalized than "social support."

Hamilton insisted Honikman formalize PSI quickly. "You should really set up the international cover society . . . it would be desirable to get the International Society on the books as a non-profit." He offered to reimburse Honikman if the incorporation application cost anything. Honikman did not actually do the paperwork until 1989, but PSI was its own organization in 1987. Hamilton was full of suggestions from the start. PSI needed a regular publication, something to make it seem stable and ongoing. "Just a little xeroxed-typed mailer would help to maintain the integrity of the over-all group," he explained. Additionally, Hamilton pushed for a clear relationship between PSI and its medical allies. "I can't overstress the importance of lining up 200-plus patient-approved doctors throughout North

Figure 5.2 A 1988 meeting about postpartum mental illness hosted by Patricia Neel Harberger in York, Pennsylvania. Back row: Carol Dix, Dr. James Hamilton, Nancy Berchtold, and Dr. Ric Fernandez; front center: Jane Honikman. Courtesy of Jane Honikman.

America," he explained to Honikman.[39] Hamilton imagined the relationship would simultaneously lend professional legitimacy to PSI and encourage doctors to pay more attention to postpartum illness.

The relationship between Honikman and Hamilton at the founding of PSI offers a window into the relationship between psychiatry and patient-activists in the 1980s. "You know, he was the driver. He was the force. That's obvious, right?" Honikman asked me.[40] In a sense, this was true. Hamilton encouraged Honikman to think about postpartum depression as a mental illness, to present at the 1984 Marcé meeting, to hold her 1987 conference, to create PSI. When speaking to the organization he quietly helped create, he was always effusive in his praise for the women. "Support groups are not just service arms of some great psychiatric research community," he told a PSI meeting in 1990. "Support groups supply a large part of the brains and a large part of the energy which impels progress in this long-neglected area. You also provide an enormous part of the heart which warms and nourishes patients through postpartum illness."[41] Hamilton was energized by the grassroots support group movement. He believed it was the best tool to make the changes he desired in American psychiatry and the *DSM*. PSI and DAD had their own goals, though, and as they grew they had to negotiate the relationship between survivor-activists and medical professionals.

Balancing Professionals and Self-Help

As part of a grant application Honikman wrote in 1989, she clarified her thoughts on the "separate but equal" roles of "self-help volunteers" and medical professionals within postpartum advocacy: volunteers could provide "support, understanding, education, information and reassurance" but were not therapists. Medical professionals, encompassing doctors, clinical psychologists, social workers, and counselors, had their own role to play. Individual patients paid them to address their needs. The "comprehensive care" model Honikman envisioned for PSI included medical professionals as "supplementing a network of friends and family members which surrounds the mother, baby and its father."[42] Her concept that medical professionals should supplement a community care model rather than the other way around was notable, both welcoming of medical professionals and setting limits with them. Berchtold and DAD also began with an approach in which professional and self-help work complemented one another; they valued the role of nonprofessional women and self-help, but also sought out guidance and support from psychiatric professionals.

The balance of power between psychiatry and the self-help movement was being negotiated in those early years. Hamilton was effusive about the importance of support groups and the self-help movement, but always conceived of them as in service to psychiatry. His investment in peer support was sincere; in inpatient settings he had observed how women further along in recovery could help sicker women. But he primarily saw postpartum support groups like DAD and PSI as pressure groups. They could influence psychiatry and mental health providers, and maybe influence insurance companies or the courts. For him, psychiatry and its needs remained at the center and the women of the movement seemed compliant.

At one point, Hamilton asked Honikman and Berchtold to prepare a chapter about support groups for an academic book he was co-editing. Honikman recalled getting disappointed feedback on a draft from him: "And I thought, Oh. I didn't do a good job. And nothing that I had written related to what he wanted. Because again, I was in over my head."[43] Hamilton gave suggestions about better mobilizing women's stories. He especially wanted their emotional "cries." If bad doctors or therapists had thwarted the cries, all the better. He asked Honikman to include more stories of "women trying to . . . let people know that something really bad was happening" and then being offered advice like "take an aspirin, or go out to a movie therapy."[44] This was not inauthentic; women received this kind of terrible advice regularly—although perhaps not as frequently as earlier in Hamilton's career. Hamilton's insistence on this narrative, though, was consistent with his belief that the most important function of postpartum illness support groups was advocacy aimed at improving psychiatry itself. In the case of this edited collection, Hamilton's co-editor, Patricia Harberger (a nurse practitioner), took over and became first author on the support groups chapter.[45]

The dream of a complementary relationship between medical professionals and patient-activists had echoes of the dream of feminist health activists from two decades before, but with some critical departures. Women would help women; families would help families. Medical professionals were important but also accountable to a lay postpartum community. They would name and discuss postpartum mental illness and take women's suffering seriously. For women with less severe problems, there might be no medical intervention at all. Penny Hanford of the Pacific Post Partum Support Society, for instance, was emphatic that "our basic philosophy . . . is that the *women are the experts here.*"[46] That organization did not have any medical professionals in it by the late 1980s and was uncomfortable with what they saw as an over-prescription of antidepressants by physicians.

American organizations like PSI and DAD were never as critical of psychiatry as the Pacific Post Partum Support Society in their discussions of complementary postpartum treatment. They and most of the smaller support organizations included medical professionals in supportive or even leadership roles. In fact, some members of the audience at the 1987 conference expressed anger at Penny Hanford's non-medical approach. One male medical professional spoke up, arguing that "people who are doing that [providing therapy] should be knowledgeable and trained in doing that." He clarified: "I mean not just experiential."[47] At once the experiential knowledge of postpartum women was valued as evidence of medical neglect and derided as inadequate knowledge in an era of professionals.

The culture around depression specifically, and psychiatry more generally, changed substantially over the course of the 1980s in ways that encouraged PPD activists to also choose professionals over personal experience. Medical professionals eventually came to dominate some of PSI and DAD, but it was no hostile takeover. The emphasis on medical language, especially hormonal language and later discussions of "brain chemistry," was a reflection of a rapidly changing language of mental illness in the broader culture.[48] Women with post-

| 117

partum mental illness eagerly adopted psychiatric language themselves. When postpartum parents wrote letters to Jane Honikman in
the 1970s, they typically told her about their stress and lack of pre-
paredness, and discussed a need for peer and community support.
Now, in the late 1980s, they wrote in the language of mental illness.
"I am currently taking 20mg. a day of PROZAC, a new, 'user friendly'
anti-depressant," one woman wrote to Honikman. "It's been in my
system for about 1 month now and I am starting to feel like a human
being again, thank God!"[49] Another wrote: "Jane, it's amazing to me
how little doctors know of P.P.D." It took her ages to find "a private
physician who is also a psychiatrist who treats P.P.D." The increased
visibility of PPD through the support group movement had encouraged her to identify her problems specifically as a psychiatric illness,
postpartum depression, and to seek specialized medical care.[50]

Women embraced the language of illness and the growing role of
healthcare providers in the movement. The grassroots momentum
continued to build in the late 1980s, but the complementary model
that won was closer to Hamilton's, and its aims were primarily improving the medical profession's treatment of postpartum depression
rather than a belief that women's support groups on their own were
curative. "I can type, stuff envelopes, talk to women going through
this—ANYTHING to help this cause!" one woman offered to Honikman in the late 1980s. While conceding she was "no PhD," she desperately wanted to help to make sure "the medical community stands
up and takes notice of this condition."[51]

118 | Nancy Berchtold also understood the support group movement as
comfortably enmeshed in the medical model. Telephone volunteers
and support groups provided women with role models for recovery
and reminded them they are not alone. This included not being alone
in treatment strategies and psychopharmaceutical use. As Berchtold
saw it, a woman in a postpartum support group "hears from other
women that medication is normal and common" and has a space to
"discuss side effects." This could even go so far as increasing medical compliance: "They will learn from other group members the
importance of taking the medication as prescribed, even when the

symptoms seem to abate after a few months." Likewise, Berchtold was explicit that support groups "are never a substitute for a doctor's care" and that women needed to "receive the proper medication and therapy" for their postpartum illness.[52]

At the same time as these support groups and suffering women adopted medical language and explicitly medical orientations, the investment of clinical psychologists, social workers, and other professionals in postpartum mental health grew. For those who were not research oriented enough to fit into the Marcé Society, PSI especially became a new professional home. Honikman recalls the organization was really starting to change by around 1990. By then the annual conference was run "through that doctor's association with a professional institution, a hospital or a school, or something like that. And it was no longer, like, Jane and Nancy . . . up in Seattle."[53]

This was not wholly a lament. The postpartum support movement had its grassroots, feminist origins. Berchtold and Honikman both used their home phone numbers as their organization phone numbers for years. Both had been involved with 1970s social movements, and both had been influenced by *Our Bodies, Ourselves*. But this was not 1969. In the late 1980s, the movement was still small enough for Honikman and Berchtold to name everyone in it, but by the 1990s that was impossible. The postpartum support movement grew and formalized against a backdrop in which medicalization was the norm and feminism was embattled. Accordingly, postpartum activists distanced themselves from the controversies of women's health and embraced the legitimizing power of the psychiatric model.

6. The Problem of Diagnosis

"Dr. O'Hara," an activist spoke up at a small Pennsylvania meeting, "don't you believe in postpartum depression?" Psychologist Michael O'Hara had been a leader in the subfield of postpartum depression since the 1980s. He had served as the president of the Marcé Society, which awarded him a medal for lifetime achievement. He had written several key articles in perinatal psychology, with thousands of citations each. Despite O'Hara's curriculum vitae being full of postpartum depression, whether he "believed" in postpartum depression as a distinct mental illness was an uncomfortable question. At scientific meetings, he said it was "not a question of belief, it's a question of what's the evidence for the phenomenon."

O'Hara told me this story as a way of clarifying the relationship between postpartum researchers and activists or "nonprofessionals." For him, like many prominent postpartum researchers, navigating these relationships with advocates has long been part of his work. The postpartum activists inspired and challenged the psychiatric and psychological researchers. The Marcé Society benefited from the existence of groups like Depression After Delivery and Postpartum Support International, which proved there was a consumer demand for postpartum research. And those consumer groups needed the legitimacy provided by psychiatry and psychology.

The details of that relationship, though, could be difficult to negotiate. O'Hara emphasized the value of nonprofessionals while admitting that some professionals found them "disruptive" when they were "clamoring to be heard." Questions like whether O'Hara believed in postpartum depression hinted at the complexity of the relationship. "I've got to be very careful in answering this question," O'Hara realized, "because she and many women like her had a big stake in believing in this [as a discrete disease], because it really represented an explanation for their misery after childbirth."

For O'Hara, the question was about diagnosis and etiology, about the difference between "postpartum depression" and "a depression in the postpartum period." The reality of depression was never in doubt. And there was no question that O'Hara "believed" in depression; he lost his own mother to suicide, prompting his career in psychology. But did he believe postpartum depression was substantively different than other depressions? Did he believe it was a discrete disease? For activists in the 1980s this was not an academic issue. To question the standalone nature of postpartum depression at a moment they were looking to diagnosis for legitimacy felt like calling its realness into doubt, like a denial of women's suffering. Out of a longer history of needing to prove this realness—of rejecting psychoanalytic insults, of finding their depression underdiscussed and understudied—activists committed to the diagnostic language of postpartum depression.

Activists and researchers both contributed to the success of the phrase "postpartum depression" in the US beginning in the 1980s. Activists debated how to refer to this constellation of postpartum illness, from psychosis to blues to anxiety, in a simple and accessible way. "Postpartum depression" offered a partial solution. The adoption of the term, though, was a political choice that grouped together women with very different experiences. It implied that postpartum status was more distinguishing than specific symptoms.

Why did advocates, and some researchers, emphasize the specificity of the disease? And why couldn't they get the American Psychiatric Association to agree? As the association undertook work on a new *Diagnostic and Statistical Manual* (*DSM-IV*), set for release in

the early 1990s, they debated and ultimately rejected a separate diagnosis of postpartum depression. The fight over the diagnosis, and
the stakes imagined on both sides, highlights conflicts between the
interests of psychiatric "consumers" or activists and the interests of
psychiatric professionals. Women's health advocates adopted the diagnostic language of postpartum depression even when psychiatry
split on the issue.[1]

Naming Rights

For decades Americans referred to the "baby blues," whether discussing mild tearfulness or psychosis. When psychiatry and psychology described postpartum mental illness in the 1980s, the terms were
not uniform. Postpartum depression, mania, stress, mood disorders,
childbirth-related psychiatric illness, puerperal depression, maternal
depression. Activists wanted a simpler term, something inclusive and
media friendly. "Postpartum depression" and its shorthand "PPD" became this simplifying term. Grouping blues, depression, anxiety, and
psychosis under this one umbrella was a political more than a psychiatric decision. It implied someone experiencing postpartum psychosis had more in common with postpartum depression than they
did with other psychoses; that the postpartum onset of the mental
illness was its most critical component. This approach allowed postpartum advocacy groups like Depression After Delivery and Postpartum Support International to create a wider base of involved women.

Carol Dix took credit for introducing "PPD" in 1984. She imagined | 123
it would come to serve as an umbrella term for postpartum mental illness.[2] It would be easy to grasp, she explained, like PMS, while avoiding the "jargon of the trade." She liked the umbrella of PPD, which
she felt could also include some subclinical distress. For her and postpartum activists, simpler language might increase their visibility and
ability to communicate their message. Jane Honikman explained that
if they could "simplify the language," then the activists could all "say
the same definitions" and present a more coherent front.[3] James
Hamilton also pushed for simpler and clearer language, especially

for a general audience. Postpartum depression could be a general term for all psychiatric illness after childbearing, including mild depressive syndromes and major psychoses.[4] Hamilton rejected the older term "puerperal," which seemed both dated and too technical. Postpartum, he reasoned, would "save us from teaching millions of people a new word." Besides, he reasoned, even "half of the psychiatrists ... pronounce 'puerperal' incorrectly."[5]

At the same time he encouraged umbrella terms, Hamilton worried about balancing inclusivity with paying attention to psychosis. "The broad popular use of 'Postpartum depression' and its acronym PPD may be very good for our needed public relations," he wrote to a Marcé Society colleague, but it cannot be "confused with suicidal depressions and florid infanticidal psychosis." PPD was more appealing and less frightening than psychosis. But Hamilton believed there were also legal and insurance-related reasons to codify the phrase "postpartum psychosis" in the *DSM*. The word "'psychosis' will be of enormous help in getting fair trials," he argued. He had ideas about how perinatal psychiatrists might distinguish illnesses, and emphasized the differences between psychosis, severe postpartum depression, and depression with psychotic elements. "The problem is," Hamilton wrote, "that people who are not psychiatrists ... are very confused by the peregrinations of our gobbledegook psychiatric argot."[6]

We Are Neglected Because We Have No Name

As the APA undertook revisions on the *DSM* in the late 1980s, activists and some psychiatrists wanted a seat at the table for postpartum illness. Postpartum psychiatry, James Hamilton argued, was "a grossly neglected area ... precisely because we have had no name."[7] But this required clarity. You could not argue that your psychiatric disorder belonged in the manual if you could not clearly define what it was, and what it was not.

In 1986, the Marcé president and treasurer, Channi Kumar and Ian Brockington, wrote to the *DSM-III* chair, Robert Spitzer. Aside from Hamilton, Marcé leaders were skeptical that a postpartum depression or psychosis met the requirements for a standalone diagnosis. Still, they wanted to argue for including postpartum diagnosis in the manual in some capacity. Even Marcé members could not agree exactly what this should look like, and how to handle basic components of a definition like how long after childbirth it would apply.[8] Hamilton showed the most optimism of the Marcé men. He had lunch with Spitzer and came away with the impression that postpartum disorders were on track for the *DSM-IV* "with the situation things, like premenstrual dysphoria and sleep disorders."[9]

Then Allen Frances replaced Spitzer as the *DSM-IV* chair. Whatever influence Hamilton believed he had on Spitzer, he did not have on Frances. Hamilton's crusade intensified. The *DSM* was not simply mis-categorizing postpartum psychiatric illness, he emphasized, but omitting it. Only offering general diagnostics like brief psychosis and depression, not postpartum psychosis or postpartum depression, was "nomenclature censorship."[10]

Hamilton figured that even if the APA would not listen to him and the Marcé Society, it might listen to activists. Postpartum support groups, he explained, were "the most positive development in this whole field." Women told women they "know all about it." And that they "had it."[11] Their language, that they had "it," all built on the idea of postpartum depression as a discrete disease.

Women in the support groups adopted this diagnostic-ish language, referring to postpartum depression and PPD. So, it frustrated many of them to learn that that language was not official. The lack of official classification, Carol Dix wrote, led women to "come to the not unusual deduction—the problem is me."[12] Some activists argued that official classification could force doctors to take postpartum mental illness seriously. Doctors need "to reassure the patient that her symptoms are those which have been experienced by others," one woman at a 1987 meeting explained; they need to tell women their symptoms "fit into a known condition, a condition which can be helped."[13] Specific diagnostic language could validate.

The need for that legitimacy and certainty came in part from a history of psychodynamic approaches, which blamed women's personalities and neuroses for their postpartum problems. Psychoanalysis often asked women to reach into their childhoods for trauma or early evidence of their maladjustment. One woman recounted her experience in the 1970s, when the state placed her baby in foster care while a psychiatrist insisted she had lesbian tendencies and hated her parents. Another bounced from one doctor who didn't take her "blues" seriously to another captivated by her "deep-rooted sexual problems."[14] In contrast, a postpartum depression diagnosis was an illness, not something inherent to them. In this context, official diagnosis felt liberatory. But, at least for the moment, that liberation was unavailable.

Lobbying for Postpartum Depression

In 1988, James Hamilton addressed a crowd of postpartum activists in Princeton, New Jersey. He had a very specific request: they needed to help him get postpartum depression into the *DSM*.

Hamilton had long encouraged support groups to lobby. Back in 1984, he encouraged Jane Honikman and a British postpartum activist to use that year's Marcé meeting to "announce ... the beginning of an international movement." He said this movement was "not a medicine dominated movement," but the idea was his, and he imagined announcing it at a medical conference.[15] But Hamilton wanted the consumer activist group to challenge the medical establishment, as they also pursued medical validation. "I think that you could say, for the U.S., at least, that this field has been totally neglected by male-dominated medicine," he suggested. He added "that you could claim a lot of support and interest from feminist sources" if they adopted this narrative of the ignorant, sexist doctor.[16]

The women did not announce any such movement at the 1984 meeting. Jane Honikman delivered a paper that was not a screed against medical sexism. Instead, she emphasized the importance of shoring up the family in an era of social change, the ongoing societal shift away from the extended family and the supports it offered parents, and the efforts of support groups like hers to fill those gaps.

Honikman spoke of parents experiencing isolation and stress, and the importance of parents finding a space to give and receive emotional support.[17] She did not use the language of postpartum mental illness, and was careful to emphasize "parents" and "family" rather than motherhood specifically.

After the conference, Hamilton asked Honikman to write up a summary of the "non-medical" papers, including her own. He gave clear notes on the "two ideas I want to get across," which again involved framing the work of new parent support groups as a battle against psychiatry and obstetrics. Hamilton's first theme was the "terrible helplessness" of people who could find no one who would legitimize their concerns, and their relief when someone finally did. The other theme was "the fact they are really angry at the neglect and stupidity they have received from doctors."[18] His concerns were not at odds with the actual points Honikman made, but they were more rooted in Hamilton's imagination of an organized postpartum support movement and what it could do.

He continued to nudge Honikman toward this kind of organization until she founded Postpartum Support International in 1987. As Honikman jokingly recalled it, "Dr. Hamilton was . . . [laughs] he was the puppeteer. I was just doing his bidding . . . he had so much faith in me, I had so little faith in myself." Hamilton seemed sincerely invested in lay postpartum activism, while also using that activism to serve his own goals. As he wrote to fellow Marcé psychiatrist John Cox, these women were "our new Army, the self-help, ex-patient groups."[19] And these postpartum activists, mostly moms working through recent or current mental health crises, found his belief they were important flattering. "Can you imagine my amazement when he reacted with sincere interest when I described our PEP group?" Honikman asked an audience of fellow postpartum activists.[20]

Defining the Stakes

As the postpartum activists and professionals organized to found Postpartum Support International in 1987, they did so against the backdrop of a well-publicized infanticide case. In January 1985, Penn-sylvania mother Sharon Comitz killed her month-old son but claimed someone had kidnapped him.[21] She pled guilty but mentally ill. The judge sentenced her to eight to twenty years in prison for third-degree murder. Comitz and her defenders argued she was suffering from postpartum depression. Her husband, Glenn Comitz, led a campaign for Sharon's early release from prison because of her mental illness. The frequent use of "postpartum depression" when describing Sha-ron Comitz's case shows how confusing the language still was. Even postpartum activists like Nancy Berchtold described the Comitz case in that umbrella language of depression. "Post-partum depression is not something concocted by criminals to elude justice," Berchtold argued.[22]

Glenn Comitz teamed up with Daniel Katkin, a Pennsylvania State University criminal justice professor involved in the case, to organize a postpartum depression conference. They wanted to bring atten-tion to postpartum mental illness and hoped that a large event would bolster Sharon Comitz's case.[23] While postpartum support groups rallied behind Sharon, they were wary of the conference. Carol Dix wrote to Jane Honikman to complain about it, saying she and Nancy Berchtold had the same reaction: "they're expecting people to pay $225 for the 3 days; it's not over a weekend. So all in all cuts out the poor every-day working, or non-working women!" She wrote to the organizer to express her frustration. She lamented they were "after being the Marcé here," meaning they would be aiming their work at professionals; they were not for the support group movement. "Let's keep ourselves clear of them," Dix explained. "Stick to the women struggling away out there."[24]

In the end, both Honikman and Berchtold attended the conference despite their reservations. This kind of interest in postpartum issues was too rare to pass the opportunity up. The support group move-ment saw Sharon Comitz as a woman like them. While Berchtold never considered killing her daughter, she said that the Comitz story "could have been me." The activists saw a wronged woman who could not get the courts to take her obvious postpartum mental illness seriously. They also saw her victimized at other points, through the typical lack of postpartum mental health screening, education, resources, and support. They understood those problems deeply.

At the conference, presenters detailed the importance of a postpartum diagnosis. James Hamilton recounted that the participants were unanimous about organizing to get the American Psychiatric Association's attention. We "are derelict if we wait passively until *DSM-IV* appears," Hamilton explained. To him, the most urgent matter (besides, perhaps, freeing Sharon Comitz) was to use media and psychiatric interest in the Comitz tragedy to influence the APA's process.[25]

The prosecution's psychologist described Comitz as not psychotic, but narcissistic, with a "passive-aggressive personality." Media coverage explained how postpartum depression "is not currently recognized as a mental illness."[26] It provided a clear challenge to psychiatrists who justified the lack of a postpartum-specific diagnosis with the fact that diagnoses like "psychosis" or "depression" could suffice. The same fear that activists brought to Michael O'Hara was clear in the court setting. In court, people concluded from the lack of a diagnosis that postpartum depression was not a "real" diagnosis. To Hamilton, that showed that the lack of a separate diagnosis was straight up medically wrong. Postpartum psychosis seemed a more "mercurial" psychosis than others, he argued, and a woman could cycle dramatically between psychosis and lucidity. An expert witness unfamiliar with the distinction could easily misdiagnose. From their opposite positions, both Comitz's prosecution and her defenders suggested postpartum mental illness needed to be standalone to be real. The Comitz conference and court case did not change the *DSM*, but it made the stakes of *DSM* language clear. | *129*

You Have the Power to Do Something

Postpartum depression and psychosis did not make the 1987 *DSM-III-R* revision manual, and their chances for the *DSM-IV* were uncertain. The *DSM-III-R Case Book* included a strange case study that briefly referenced the issue. In the case, "Postpartum Piety," a

Nigerian woman named Zela is hospitalized for weeks after child-birth because of hemorrhaging and other complications. Amid this, she says she is a sinner, not a good Christian, and must die. Her Nigerian psychiatrist diagnoses her case with a postpartum psychosis, gives her an antipsychotic, and discharges her.[27] They readmitted the woman a couple times, each for recurrences of the religious delusions when she stopped taking the antipsychotics.

The *DSM* casebook authors did not deny that Zela's psychosis had a postpartum onset. They argued that postpartum onset did not characterize the illness, though. It initially should have been described not as a postpartum psychosis but as "psychotic symptoms and emotional turmoil shortly after, and apparently in response to, a markedly stressful event [the hemorrhaging], that are not due to a known organic factor." Given her relapses, the casebook authors then reasoned the diagnosis should be changed to a schizophreniform disorder. The casebook made it clear that postpartum mental illness was not a standalone diagnosis. They rejected the African treating psychiatrist's use of postpartum-specific language, "because a specific organic factor has not been identified," and reiterated the preferred language of the *DSM-III-R*.[28] In the African case study, the *DSM* casebook authors go out of their way to describe the supposed backwardness of "even highly educated Nigerians" who might seek treatment from traditional or spiritual healers before psychiatrists. The point, it seems, was that both the African psychiatrist who submitted the case and the diagnostic language he applied were out of date. Postpartum psychosis was no closer to the *DSM* in 1987 than it had been in 1980. Advocates needed a new strategy to influence the *DSM-IV*.

Hamilton had been writing to the APA on the issue since 1977, keeping up "a fairly steady barrage ever since." After a conversation with Channi Kumar and Barbara Parry, Hamilton agreed to back off his "heckling."[29] He would personally "keep a discreet distance" during the lobbying. In his place he proposed Parry serve as the head of a Nomenclature Task Force of the Marcé Society. In a letter to a male Marcé colleague, Hamilton described Parry as "bright, scholarly, low-key . . . and very attractive," making her a useful intermediary.[30] She can handle Robert Spitzer (who was still the *DSM* task force chair at that point), he wrote.

While Hamilton was eager for Parry to "work on the bastards with sweetness and light," he was also becoming pessimistic about their chances.[31] The *DSM* was too entrenched, and it was "inordinately difficult to budge a system of classification which is almost a half-century old." He remained suspicious of the authors' motives. The book "yields the APA millions of dollars" since the diagnostic manuals "must be bought in quantity by hospitals and are essential for every psychiatrist for his billing." Hamilton hated the power this gave the *DSM* committees. The "Task Force on Nomenclature have always been the little darlings, because they paid the rent, not to say the expense and travel expenses of hundreds of APA officers," he complained.[32] The task force, Hamilton reasoned, was afraid of change and was disincentivized from making changes or challenging the discipline. Other psychiatrists wielded only so much power over the task force.

Now Hamilton had an additional plan. A postpartum group might have more sway if they directly lobbied the APA as consumer activists. In June 1988, ahead of the second annual meeting of postpartum support group activists, Hamilton approached Honikman. What the emerging postpartum organizations needed, Hamilton told her, was a task force on "Social Responsibility." They needed to make the issue of diagnosis more human and emotional, to convince the *DSM* task force this was a "life-or-death" situation. Hamilton needed Honikman on that social responsibility task force, either chairing or at least in a position to goad the chairperson.[33]

With their postpartum support group organization, they could "undertake a power play which has a very good chance of knocking out the APA task force [on mood disorders]." That required Honikman and the other support group leaders to get very serious. They would need to write letters on official stationery asking about the APA task force's plans for postpartum psychiatric conditions in the *DSM*. Hamilton instructed that later letters should explain "you are convinced of the culpability of the nomenclature system" in the mistreatment of postpartum women with mental illness. As the correspondence continued, Hamilton schemed, you must "let it be known that you are considering a class action suit against the APA" and then actually consult with lawyers. They could threaten to sue in the name of current patients, which "could quickly run to $100 million." Or they could threaten to represent past and future patients, in which case "the sky is the limit for damages." With these direct, material threats, he concluded, "the APA will say, 'Wait, let's talk about this.'"[34]

He asked Honikman to convince conference attendees of the incredible importance of the *DSM* to their concerns. They needed to agree that *DSM* diagnosis was, in Hamilton's words, a "life-or-death" situation. At a conference, Hamilton proposed the task force idea to the full audience. "You have the power to do something," he told them. "You, and those you represent, have been harmed by the current terminology . . . you are being harmed by these policies now, and future members of your network will be harmed by them."[35] Hamilton directed the women to tell the APA that they were "convinced of the culpability of the nomenclature system" in their struggles getting postpartum attention and treatment.[36] He emphasized their powerful voice, and then laid out his proposal for a task force composed of "the most able and the angriest of your members." The group would have the primary responsibility for "eradicating this monstrosity of institutional stupidity, this perversion of nomenclature which now threatens a second Dark Century for the victims of postpartum psychiatric illness."[37]

The American Psychiatric Association, he explained to the postpartum activists, was largely their enemy. Only a small number of the APA's members knew or cared about postpartum matters, and those members had little influence over the *DSM*. Without the help of activists, Hamilton said, we will fail.

Limits of a Consumer Movement

This 1988 meeting was only the second annual conference for postpartum support groups. While Postpartum Support International would eventually become a large organization, it was not yet. It was basically an annual meeting and a quarterly newsletter written by Jane Honikman. PSI would not trick the APA into believing it was a large, litigious consumer group. Nor did the members really want to.

After the 1988 meeting, Honikman and two other central activists privately discussed the task force issue. One of them was Angela Burling, who had killed her infant son years earlier while experiencing postpartum psychosis.[38] A jury acquitted Burling because of her psychotic state, but her acquittal was unusual. The potential stakes of diagnostics were clear to her. She agreed to pursue the issue with the APA, though not in the form of Hamilton's threatened lawsuits. Instead, she wrote a personal letter. In it, Burling described how a better *DSM* definition of postpartum psychosis and postpartum depression "will give validation to what thousands of women experience." It will help physicians know what to look for, and protect women who suffer so severely they commit infanticide.[39]

While Burling cared about the *DSM*, most postpartum activists either did not understand or did not prioritize it. Honikman told Hamilton that most of them did not understand the significance of his idea.[40] Hamilton regretted he had not made a handout for them when he spoke.[41] Nancy Berchtold understood, and attributed much of her education on *DSM*-related issues to Hamilton. But she also had a bit of a filter for Hamilton, whose talks and schemes did not always align with those of the support group movement. She joked about a four-page "very academic" letter he wrote her about the relationship between diagnosis and insurance. She understood his points, but they did not translate to action points for her. It was typical of both Hamilton's passion and tunnel vision about the *DSM*. Hamilton had substantial influence with the support group movement, but they were not the pawns he envisioned.

Hamilton pushed the activists to frame the problems of postpartum women in terms he thought would be most persuasive to the APA. Again and again he emphasized how women were victims of psychiatry, and victims of bad doctors. He told them to make sure their groups continued to "collect gruesome stories of bad care and bad results."[42] Hamilton's investment in improving women's treat-

| 133

ment seems genuine, but he also tried to use women's pain as currency in his campaign.

The DSM-IV

Ultimately, neither postpartum depression nor postpartum psychosis made it into the 1994 *DSM-IV*. At least not in the form Hamilton, the Marcé Society, and the postpartum support group leadership had hoped.

It was the job of the *DSM-IV* Mood Disorders Committee to make recommendations on where different mood disorders belonged in the *DSM*—if at all. Postpartum depression fell under their purview. Dr. Ellen Frank, a psychiatrist and professor, took the lead on the question of postpartum depression. Her job was to examine the evidence and bring it back to the other five members of the committee.

The Mood Disorders Committee, like the rest of the *DSM-IV* revision work, prioritized empirical evidence. The 1980 *DSM-III* had already moved in that direction, purging most psychoanalysis and countering the criticism of the discipline pervasive in the 1960s and 1970s. The *DSM-IV* was even more invested in this approach to diagnosis.[43] They deprioritized clinician, patient, and popular understandings of illness in favor of empirical research.

At the same time that it considered the question of postpartum mental illness, the Mood Disorders Committee was managing the more public and more obviously political question of whether they should include PMS (Late Luteal Phase Dysphoric Disorder, or LLPDD) in the new edition. Some women argued that adding LLPDD pathologized women, while others argued that the diagnosis was critical to accessing research and treatment. The LLPDD arguments echoed concerns over postpartum depression, but the level of controversy was quite different. Feminist protestors stood outside APA meetings, saying LLPDD pathologized women.[44] With the backdrop of this PMS fight, though, the already-empiricist committee emphasized its non-political, evidence-only approach to diagnostic questions.

This strict empiricism meant strict limits on what the committee accepted as meaningful research on postpartum depression. The committee prioritized data, especially data based on over fifty cases. They avoided using anecdotes as evidence.[45] The *DSM-IV* considered case studies less rigorous than controlled experiments. Much of the existing postpartum depression literature were clinical case studies with tiny sample sizes. But the rejection of "anecdote" had a second meaning in this context. It also hinted at the ways they would not consider postpartum activists' personal stories. These activists had spent years telling women's stories of postpartum distress and medical indifference. For most of them, the primary motivation was not *DSM*-related. James Hamilton, though, had been encouraging activists to frame those stories to influence the *DSM*. The Mood Disorders Committee, however, didn't care about stories.

By 1989, the public and the profession knew postpartum depression. They might not be able to precisely define it—it seemed no one could—but it was a very different context than the *DSM-III* preparation ten years earlier. Ellen Frank says she assumed she would find scientifically acceptable evidence that postpartum depression merited a *DSM* entry. When Frank and her graduate student, Daniel Purdy, evaluated the literature, though, they did not find it. They could not find enough evidence, up to their standards, for either postpartum psychosis or non-psychotic postpartum depression as stand-alone diagnoses.[46] Their literature review didn't show "a unique and consistent constellation of diagnostic validating criteria." Postpartum depression was not different enough from other depression, postpartum psychosis not different enough than other permutations of brief psychosis.[47] Purdy and Frank conceded there was something there to watch in future research, and that there were some features of postpartum psychosis like confusion and disorientation that differed from other psychoses. Frank agreed that the *DSM-III-R* treatment of the postpartum was "extremely unsatisfying," and that the new edition needed to offer more recognition.[48] But not as discrete diagnoses.

Ironically, many problems Purdy and Frank outlined owed to the lack of diagnostic language itself. They found a variety of studies unusable because of their different definitions of when the "post-partum" period ended, and because of their different thresholds be-tween blues and clinical depression. Frank lamented that assessing the research was like comparing apples and oranges. For advocates like James Hamilton, this reasoning was infuriating. Yes, Hamilton agreed, this literature was hard to analyze. But this should not under-mine the creation of a new *DSM* category; it should *encourage* it. If re-searchers had a shared postpartum language, then their postpartum research would be more clearly in conversation. Hamilton wrote to Frank to make another point as well. The apples-to-oranges issue, he wrote, "carries into hospital diagnoses and into the courtroom, where judges and juries have a very difficult time with postpartum nomen-clature."[49] A clear *DSM* definition of postpartum mental illnesses would allow researchers and jurors to compare apples to apples.

Other psychiatrists who sided with Hamilton made similar points to Frank. If the *DSM* did not offer clinicians a way to label patients as postpartum, researchers could not link postpartum depression case files. This made it harder to do the kind of large-sample research the Mood Disorders Committee considered acceptable evidence. Psychi-atrist and Marcé member Raphael Good explained it as a "chicken-egg" problem.[50] Despite the vocal Marcé opposition to the *DSM* status quo, though, it seems many psychiatrists were fine with it. Frank and Purdy surveyed the first authors from twenty-one recent studies they considered the best on the subject, asking if they believed the existing (*DSM-III-R*) diagnostics were acceptable. Only twelve of the authors responded, and Purdy and Frank said most were fine with existing definitions or just wanted a little more specificity.[51]

Instead of a new diagnostic category, Frank and the Mood Disor-ders Committee introduced a "with postpartum onset" modifier. It could be added to a diagnosis of major depressive disorder, bipolar I, or brief psychotic disorder. The modifier did not change the diagno-sis, but it made the postpartum status of the patient clear.[52] Modifiers required a lower standard of evidence, and required far less empir-ical evidence for adoption.[53] Frank presented the modifier as an en-tering wedge: the modifier would encourage postpartum depression research. In the meantime, she explained, part of the motivation for the modifier was that since "the idea of PPD does go back at least for centuries . . . there's probably something there."[54]

Postpartum patient activists understood the modifier compromise as an insult. It was yet another challenge to the legitimacy of their suffering. The modifier had many limits, especially in terms of its definition of how long the "postpartum" lasted. The modifier was supposed to be applied for illness that began within four weeks post-birth. Such a limited window was controversial, since some psychoses and most depressions began later. In practice, psychiatrists use the modifier long past four weeks, part of a common "fudging" of *DSM* specifics.[55] Even today, psychiatrists and consumer activists continue to push for a longer window for the onset modifier, arguing that three, six, or twelve months postpartum would be more appropriate.[56]

The addition of the onset specifier, though, was at least a partial victory. Once the Mood Disorders Committee revealed its conclusion in 1990, four years ahead of *DSM-IV* publication, Hamilton lamented that "I don't think it likely that we have won much." Still, he conceded, "some mention of mood disorders may help a little."[57] He accepted the compromise more as the *DSM-IV* publication date neared. Hamilton now told Ellen Frank that his "first and main goal was to have postpartum illness somewhere in *DSM-IV*."[58] While an onset specifier was not what he had in mind, maybe it could indeed be an entering wedge.

At the 1990 PSI meeting in St. Louis, participants tried to make sense of the preliminary decision to include a modifier but not a diagnosis. Psychiatrist Christa Hines argued that the decision was evidence of how far behind the rest of the world the US was on postpartum depression. The qualifier will help, she allowed, but did not fix the underlying problem of the *DSM*'s obsession with symptoms rather than causes.[59]

When PSI held their meeting in Pittsburgh the next year, Ellen Frank gave an update. She confirmed the decision of a postpartum modifier, which Frank tried to describe as a step forward. She contrasted the empirical approach of the *DSM-IV* task forces with previous versions. The earlier *DSM*s "were essentially put together in smoke-filled rooms," she said.[60] Not this *DSM*. This one was based in literature reviews and data reanalysis, this one had explicit standards for adequate research. Their reviews of the literature, though, suggested non-psychotic postpartum depression mostly presented like other non-psychotic depressions, and postpartum psychoses largely presented as other psychoses did. Frank emphasized the acceleration of research in the area, including around postpartum anxiety, and the possibility that some future *DSM* taskforce might find adequate acceptable evidence. Just not the *DSM-IV*.

Frank explained what the Mood Disorders Committee planned to do about postpartum disorders in a way that underestimated the audience's understanding of the subject. Even by 1991, PSI meetings were full of clinician-activists, not just consumer-activists. Frank still told the room what the modifier meant. There would be some kind of textual discussion of postpartum disorders in the manual, she offered. To emphasize the significance of this, she added that the draft version was "almost one full printed page." Then she told PSI members how course specifiers work. "Disorders are assigned numbers," she explained, and with the specifier there would be a special digit added after the decimal point to mark postpartum onset. They planned a similar decimal addition for disorders with "seasonal onset," she explained, though the implied equivalence couldn't have helped her case with that crowd. With a decimal, she argued, researchers would be able to pull relevant medical records. And clinicians picking diagnostic codes for a patient, she optimistically imagined, would have to reflect on whether to add on another decimal. In the process, they might even recognize the postpartum onset of a case where they had not considered it before.

This was, however, a difficult crowd. Getting a decimal was something, but Frank would not convince them that a decimal was *almost* as good as a diagnosis. One account describes the audience's frustrated and "very pointed questions."[61] Psychiatrist Barbara Parry noted that Frank "basically got booed out of the room." The meeting had "so many people in that room . . . who had either experienced postpartum depression or anxiety or knew someone who had . . . or who was a clinician working in that area or a researcher."[62] Frank could discuss the literature review all day; she would never convince attendees that the evidence did not support creating a postpartum depression or postpartum psychosis diagnosis.

Parry also recalled how a member of the *DSM* Mood Disorders Committee confessed that she had never actually seen a patient with postpartum depression or psychosis. While Parry also did empirical research, she still valued anecdotal and narrative evidence. Reading the literature, she implied, was not enough to grasp what the disorder meant. Why were people without postpartum patient experience making this decision?

More than that, Parry argued, there was ample empirical evidence that postpartum depression was a discrete diagnosis. Women with postpartum depression often presented differently than with other depressions, Parry explained, and postpartum psychosis might require different treatment than other psychoses. For example, Parry prefers using first-generation antipsychotics with postpartum psychosis patients instead of the more popular second-generation antipsychotics, because she thinks they work better for such cases. She understands postpartum psychosis as different than other psychosis. The *DSM-IV* committee was not in tune with clinicians, researchers, or the public, Parry argued.

Ellen Frank juxtaposed her approach with those of postpartum consumer activists especially, whose arguments seemed more emotional and personal. Frank explained she was an empiricist and had to follow the data. Groups of angry women with postpartum mental illness were hardly a reason to change the manual. Instead, Frank saw the mainstreaming of postpartum depression as a reflection of cultural rather than scientific concerns. Many women considered postpartum depression a less stigmatized version of depression, Frank reasoned, and the "fact that their depression was 'unique' was very important to them." But emotions do not change the data, she explained.[63]

| 139

Before, when James Hamilton told women how the *DSM* had wronged them, it was more abstract. Some women had problems getting insurance after being diagnosed with a condition more stigmatized than postpartum depression, others understood the *DSM* was partially to blame for their doctors' lack of training in postpartum illnesses. But it was distant. After the Mood Disorders Committee rejected postpartum depression and psychosis as standalone disorders, though, the problem became less abstract. PSI published Ellen Frank and Daniel Purdy's twenty-six-page explanation of their decision in their 1991 conference proceedings.[64] Depression After Delivery organized a letter-writing campaign aimed at two federal funding agencies, the National Institute of Mental Health (NIMH) and the National Institutes of Health (NIH). They requested more federal funding for postpartum mental illness. The problems of popular and diagnostic naming came together.

What Exactly Are Postpartum Disorders?

On the same 1991 panel as Ellen Frank, psychiatrist Katherine Wisner also spoke. She never mentioned the *DSM*, but her talk focused on a related issue: defining postpartum mental illness. To prepare a talk on postpartum disorders, she told the audience, she "had to answer the question for myself, 'What exactly are postpartum disorders?'" This was not so simple. "After five years of dedicating my work to clinical work and research with women with postpartum disorders," she told them, "I have to confess to you that I do not know the answer to this question."[65]

She described the complex presentations she saw in patients. Many had previous histories of mental illness, or undiagnosed depression before they were pregnant. Wisner described women in a long-term study she was running whose depression never seemed to let up, women whose "postpartum" depressions lasted five years. A woman who recovered from postpartum depression relapsed four years later and asked Wisner if this was postpartum depression again, despite not having another child. These were questions that put some postpartum activists on edge. Noting a woman's preexisting mental health problems often felt like undercutting the distinctness—and thus the legitimacy—of postpartum depression.

But even as Wisner raised these hard definitional questions, no one questioned her intent. Frank was an outsider who did not seem to understand them. Wisner had been closely allied with postpartum advocacy groups for years. She served as a medical advisor to a Pittsburgh support group chapter. The audience could be confident that she was not bringing up these definition problems to undercut their activism, but to encourage more conversation and more research. Wisner might question definitions, but activists trusted her, she would never question their legitimacy. Wisner was, Michael O'Hara explained to me, a mother of postpartum depression research in the US.[66]

The *DSM* Mood Disorders Committee had demanded more data, Wisner explained, but "the reality was ... there was a huge advocacy group with this experience." Wisner echoed James Hamilton's description of these women's experiences as "part of the data." As postpartum advocates, psychiatrists, and psychologists made alliances, they had to address hard questions about defining postpartum mental illness. They had to manage simultaneous goals of talking about postpartum illness in ways that made it widely understandable and media friendly, and also talking about it in ways that were precise enough for the *DSM*. And, as always, they had to address it while trying to prove the legitimacy of their illnesses and their cause. The alliances that stuck were often those that took postpartum patients' stories seriously, which meant taking them as data.

7. *The Postpartum Professional*

Shoshana Bennett had the perfect pregnancy. She swam a mile a day. She read all the pregnancy books. Bennett took prepared childbirth classes. She was a teacher with a BA in psychology, as well as an advanced degree in special education. She seemed unusually prepared for motherhood. So prepared that she approached it with sky-high expectations. Bennett was going to ace motherhood, just as she had always aced everything else.

But there is no such thing as "acing" motherhood, and Bennett plummeted after she delivered in a frightening and unplanned cesarean in 1983. She felt lost, a shell of her old self. The people who were supposed to support her all compounded the problem. Her mother-in-law, a postpartum nurse, told her to think of the baby, not herself. A friend called her to check in on how the birth went and lamented Bennett's failure at "natural" birth. No one seemed interested in how Bennett was doing. She felt like a vessel and a "nonperson." She wanted people to ask about the baby, sure, but she also wanted them to ask about her. They did not.

Bennett had trouble bonding with her baby and felt emotionally numb. Still, determined to ace it, she pretended things were okay even as nightmares and scary thoughts overwhelmed her. When she finally consulted a therapist, it was not helpful. "She knew nothing,"

Bennett said. "She was quite psychoanalytic." The therapist was inventing issues from her childhood. But her childhood was not the problem. Bennett's other point of medical contact was her obstetrician, who was equally useless. "Oh, all new mothers go through this," the obstetrician told her. Echoing decades of baby blues advice, he suggested she do "something nice for yourself and it'll pass." Leaving his office, she contemplated suicide.

It did pass, but only after two and a half agonizing years. Bennett says the long depression caused bonding problems with her daughter that it took years to make up for. Then she had another child. Not only did her suicidal depression return, but she also found that her ongoing issues with obsessive-compulsive disorder got much more severe. As she suffered through this second bout of postpartum illness, though, she caught a snippet of a television program that mentioned "postpartum depression." The diagnostic language opened a new world for her. Now, she could do all the things her straight-A self knew how to do. Research, educate herself, and then educate others. What's more, she was mad. She simultaneously felt relief and "utter rage," wondering why no one intervened in her suffering. "If this was so common," she asked, "where the heck were the professionals?"

Bennett's story is a little different from other postpartum activism stories of the 1980s, though. Her own postpartum mental illness highlighted a psychiatric and psychological lacuna. Where were the postpartum specialists? Why was it so hard to find a professional who got it? And so her experience led her not only to founding a self-help group, it also led her to become "Dr. Shosh." She would be the postpartum-specialized psychotherapist she wished she had.

She was not alone. A number of women became postpartum-specialized therapists in the late 1980s and 1990s. Most of these therapists experienced some level of postpartum distress themselves, which sparked their interest in it. These were women who were already psychologists before their pregnancies, or at least had some psychology background. Their choice of specialization came out of their lived experiences. Their commitment to postpartum mental health was both professional and personal.

As the large postpartum activist organizations of the 1980s formed, they did so with psychiatrists. Psychiatric advisors like James Hamilton and Ric Fernandez lent guidance and legitimacy to Postpartum Support International (PSI) and Depression After Delivery (DAD). They mostly stayed out of the spotlight in these groups, though. Perinatal psychiatrists had the Marcé Society as their professional home. For this new type of postpartum professional, psychotherapists like Dr. Shoshana Bennett, self-help activist organizations also became their professional homes.

Postpartum clinicians occupied a messy space between activism and professionalism. This was characteristic of women who entered medical professions in large numbers in the 1980s. It was a path enabled by the women's health movement, but most professionals did not feel indebted to it.[1] Some, like Bennett, identified as activists. Others did not use that language, and saw themselves as clinicians first. However they framed it, these were therapists who sought large-scale change. They wanted to change therapy, to provide a service they felt did not exist, to fill a therapeutic gap. And they wanted to do this against a backdrop of medical sexism, of obstetricians who downplayed postpartum distress and psychiatrists who drew on psychoanalysis to blame women. Many of these new therapists were motivated by their own postpartum mental health crises and subsequent difficulty finding specialized help. Diana Lynn Barnes, another psychotherapist and Postpartum Support International leader, described how "she was really driven by the horror" of her postpartum experience. "I mean, I never even heard the word postpartum depression," Barnes explained. "I was seeing countless doctors for treatment because nobody knew what to do with me and I was getting all these different diagnoses, and I never really even heard the word postpartum depression until [my baby] was a year old. So it became . . . unbelievably clear to me upon the heels of my recovery that this was an area where there was such a gap in understanding and information." Barnes, and the other women featured in this chapter, all wanted to help the individual women who came to them, but also to help women more broadly. This meant writing books, making television and radio appearances, and sometimes engaging in legal advocacy. They did not imagine a total revolution in motherhood, but they wanted expectations adjusted, especially around the expectations of white middle-class mothering.

Characterizing them as activists, or even activism-adjacent, is incomplete. These were therapists who wanted social change, but they were also entrepreneurs. Most were in private practice, often by themselves. This was not solely a labor of love. But why would we expect it to be? Passion still motivated these clinicians' work, but they were also making a living. Most had hustle, and career goals. Each time they published an article or book, appeared on television, or convinced an obstetrician to take postpartum mental health seriously, they educated and raised awareness—while also building up their own practices. They were creating a whole new specialty. They were postpartum professionals.

The emergence of the postpartum professional is critical to understanding the history of organizations like Postpartum Support International and Depression After Delivery. Postpartum professionals *became* these organizations, especially PSI. Most postpartum professionals of the late 1980s and early 1990s were members of DAD or PSI. For some that was a membership on paper; others served on the board. Eventually, postpartum professionals came to lead both organizations, replacing nonprofessionals like Jane Honikman and Nancy Berchtold.

As more women therapists joined organizations like PSI and DAD, psychological thinking became critical to them. Psychology as a discipline typically framed itself as "depoliticized" and "value-neutral" and emphasized the importance of empowering the individual woman over structural change.[2] That meant that even as therapists consistently acknowledged larger problems, including expectations about maternal instincts and the difficulty of managing work and home lives, they saw solutions as lying with individuals. For example, in response to unreasonable expectations, women must "set limits"; monitor their sleep, diet, and exercise; and work on "identifying and understanding your feelings."[3]

I tell the stories of three "postpartum professionals": psychologists Shoshana Bennett, Susan Feingold, and Ann Dunnewold. I focus on their work in the 1980s and 1990s, though all are still working today. In the late 1980s or early 1990s, as they were starting out, all three did extensive mass media appearances, including on shows like *Oprah* and *20/20*. The three women all wrote self-help books aimed for a general postpartum audience, including *The Postpartum Survival Guide* and *Postpartum Depression for Dummies*. All had affiliations with PSI or DAD (or both) and came to hold significant leadership roles in them: two served as president of PSI, and one served as president of DAD.

These clinicians navigated between organizational leadership, education, writing and promoting self-help books, and treating patients. They were so much more than a distant world of therapists in private offices. But they were also those therapists notably treating mainly white, middle- to upper-class patients—a clientele that undoubtedly shaped their own understandings of the postpartum. And that in turn reshaped the movement. But they weren't the only postpartum professionals who emerged at this moment. Dozens of others followed similar paths, becoming postpartum professionals who professionalized postpartum activism.

The Survivor-Therapist: Shoshana Bennett

Bennett, as we saw, became a postpartum-specialized psychologist when she could not find adequate diagnosis or treatment for her own | *147*
postpartum depression. Her journey stands out, though, because before she became a therapist she became a grassroots activist. Even today, she identifies herself first as a "survivor of postpartum depression and anxiety," and second as a clinical psychologist.

Bennett's first step was to create a postpartum self-help group in the San Francisco Bay Area. She put up two fliers advertising it, one at a Safeway and one in a pediatrician's office. The fliers asked women if they were feeling overwhelmed or stressed. She was careful not to use the word "depression," which she thought might scare mothers away. Perhaps her caution worked, because she had no trouble getting people to show up. "I'm almost embarrassed to say how effortless it was," she explains.[4] At first, Bennett held weekly meetings in her living room for between five and fifteen women. The group grew, and soon Bennett ran groups at several medical facilities. She was not yet a licensed therapist, but her bachelor's degree in psychology shaped her approach. The groups were therapeutic, she explains, but were not therapy groups. She ran the groups "as a survivor," still somewhat depressed herself. Like many women in postpartum support group contexts, Bennett says helping other women was therapeutic for her.

Her groups were "women helping women," she explained—not unlike earlier consciousness-raising groups. "There wasn't somebody sitting there who had all the answers, you know, that everybody was looking to." Although Bennett led the groups, she did not frame herself as the expert. This was in part because she was not yet licensed and set limits on what she thought was appropriate for her to do. Bennett, who identified as a feminist at the time, considered herself "part of the circle" as women opened up about their experiences around this taboo women's issue.[5]

Bennett's group, Postpartum Assistance for Mothers, was born in 1987. Depression After Delivery had been founded in 1985, while Postpartum Support International also launched in 1987. Around that time, Bennett met Jane Honikman and got a little involved in the development of PSI, but Postpartum Assistance for Mothers remained an independent organization. Sociologists might describe these groups as a political movement cohort or a political generation; certainly something was going on that made the late 1980s such a moment for all these groups to spring up independent of one another.[6] Bennett described her excitement at getting to know Honikman, and how they "both had this fire" about postpartum activism. Besides running the groups, Bennett began doing in-service trainings for doctors from the place of a survivor and advocate.

Bennett's fire was at this intersection between the activist and the therapeutic. She continued her studies and began a clinical counseling PhD, ultimately becoming "Dr. Shosh." The transition from support group organizer to clinician seemed natural to her. While she emphasized the equal role of all women in the group, the reality was that women stayed after meetings to get additional advice and insight from her. These "mommies were asking for more" from her, she explained. Many saw their own therapists but felt they "didn't know what the heck they were doing." Like most of the postpartum professional women coming out of the late 1980s, Bennett was driven by that gap between what women needed and what the medical professionals around them could provide. Once she had the degrees, she began doing larger trainings and postpartum education for doctors, lactation consultants, and doulas. Instead of one hospital bringing her in to speak as a survivor, now national organizations brought her in as a PhD who could provide training. The degree opened doors.

When Bennett wrote her first book, it opened even more doors. In the late 1990s, she met Dr. Pec Indman, a psychotherapist in San Jose, California, through Jane Honikman and PSI. The two began writing a book together in 1999, and self-published *Beyond the Blues* in 2001. The women framed it as "something for a diaper bag," a book of seventy pages or so that would not overwhelm a depressed person. The book opened up other opportunities for both women, including media appearances. Bennett appeared on the local news whenever there was a relevant tragedy, and also made appearances on national programs like *20/20*, the *Ricki Lake Show*, and *The Doctors*. She became more involved with Postpartum Support International, and served a term as president of that organization from 2004 to 2006. Later she wrote other self-help books, including *Postpartum Depression for Dummies* (2007), *Pregnant on Prozac* (2009), and *Children of the Depressed* (2014). Those first two books feature both her activist credentials and her professional credentials on the cover. This framing of her expertise is illustrative of the way she straddled these worlds.

Alongside her advocacy work, Bennett built up a postpartum-specialized private practice. The specialized care she provides is expensive, and she does not accept medical insurance. "This is when you use up some savings," she tells mothers, and "pay somebody who

Figure 7.1 Postpartum advocates at the 2007 Kansas City Postpartum Support International meeting. Left to right: Dr. Pec Indman, Dr. Shoshana Bennett, and Dr. Diana Barnes. Courtesy of Jane Honikman.

really knows what they're talking about with this particular specialty." Like you would if your child needed help that insurance would not cover, she adds. The existence of such savings, whether for oneself or one's child, is certainly not universal. But Bennett's choice was typical of the emerging postpartum-specialized psychotherapists.

In the late 1980s and early 1990s, there was very little insurance coverage at all for outpatient mental health treatment—and coverage of pregnancy was erratic. In the 1980s, Medicaid coverage for pregnancy was determined by the states.[7] While most low-income people can access Medicaid while pregnant—the result of a 1992 federal law—many lose access after the immediate postpartum period. This has improved only recently, and depends on where people live. Medicaid benefits for low-income Americans have inconsistent support for mental and behavioral health, especially for outpatient services.[8]

Since Medicaid rarely covered anything like private postpartum psychotherapy in the late 1980s and early 1990s, and private insurance covered it minimally or not at all, there was little incentive for private psychotherapists to accept either. (Moreover, small private practices without billing specialists often felt unprepared to deal with insurance paperwork.) The legacy of this history is clear throughout behavioral healthcare, where many therapists and psychiatrists do not accept private insurance and even fewer accept the low reimbursement rates of Medicaid. This is especially true in a niche like postpartum therapy. Bennett emphasizes that today many self-help and support groups are free, especially those run outside of medical practices. While the support groups are not meant to replace psychiatric care, sometimes they are the only accessible resources.

When she first tried to get local psychiatrists on board with postpartum treatment, Bennett joked that she "didn't care if they saw dollar signs in their eyes"—at least they could provide services. Psychotherapists need trustworthy psychiatric contacts for patients who need medication or who are experiencing postpartum psychosis. Nearly forty years later, Bennett now sees many psychiatrists and other MDs interested in postpartum mental illness for the "right" reasons. But, then and now, money is inseparable from the work of crafting a professional postpartum niche. This is what made postpartum depression messaging and advocacy as successful as it was: it was well suited for a 1980s context, a logical passion project for ambitious working mothers who understood postpartum depression.

Toward Self-Care: Ann Dunnewold

While Bennett earned her PhD after her postpartum depression, Ann Dunnewold already was a working psychologist with a PhD when she got depressed in the mid-1980s. She described having a "great baby" who slept well, yet still experiencing emotional turmoil postpartum. Even though she was a clinician, she did not understand her own reaction. "So I said what's the matter with me," Dunnewold recalls, "which I think most every mother does who finds that it's not the most wonderful thing that they thought it was going to be."

She knew how to research and how to interpret what she read. But what was there to read? She only found one useful book, Carol Dix's *The New Mother Syndrome*, but still hungered for more information. What must this be like, she wondered, for parents who did not have the skills and resources she did? This was before an easy internet search, and at a time that a woman might not have ever heard of the phrase "postpartum depression" to use in a search of a library card catalog. Even if she had, it would not turn up that much. So where could a struggling mother turn?

Dunnewold looked to her profession. She searched for a professional home aligned with her new interest in postpartum depression. In 1990, she stumbled across Postpartum Support International and its fourth annual conference, held that year in St. Louis. Her commitment to PSI was almost immediate. She explains, "I was hooked because here were my people."

Through PSI she met Dr. Diane Sanford, a St. Louis–based PhD psychologist and clinician. Sanford's personal experience with postpartum depression had set her on a similar path. Dunnewold and Sanford put together a postpartum panel for the annual conference of the American Psychological Association. The crowd appreciated the presentation, Dunnewold thought, and a publisher reached out to them. Dunnewold spent all day in her private practice saying the same things again and again to people, she explained, so a book seemed like a way to reach more people with those same ideas.

Dunnewold, whose private practice was based in Dallas, increased her outreach. While the American Psychological Association talk went well, it was not quite the right audience. The people who cared most weren't psychologists but were in childbirth-specific fields. Dunnewold trained nurse midwives, lactation consultants, and birth educators on how to recognize and handle postpartum distress. While private practice remained her "bread and butter," her larger impact came through her work in PSI, her co-authored self-help book *Postpartum Survival Guide* (1994), and these medical trainings. After that book came out, she had many more medical speaking gigs, including before the American College of Nurse Midwives and the

Association of Obstetric and Neonatal Nurses. Dunnewold explained to her audiences that postpartum clinical psychology was not just regular psychology that happened to be about the postpartum. Instead, it was something unique. Dunnewold emphasizes the importance of the special postpartum depression niche that developed in clinical psychology in the early 1990s. It was not simply that this was a group of therapists, mostly women and mothers, who would listen in ways other clinicians did not. It was also about specific approaches to treatment that emerged out of treating postpartum women.

At the 1992 PSI meeting in San Diego, Dunnewold met psychologist Dr. Susan Hickman. Hickman was an established postpartum psychotherapist in San Diego. A depressed friend had nudged her to start up a free support group for postpartum women in 1984, and her work had straddled the lines between advocacy and psychotherapy since then.[9] Hickman later opened the Postpartum Mood Disorders Clinic with her husband, Robert Hickman. Hickman also served as an expert witness in postpartum psychosis–based infanticide cases. She emphasized the biochemical origins of postpartum psychosis especially, fighting the perception that women with postpartum

Figure 7.2 Psychologist Dr. Ann Dunnewold in front of a chalkboard at the 1999 Postpartum Support International Board Meeting in Vancouver. Courtesy of Jane Honikman.

psychosis had "moral defects." Instead, they "are highly functioning, normal, all-American girls who go crazy and harm their babies after they give birth."[10] In making this argument, she sought particularly to combat the bias that often led lower-income mothers to receive harsher penalties than higher-income ones.[11]

Hickman mentored many emerging postpartum psychologists, including Bennett and Dunnewold. Dunnewold describes how Hickman helped crystallize her own approach to postpartum patients. "When a house is on fire," Hickman explained in a quote that is now repeated often in PSI, "you put out the fire first before rewiring the house."[12] Like Bennett, who had been frustrated with a psychotherapist who wanted to get to the childhood root of her troubles, Dunnewold rejected psychoanalytic approaches, which were largely out of favor by the late 1980s anyhow.

What they moved toward was a talk therapy infused with some feminist ideas, but not explicitly feminist. It emphasized women's experiences, particularly in the present, but within an individual framework. These therapists acknowledged power and larger structures but did not seek to fix anything other than the woman in front of them. One founding postpartum therapist explained she had never considered herself a feminist, and in the late 1980s and early 1990s "feminism was viewed to be a bit more radical, edgy, even aggressive at times."[13]

This acknowledgment of inequalities alongside a rejection of feminism, sometimes described as a "post-feminist" politics, was hardly unusual. It came arm-in-arm with the recognition that some cultural norms *did* oppress women. This could be the norm of "the supermom of myth and TV shows," and it could be the old-fashioned therapist who assumed a deep-seated pathology in the depressed mother.[14] As Dunnewold saw it, talking about when you were four was not the most urgent need of the postpartum woman. What women needed in a postpartum therapist was "an active problem solver." This was not the time to unpack a woman's personality and neurosis through Freudian navel-gazing, but along the same lines, it was not a useful time to challenge broader political cultures.

These postpartum therapists saw the need to focus on the individual, actively suffering woman in pragmatic terms. You can't ask women to process their childhood and achieve insights if they are sleep deprived, or if they aren't eating, Dunnewold explained. While it might seem obvious now, she emphasizes how not obvious it was to these women's previous therapists. Things have changed a lot since then, Dunnewold explains, but in the early 1990s she regularly had new clients who came to her after yet another therapist only wanted to interrogate how they felt about their mothers. The therapists weren't talking about concrete life skills or self-care, she explained, and so they weren't helping postpartum women.

The emphasis on self-care as a practical and immediate way of addressing postpartum depression was a departure. Dunnewold credits Jane Honikman with pushing conversations about both peer support and self-care through her leadership in Postpartum Support International. Those conversations influenced professionals within PSI. "You know," she says, "nobody was really using that term self-care until the early '90s." Did postpartum therapy help spread the idea of self-care as an important part of mental health, as Dunnewold says? It is hard to know exactly, but it is clear that postpartum therapists were at the front of the trend toward articulating its therapeutic value.

Now, there was already a long history of self-care-oriented postpartum advice. For decades, popular writers and psychiatrists alike told distressed women to get new hairdos and dresses and go to the movies with their husband. Coming from those sources, the advice was condescending and dismissive of women's suffering. The role of self-care in this new, woman-dominated postpartum specialty was a response to the rise of attachment and child-centered parenting in the 1980s and beyond. For middle-class women, the pressure to sublimate their identities into motherhood was enormous. Postpartum therapists of the era almost universally agreed this contributed to depression and anxiety among their patients. In this context, self-care served as a way of asserting one's selfhood and independence. This could be one of those steps toward "putting out the fire" before trying to go deeper.

Here, self-care was a strange marriage of conservative baby blues advice of the 1960s and women's health rhetoric of the 1970s. But it is unclear how conservative or liberatory the concept of self-care is. In 1988, radical Black feminist and poet Audre Lorde wrote that "caring for myself is not self-indulgence, it is self-preservation, and that is an act of political warfare."[15] The line, which reflects Lorde's response to both her breast cancer and living in a racist system more generally, was not cited in any of these postpartum books from that moment. Postpartum professionals and the postpartum movement were still overwhelmingly white and unlikely to have been reading any Black feminist theory in the 1980s. The circulation of languages of self-care in very different circles echoed 1980s politics, but was Lorde's self-care the same as Dunnewold's?

Self-care as political warfare would be a stretch for the postpartum professionals. Today, a larger literature argues over whether self-care can truly be political or is doomed to be a neoliberal façade. Self-care is seen as neoliberal by some because of its emphasis on individual comfort and well-being (often through consumption) over systemic change.[16] In the realm of postpartum therapy of the '80s and '90s, there were bits of both at work. Restoring individual middle-class white women to their roles as mothers, especially through consumption, is a somewhat conservative politics. But they also argued that motherhood itself needed to be—at least moderately—rethought in ways that emphasized women's needs outside motherhood.

Dunnewold worked closely with Honikman to establish trainings in postpartum depression for medical professionals, especially for mental health professionals. She explained they "combine[d] my sort of practice kind of approach with her peer support kind of approach." The trainings began around 1993 as a PSI project, and the two women's combination of clinical and activist work perfectly encapsulated where the organization was. They affiliated with the University of California at Santa Barbara extension program to offer continuing education credits for their trainings and encourage attendance. The affiliation also meant Dunnewold was now paid for her time.

That core course that Honikman and Dunnewold developed grew

wildly, not unlike Postpartum Support International itself. By the 2020s, the course had gone from a dozen or so attendees to hundreds in online trainings. Dunnewold describes the trainings as a way of raising awareness among mental health professionals and a "scattering" of obstetricians and psychiatrists. The trainings were helpful in pushing the larger PSI argument that postpartum depression and anxiety could not be treated the same as other depressions and anxiety. She explains this is not only because of hormonal differences, but also because of role changes, societal expectations, and what a "unique life transition" the postpartum is, from "an adult developmental point of view."

In 1996, Dunnewold was elected president of Postpartum Support International, with Honikman's strong support. It seemed that picking a psychologist, rather than a nonprofessional, was intentional. Honikman herself had gone back to school to earn an MS in psychology, though she did not pursue a clinical path with it. Honikman occasionally lamented how overwhelmingly filled with professionals PSI was becoming, but more often she encouraged this professional takeover. If the goal had been to get clinicians to take postpartum depression more seriously, what could be a greater sign of success than this?

Dunnewold saw her role as PSI president as bringing more clinicians, from a diversity of professions, into the fold. It shouldn't just be an organization of childbirth support people or educators or nurses, she said, and it was also not just an organization for social workers or psychologists. It would be all those professions working together. While Dunnewold did not think anyone—not even Honikman—had masterminded the specific succession of PSI presidents, she recognizes that the list of early presidents seems like "a real concrete effort to sample from all the different kinds of professions that were involved with the organization." She had been preceded by Canadian support group organizer Eileen Beltzner, and advocate Sonia Murdock served a term from 2000 to 2002. After her, the presidency was mainly held by postpartum professionals: psychotherapist Diana Lynn Barnes served a term, followed by Shoshana Bennett. Then

| 157

clinical social worker Susan Dowd Stone took the reins. PSI was thriving, and through its trainings and outreach, PSI was influential. And PSI was also profoundly professional.

Susan Feingold: From Private Practice to Advocacy

Susan Feingold had her first child in 1982, and then her second ten years later. The first postpartum was fine, but after the birth of her second child she experienced severe postpartum depression and anxiety. Feingold had a PsyD degree and was working as a staff psychologist at a Chicago Veterans Administration hospital during that second pregnancy. During a required CPR class, the instructor demonstrated the Heimlich on her, despite knowing she was pregnant. The result was contractions, preterm labor, and bed rest for the rest of her pregnancy. Her son was fine, but after his birth the possibility the Heimlich incident had disabled him in some way yet to be revealed haunted Feingold. She had obsessive thoughts and could not eat or sleep well. Feingold had no name for how she felt. She just knew she was in some kind of "living hell."[17]

Like so many women, Susan Feingold sought psychological help but struggled to find a decent provider. She saw a psychiatrist who told her she probably had some unresolved issues with her mother. Feingold was unconvinced. Since she was herself a psychologist, she researched and read all she could about her feelings. After she self-diagnosed with postpartum depression, Feingold told her primary care physician what she thought was going on. The doctor disagreed, suggesting the problem was probably sleep deprivation and too much on her plate. Maybe she should take a vacation with her husband.

Her doctor didn't mean to be unhelpful, Feingold reflects, but she did not have a medical explanation for the problem. But a doctor should not derail someone in need just because they don't "know the heck what they're doing," whether because they take an unhelpful psychodynamic approach or because they are skeptical of a postpartum depression diagnosis. So, once Feingold recovered, she left her job at the Veterans Administration and began a specialized private

practice. Her colleagues told her that the specialization was too narrow, that there were not enough people with the problem, that she
could never build a full-time private practice this way. "It's just too
rare," they told her. They were wrong.

She found her not-so-rare clients first by writing for free local
publications like *Chicago Parent,* where she could "get her name out
there." She also started up a free postpartum support group, originally at a YMCA, and ran it for eighteen years. This allowed her to
help women outside a private practice setting, but also served as a
private practice feeder for mothers who needed additional support.
In the early days of her practice, she also went to obstetricians' offices to convince them to refer patients. Many turned her away, and
she "felt like a used car salesman or a drug rep." Really, the message seemed to get out in the opposite direction, Feingold reflects.
Her earliest patients told their obstetricians about Feingold's practice, and that was what got the obstetricians' attention. At that point
they started calling, referring patients, and asking her to give hospital
talks. From there, her practice snowballed.

Around that time, Feingold learned about Nancy Berchtold's organization, Depression After Delivery (DAD). A neighbor saw a small
newspaper article about this group, about Berchtold and her psychosis, and gave the clipping to Feingold. "That was a life-changing
thing," Feingold says. Today she has the clipping framed. At that
moment, she learned that her private practice and her professional
journey were part of something larger.

Even though she knew from her own growing client list that post- | 159
partum depression was common, it surprised her that there was a
whole organization. At that time, around 1992, she saw DAD as "very
grassroots." She got involved immediately, and ended up on their
board quickly. She became president of DAD in 1994, just two years
after her own postpartum depression. Like many postpartum professionals, she occupied a role in DAD as both someone recovered from
postpartum depression and someone professionally invested in it.

During her two-year term as president, Feingold worked to bring
other professionals on board. Like Dunnewold at PSI, Feingold

noticed the professional members of DAD were mostly nurses and therapists. A couple of social workers, a couple of psychiatrists, but not other kinds of medical specialties. Feingold asked her own OB-GYN to join the DAD board, and she agreed. Feingold also recruited pediatricians and general practitioners. The organization still had a mix of members, and many non-medical professionals were regular members. Medical professionals, though, dominated the leadership.

Feingold remained involved in DAD, but pulled back some after her presidency to focus on her private practice and her children. She wrote a book on postpartum depression published in 2013, *Happy Endings, New Beginnings*. But what brought her back to these postpartum organizations was not her investment in depression, but a newfound interest in activism around postpartum psychosis.

Feingold rarely saw women with postpartum psychosis in her office. This was in part because of how rare postpartum psychosis is, and in part because psychosis is more immediately treated with hospitalization and psychopharmaceuticals rather than psychotherapy. She treated some women after their bouts of psychosis, as they processed their experiences, but most of her patients were depressed or anxious rather than experiencing psychosis.

In 2003, Feingold was approached about an infanticide case up for appeal. Debra Gindorf had tried to kill herself and her two young children in 1985, but only the children died. Gindorf had lived in poverty in Zion, Illinois, recently divorced from an abusive husband. She had no job, no car, and no phone. Still, while postpartum with her youngest, she knew something was wrong. She walked to a hospital to get help, but the hospital turned her away. Gindorf asked her mother to take care of the children if she were to die, and her mother refused. So Gindorf went to kill herself and the children. When she found the children were dead but she was still alive, she walked to the police station and turned herself in. They sentenced her to life without parole.

By 2003, over fifteen years later, the parole board was sympathetic. Even the psychiatrist who testified against Gindorf originally now

advocated for her. In Illinois, though, this sentence commutation required the governor's approval. Governor George Ryan ignored her
request for a pardon or commutation. When Governor Rod Blagojevich took office, Gindorf again petitioned. That May, Blagojevich
declared it "Postpartum Depression Month." Yet he declined to act on
her petition. Only when yet another governor, Pat Quinn, took office
in 2009 was Gindorf released and granted clemency.[18]

This case was Feingold's first involvement with the legal system
around postpartum psychosis, and it was almost another decade
until she got involved in the issue again. In 2017, she read an email
on a Postpartum Support International listserv. Advocates needed
some professionals with PhDs to testify before a subcommittee in
the Illinois House to support House Bill 1764. That bill argued that
courts should consider untreated postpartum depression or postpartum psychosis as mitigating factors in crimes. It also allowed women
convicted for related felonies who had not presented their postpartum illness at trial or sentencing to now do so.[19] Two Illinois women
incarcerated for infanticides committed during their postpartum
psychoses, Paula Sims and Janet Jackson, originally drafted the law.
Feingold and her partner, criminal attorney Barry M. Lewis, together
advocated for the law.

"I'd never been an advocate," Feingold recounts, and "hadn't been
even political since the '70s and the Vietnam War." But the compelling bill, and memories of the terrible legal treatment of Debra Gindorf, compelled her to drive to the state capital to testify.

The law was enacted in 2018, the first criminal law in the US to
center the role of postpartum mental illness in crimes committed.
The law has since become a model for activists in other states. It also
started a new chapter in Feingold's career, including a new relationship with Postpartum Support International, where she joined the
advisory council. While she maintains her postpartum depression-
oriented private practice outside Chicago, she increasingly focuses
her energy on advocacy for women who commit crimes related to
their postpartum mental illness.

Grassroots Professionals

Susan Feingold, Shoshana Bennett, and Ann Dunnewold all knew the hell of postpartum depressions personally. When they sought help, they realized how little most medical professionals knew about postpartum mental health. They all created their own specialties in postpartum mental health, especially postpartum depression and anxiety, in the late 1980s and 1990s. Along the way, they got involved with the main postpartum activist groups in the US, Postpartum Support International and Depression After Delivery. Each had a different relationship to activism and advocacy, and that relationship changed over each woman's career.

Other specialized therapists emerged these same years, with more limited ties to PSI and DAD. Karen Kleiman, a social worker, built the Postpartum Stress Center in Pennsylvania in 1988 in response to the dearth of medical professionals who "got it," a near universal motivator for postpartum professionals of the time. Kleiman became a member of DAD, but never got seriously involved with the group. She was adamant she was not an activist, which she associates with compromising her individual beliefs for group messaging. Still, besides private practice, she has emphasized awareness and education, writing eleven books about the postpartum. Kleiman's story is important even though—or because—she remained on the outskirts of organized postpartum work. Postpartum professionals were not all involved in PSI and DAD, but by the mid-1990s, PSI and DAD were both led by postpartum professionals.

The composition of PSI especially shows the rise of the postpartum professional, as well as the thin line between career-building and advocacy for many of those professionals. By its fourth annual conference, it had become hard to explain exactly what the organization was. Feingold differentiated PSI from the Marcé Society by emphasizing how Marcé was the scientific arm of postpartum work, "very sophisticated, well-respected." She started to describe PSI as "more grassroots," but amended that PSI was also focused on "professionals as well." The line between the groups was more a line between researchers and clinicians than it was between professionals and grassroots activists. For Bennett, who began by founding a support group and then became a clinician, the professionalization of PSI offered evidence of its success. "So, now, when I look at the PSI conferences," she explained, "and I see doctors coming and I see physicians' assistants and I see nurses coming, as well as many other types of professionals, that just—I mean, it's fabulous."

Shoshana Bennett's journey from the grassroots end to a more professional existence paralleled PSI's path. And PSI's path was not unusual either. The origin story for this emerging generation of postpartum therapists echoed earlier feminist agitation. The motivation sprang from a widespread lack of understanding about women's health and challenged professional norms. It reshaped conversations within clinical psychology rather than simply adding women in, and there were plenty of more standard "activist" moments sprinkled in. Feingold's work as an expert witness combined a commitment to advocacy with expertise. The self-help books and media appearances made by postpartum professionals offered public education and awareness raising. There are substantial limits to awareness raising as activism, but there is also much to say about their successes. These postpartum professionals often blurred the lines between self-help and professional help, awareness raising and entrepreneurship.

It is easy to romanticize the grassroots, and to lament the apparent loss of lay energy in organizations that became dominated by professionals. In this case, that energy did not disappear, but an already medically minded movement became even more medical and professional. Clinicians didn't storm PSI conferences and elbow their way into a takeover, either. The power imbalance between credentialed clinicians and lay activists was substantial, but it was a power balance that non-clinicians mostly accepted. These were not psychoanalysts calling them neurotic, these were professionals who loathed those figures as much as they did. The feminization of clinical psychology also enabled this possibility of alliances between clinicians and laypeople throughout this period. Professionals offered legitimacy. This legitimacy in part came through activist alliances with the

Marcé Society and its reproductive psychiatrists. But it would also
come from these women clinicians. And, while a Marcé psychiatrist
like James Hamilton tried to shape the consumer movement from
behind the scenes, these postpartum professionals were increasingly
on center stage: talk shows, television specials, interviews, and other
mass media.

8. *Talk Shows, Tell-Alls, and Postpartum Awareness*

In 1986, when the *Oprah* show aired only in Chicago, psychiatrist Nada Stotland appeared on an episode to discuss postpartum depression. "I don't know where Oprah got the idea or her people got the idea," Stotland said, "but I was called in because I did consultations with OB-GYN, not because I was some big expert in postpartum depression particularly." Working in a hospital setting, she had seen occasional postpartum psychosis cases, though less depression. On the show she briefly explained postpartum illness, sandwiched between women's stories of severe depression and psychosis. After her appearance, the switchboard at the hospital where she worked lit up. It was incredible, she said. When the show went national soon after, they re-aired the popular episode for the larger audience. Again, the calls poured in. The woman at the front desk of the hospital told her that the "switchboard is ringing off the wall."

Women sought Stotland out for different purposes. Most wanted to discuss their own depression. Some sought immediate help. But many of them were long past their postpartum experiences. Women fifty or sixty years old spoke their suffering aloud for the first time. This thing that they experienced, they just learned that it had a name. Women left messages about how misunderstood their postpartum pain had been, how they had hidden their struggles, and how no one took them seriously. Stotland had been the first to tell them it was all *real*.

This story played out repeatedly. Television talk shows, especially daytime ones like *Oprah*, *Donahue*, and *Joan Rivers*, became complicated sites of awareness raising. These shows almost always featured a mix of credentialed experts and women with personal stories to tell. Depression After Delivery (DAD) members appeared on these shows as survivors and activists. Although some people mocked these types of shows for their drama, superficiality, and sensationalism, they helped make postpartum depression more normal.[1] Pairing women with experts affirmed the gravity by medicalizing it.

The talk circuit had limits, though. Appearances often centered on suicides or infanticides. Tragedy and insanity got ratings. This still allowed advocates a chance to raise awareness on a massive national platform. But it also made postpartum depression frightening and unclear. Some guests discussed depression and anxiety, but the grimness of infanticide dominated. At other points, the lines between depression and psychosis blurred, and television hosts, news programs, and guests conflated the two.

As advocates took to the media, they sought to increase public understanding of postpartum depression as a common, legitimate mental illness. They could not control, though, exactly the shape their messaging took. In the late 1980s, advocates found that infanticide cases dominated every appearance. By the 1990s, news segments occasionally interviewed women who described depression and anxiety rather than psychosis. The real media breakthrough came at the end of that decade and into the early 2000s, when several celebrities spoke about their depressions. These high-profile confessions offered opportunities for activists to discuss postpartum depression without the sensationalism. Yet these efforts were complicated by Andrea Yates's 2001 postpartum murder of her five children. Media attention made postpartum mental illness seem increasingly real. It raised awareness in a way nothing else could. It also could make the postpartum seem terrifying.

The media work so important to postpartum advocates raised

awareness and gave postpartum depression a higher profile, part of their decades-long project of legitimizing the illness. But it also limited who this diagnosis was for by telling stories featuring sympathetic white middle-class mothers.[2] Support groups continued to thrive and spread. But the scale of these awareness campaigns meant they referred most women to their doctors or to self-help books, with an emphasis on this individual recovery rather than structural problems around motherhood.[3] Exposure did not bring equity.

Television Appearances in the 1980s

The 1980s brought in a new era of intimate, often confessional television. Personal problems became public entertainment on *The Oprah Winfrey Show* and *Donahue*. Oprah had 19 million viewers a day in 1990. Later in the 1990s, dozens of television talk shows, like Ricki Lake's and Jerry Springer's, centered on even more sensational topics.[4] Oprah's show remained on the classier end of the spectrum, focused on women's emotional stories.

Postpartum mental illness fit these venues, and postpartum advocates sought to take advantage of them. What critics saw as "public therapy," advocates saw as awareness raising.[5] But as perfectly suited as postpartum depression was for the medium, convincing producers of this was harder than it seemed. Occasionally shows sought postpartum depression guests, but usually it was tough to get booked. Carol Dix, author of the 1985 *The New Mother Syndrome*, worked hard to get television exposure when her book came out. She had little success until the next year. At that point, she knew DAD activists, some of whom had enthralling stories of their time with psychosis. She also knew an important truth about this kind of television: even among the hosts who considered themselves serious, sensationalism made a better pitch. This meant mundane depressions were not enough. The way to mass media was through psychosis and infanticide.

When Dix tried to get on the *Phil Donahue Show* in 1986, she pitched a panel on "normal middle-class women" with serious postpartum problems. This was not a niche feminist topic, Dix argued, this was about brain chemistry and hormones. This could come for any mother. She offered three women who would discuss their severe (but not psychotic) postpartum problems. Cheryl, for instance, was "bright, intelligent, not a feminist, just a young woman who finally accepted the experience of motherhood had taken her over the top."[6] Like much "post-feminism," the pitch was for a postpartum depression that was individual and media friendly.[7] A structural critique of motherhood and the lack of social support was not exciting television. But this medical framing suggested everyone was at risk, including the Donahue audience. This was "a new-woman post-feminist idea that could really get people talking and thinking," Dix said.[8] The producer apparently told her the subject sounded too depressing.[9] "They wanted nothing to do with her," advocate Nancy Berchtold recalled. "Nothing to do with her, nothing to do with the topic."

Six months later, in the wake of the Sharon Comitz infanticide case and the surrounding activism, Dix tried again. Dix's proposed guests—including Comitz's husband—were still "normal" and "middle class." But they would not be depressing. They would be shocking. *Donahue* booked them for May 1986.

For Nancy Berchtold, who also appeared in the episode, it was an amazing experience. The producers expressed both excitement for the sensationalism and fear about how the audience might treat the guests. In the green room before the show, Phil Donahue gave Berchtold and the other women a pep talk like a football coach. "We knew that we were going out into the lion's den," Berchtold explained. "We kind of had that feeling like we could get jumped on" by the audience. Donahue, she recalled, promised to support and protect them. He did not have to, though, because no one jumped on them. Instead, audience women raised their hands to tell their own stories of loneliness, depression, and shame.

A couple months later, Berchtold appeared on the same episode of the *Oprah Winfrey* show as Nada Stotland.[10] Both shows mentioned Depression After Delivery (DAD) but did not give contact information. People called the TV stations for information, or asked

Figure 8.1 Nancy Berchtold with talk show host Phil Donahue. Courtesy of Nancy Berchtold.

telephone operators for help tracking down Berchtold personally. The first time a national show actually flashed DAD contact information, the response was incredible. When Berchtold checked the DAD PO box, a worker told her she was going to need help with all the letters.

"They had three trays in one day, three trays of letters from people and women, families, just writing and writing and wanting to know what they could do, what they needed to do," she recalled. Some were urgent pleas for help. One woman permanently disabled by a postpartum suicide attempt wrote in for legal advice. Her ex-husband was suing her for custody of their infant, arguing that she was insane. Could DAD help her?[11] Others were requests for assistance in organizing. A woman from Cincinnati called that July, after seeing DAD on television. Then she created a DAD chapter. As the television appearances continued, so did the new DAD chapters. Southern New Jersey, Seattle, Pittsburgh, Los Angeles. The shows might have been sensational and resistant to any kind of feminist language, but they made women's health activism a national subject.

Figure 8.2 Nancy Berchtold and daughter, holding mail received after a television appearance. Courtesy of Nancy Berchtold.

There were limits to the talk show genre. In 1988, Carol Dix and Jane Honikman tried to get on *Donahue*. Dix's book was coming out in a second edition, and Honikman had just launched Postpartum Support International. They proposed an episode that would talk about postpartum depression and "the women's movement." Honikman had recently written a letter to *Ms. Magazine* about postpartum depression, which the editors ignored. It confirmed Honikman's worst suspicions about feminism focusing only on certain kinds of rights, and leaving mothers behind. The magazine did release a special issue on mothers, but it focused primarily on working women and problems of balance. Honikman fumed that there was no discussion of the postpartum. Their *Donahue* pitch did not promise psychosis or infanticide, but it did promise controversy at a moment of cultural conflict over feminism. "Quite frankly," Honikman wrote, "I think a television presentation addressing the question of the feminist 'stand' on maternal mental health would be powerful."[12] The show could challenge feminists on this point, she mused, and see if it was ignorance or fear keeping them from taking postpartum health seriously.

The *Donahue* producers were not interested in the show, but contemplated an infanticide episode. "Of course," Honikman complained, "the TV lady said 'if we can't find anyone who has killed her baby willing to go on the show, then we won't do it.'" It was "so disgusting."[13]

Postpartum activists accepted, and sometimes embraced, these media appetites. If something terrible had to happen to get them attention, they would get "ready to jump into the media's view." Beyond infanticide, they also pushed attention on mothers' suicides, divorce because of postpartum depression, and the impact of depression on child development. The latter pitch caused some concern: "I shudder to think of the damage they'll do . . . more guilt trips for mothers," Honikman wrote. She still argued the press would be worth it.[14] If the culture wars could get them booked, they could do culture wars. Bad moms and the crumbling family could be entering wedges. Getting on television or in print seemed to outweigh the negatives.

In 1989, Glenn Comitz and Berchtold went on the *Joan Rivers* show.

The segment illustrates the way conservative values about mothering structured these public conversations.[15] Joan Rivers told viewers that "for many, many women pregnancy is just bliss." This bliss of motherhood extended to the postpartum, and the first few days home. "The bonding between the mother and baby is just the most wonderful time," Rivers reminded the audience. "But there are some women that these days are just a living hell. Instead of joy they feel anxious and depressed and alone."

Rivers introduced one guest by explaining how, six weeks postpartum, the woman "cracked up" and ended up in "a mental home." They did not present the women's psychoses as part of an array of reactions to motherhood, the most extreme on a continuum. Instead, they were anomalies, outliers whose traumatic postpartum stories could reinforce the lines between normal and abnormal motherhood. The women had tried to be good white suburban mothers, or to be what Rivers called "perfect wives" and "perfect mothers." It was not their fault they could not meet the ideal.

Average, common depressions in the postpartum were not interesting television. Even "ordinary" psychosis had to be upsold. While Berchtold is resolute that she had no thoughts of harming her daughter during her psychosis, sometimes in television appearances she speculated about the possibilities if she had gone untreated. "If I hadn't been picked up, I could have harmed myself or her," Berchtold said on *CBS News* in 1988. "Luckily, Nancy was hospitalized before she harmed her child," the reporter voiced over images of Berchtold playing with her daughter.[16] Then they segued to the Comitz infanticide case.

Daytime talk also avoided politics, and emphasized the individual rather than collective nature of postpartum problems. When Glenn Comitz brought up disparities in the legal system and how they influenced his wife's case, Rivers cut him off. "Let's not talk about the legal system," she said, "it's all tricks these days." The show ended with a call for women to not be ashamed to ask for help, a bit ironic in light of how shaming the conversation was.

The sensational killer mom continued to feed American appetites for bad mothers. Men's rights groups attacked postpartum depression as a legal defense, arguing that it fit within a longer tradition of courts treating women more gently than men. As an article in one anti-feminist newsletter put it, "now they've opened season on children, claiming insanity. The ones who are insane, is the general public, if they believe this excuse."[17] Television audiences did believe some of these guests—nice middle-class white women who had shocking psychotic breaks—but the shows existed to titillate and horrify rather than to advance any feminist agenda.

The 1990s and the Postpartum Press

Television appearances around tragedies continued through the 1990s, but increasingly there was room for talk of the depressed, non-psychotic mother. In a 1993 NBC segment, a woman described feeling that "the rug was pulled out from under me" postpartum. She described insomnia and crying. The voiceover emphasized the pressures on women of the 1990s, especially the pressure to balance work with new motherhood.[18] No one mentioned psychosis or infanticide. Other segments from that year described depression and intrusive thoughts, including depression requiring hospitalization, but not psychosis.[19] They emphasized the treatability of the illness. All featured footage of recovered mothers playing with their children, emphasizing their restoration to good motherhood.

Postpartum therapist Karen Kleiman appeared on a 1996 episode of *Oprah*.[20] Kleiman had co-authored a book on postpartum depression, *This Isn't What I Expected*, which received coverage in *Parents* and the *New York Times*. The book was not at all about infanticide, looking instead at a range of maternal stresses, depressions, and anxieties. In the last few minutes of the episode, Oprah said to Kleiman, "One other thing that can happen is some women don't feel good after they have a baby." Kleiman spoke for a minute about postpartum depression—not psychosis. Even though it was just a few minutes, "Oprah tackling this conversation felt very important," Kleiman said. "Her reach is just so beyond comprehension."

Part of this inclusion of more common postpartum depression stories alongside the "killer mom" features came from a context of continued ambivalence about American motherhood in the wake of substantial economic and social change. Headlines about the second shift
and the failed supermom were ubiquitous, as American women both
critiqued and pursued the idea of "having it all." Other women gave
up on the idea, as news stories of the '90s described women leaving
corporate America for stay-at-home motherhood with a confidence
that feminism had failed. One writer described a new "feminine
mystique" of the era.[21] At the height of this post-feminist moment,
women's decisions about motherhood were discussed as individual
choices.

Mainstream media coverage about postpartum illness focused on
white motherhood. Talk show episodes almost exclusively featured
white women's personal stories when trying to set up sympathetic
narratives. Even as women of color did not see their postpartum
depression stories featured on the television shows, Black middle-
class publications began increasing their attention to mental health
and depression in this same period. Black pregnancy and childcare
books included brief references to getting professional help for baby
blues that did not go away through social support, rest, or exercise.[22]
Black magazines mirrored other mainstream magazines' depression profiles, but usually included a reference to special depression-
inducing social pressures facing Black Americans. "Experts agree
that given the racism and extreme financial pressures that many
African-Americans must contend with," a 1995 *Ebony* article explained, "it's not at all surprising that they feel depressed more often than whites."[23] Another article explained that while genetic and
biological factors mattered, the stress on Black women put them at
special risk. "We are socialized to want to take care of everybody," a
woman explained, but not to think about themselves.[24] These articles
did not discuss antidepressants, but Meri Nana-Ama Danquah's
1998 memoir of depression, *Willow Weep for Me*, did. As Danquah
struggled with her antidepressants, she recounted a woman telling
her "that when *black* women start going on Prozac, you know the

whole world is falling apart [emphasis added]." That is, Prozac was a white woman's drug. "When black women start going on Prozac, their whole world has already fallen apart," she replied. "They're just trying to piece it back together."[25]

In the 1990s, Prozac became a household word.[26] While it was far from the first antidepressant, it had fewer side effects. Psychiatrists and other prescribers reweighed the costs and benefits of antidepressants. By 1990, Prozac was the number-one prescribed drug in the country. The market was flooded with similar drugs, including Paxil and Zoloft. Books like *Prozac Nation* and *Listening to Prozac* joined a national conversation on the opportunities and risks of antidepressants. Direct-to-consumer advertising, as well as media debates over the drugs, familiarized Americans with this new landscape of medications.[27]

Feminists also debated the political ramifications of these drugs, which doctors prescribed more to women than to men. Were these drugs part of an effort to pathologize women? Or would they help women stand up to injustice, allowing them to be more confident and assertive? Middle- and upper-class white women were more likely to receive antidepressant prescriptions in the 1990s than Black women and lower-income women were.[28] These prescribing patterns echoed disparities in depression diagnosis.

By the late 1990s, pharmaceutical companies began directly marketing antidepressants as postpartum depression drugs. In 1998, Pfizer produced an awareness brochure meant to explain the ailment to potential prescribers.[29] No one introduced postpartum depression-specific drugs in the 1990s. But pharmaceutical companies came to see value in taking postpartum depression seriously. If, as experts estimated, 10 to 15 percent of new mothers had the illness, then that was a serious market indeed.

| 175

Celebrities with Depression

In the 1990s, even as media interest in postpartum depression grew, it sometimes echoed the dismissive language of decades past. A

1997 article in *People* magazine explained that "Postpartum depression isn't an option for such celebrity moms as Whitney Houston,
Madonna, and supermodel Niki Taylor." In this framing, celebrity
mothers embodied a version of the supermom. Celebrity moms had
nannies watch their babies on the movie set so they could nurse
during breaks, or they made their own schedules around their babies. Babies and their celebrity mothers wore matching designer
outfits. Celebrity moms quickly returned to their pre-pregnancy
size, proving "a woman can be a mother *and* a hot number!"[30] They
brought happy babies to galas and awards shows. A very pregnant
Demi Moore posed nude for *Vanity Fair* and boasted to the reporter
that she had breastfed her first child for two years while maintaining her filming schedule.[31] American women might have known idealized celebrity motherhoods were not accessible. But they also felt
continued pressure to live as close to the ideal as possible. The claim
that an ideal mother was too wonderfully busy for postpartum depression reinforced the worst stereotypes about postpartum illness
as frivolous.

Princess Diana's admission of postpartum depression stands out
for challenging the expectations of celebrity motherhood at the time.
The tabloids had spent years glorifying her motherhood through joy-
ous soft-focus photos of her and her babies.[32] Then, in 1995, Diana
spoke about her depression in a BBC interview watched by 15 million people in Britain and excerpted and discussed in the American
media.[33] "I was unwell with post-natal depression, which no one ever
discusses," she told the interviewer. "You'd wake up in the morning feeling you didn't want to get out of bed, you felt misunderstood,
and just very, very low in yourself."[34] She said she had treatment,
but also "knew in myself that actually what I needed was space and
time to adapt to all the different roles that had come my way."[35] After
the interview, women "jammed the switchboards" of a British postpartum group, seeking help.[36] While the revelations of the interview
were more salacious than postpartum depression alone—adultery
was the big headline—American media covered this open discussion
of depression.

Four years later, in 1999, singer Marie Osmond revealed her post-partum depression in an interview with *TV Guide Magazine*. Then, she went on *Oprah* to discuss it in depth. "It's like your eyes are in the back of your head and you just want to close them and never open them," she said, "you're just so incredibly tired." She described sitting on the floor, eating peanut butter from a jar, crying, overwhelmed. Osmond had only three weeks off work after her seventh child, she explained, and the stress of it flattened her. One day, she handed the baby to a babysitter and took off. As she drove up the California coast alone, she had no idea where she was going. She was driving away from everything, she said, "And I'm sure women can relate to this."[37]

Osmond was one of the biggest American celebrities to speak openly about postpartum depression. She reported receiving thousands of emails from women "thanking me for giving what is bothering them a name."[38] *McCall's Magazine* headlined an interview with her with tabloid flair: "Marie Osmond's Shocking Postbaby Breakdown."[39] Osmond followed up with a 2001 memoir, *Behind My Smile: My Journey Out of Postpartum Depression.*

Osmond's recovery included restoring herself not only to good motherhood but also to good wifehood. The Mormon star had gotten divorced while still depressed but now reconciled her marriage. She also took time off work, focusing on family and faith. Besides her book tour, she described spending the year preparing her oldest son for a missionary trip. Articles emphasized how much work she was turning down to stay home with her children, including multiple Broadway shows.[40] She was prioritizing family dinners and scripture reading and proudly refusing the live-in help expected of a celebrity mom.[41] Her book was important for her daughters, she said, so if they have children in the future they can recognize the symptoms of postpartum depression. And her book was important for her sons, since it could "help them know a woman as a complete, multilevel person. They will understand that a woman is different from a man, emotionally as well as physically, and grow to value those differences."[42]

Osmond's conservative take on postpartum depression reified natural motherhood. It also had the power to reach conservative and Christian mothers in a way nothing before it had. She spoke about postpartum depression when emceeing President George W. Bush's inaugural ball.[43] Utah's *Deseret News* covered Osmond's initial admission of illness, which grimly described how it had caused her "to abandon her husband and seven children."[44] After the book, and after her reconciliation with her husband, the paper showed more support.[45] Osmond's narrative did not critique the expectations of motherhood, though it challenged some of the stresses on working mothers in Hollywood.

Psychosis and Sensationalism

A month after the release of Osmond's book, postpartum mental illness made headlines like never before. Andrea Yates was a mother of five children between the ages of six months and seven years old living in Texas. She has a long history of mental illness, which included previous bouts of postpartum depression. In June 2001, Yates drowned all five children. She then called 911.[46] The horrific case made headlines around the country, and Americans seemed unable to get enough of the gruesome details. Papers ran more than a thousand articles on Yates in the first month of her trial.[47]

The extraordinary appetite for stories about Yates offered an awareness-raising opportunity. News stories covered Yates, her husband, her religion, and her health history in depth. They brought on experts, many of them postpartum psychiatrists and psychologists who had been doing media for over a decade. But postpartum advocates questioned how much of an opportunity it really was, when every conversation centered on a quintuple murder.

Postpartum Support International now had a website, run out of Indiana University of Pennsylvania, managed by anthropologist Laurence Kruckman. It had a clunky university URL and limited resources at first, though Kruckman and his wife later purchased and donated the more memorable postpartum.net address to PSI.[48] Still, the existence of the website helped establish PSI and its professional members as the "go-tos" for reporters looking for an expert.

PSI experts avoided speculating about Yates; instead, they spoke generally about postpartum mental illness. The conflation of depression and psychosis meant a confusing muddle of news reports on both postpartum depression and psychosis. One *ABC News* segment airing the day after the deaths described "a rollercoaster of emotions in the first few days postpartum." For most, the condition "clears up," the voiceover explained, but some develop a more serious postpartum depression or even a psychosis.[49] In this way, the Yates tragedy provided an entering wedge.

But overall the media coverage of Yates was not good for women. Postpartum therapist Karen Kleiman got call after call about Yates from news outlets. She would try to turn the interviews around, to be as broadly educational about the postpartum as possible. But most of what resulted "scared the shit out of women," Kleiman said. They were afraid they could hurt their children, but also afraid that if they spoke about any of their postpartum emotional problems, other people would assume they might hurt their children. Even as it made for media coverage of postpartum illness, Kleiman says, "the whole Andrea Yates piece was re-silencing moms."

Depression After Delivery activist Joyce Venis said something similar: all the emphasis on extreme cases of postpartum psychosis was stigmatizing the more common versions of postpartum depression. It made women more embarrassed to seek help.[50] And of course not everyone accepted the explanation that Yates's situation was the result of a postpartum psychosis. PSI president-elect Larry Kruckman received calls to his home after his Yates-related media appearances, including one from an angry person who called in the middle of the night to tell him he was evil. Conservative talk hosts described Kruckman as a "liberal whiner" for his medicalization of Yates's situation.[51]

Psychologist Shoshana Bennett described the stress of dealing with the media in a "psychotic mom killing child" moment. "I've always used those instances as a way to educate," she said. While there is some media that is so obviously sensationalist that she won't participate, usually she'll take the opportunities. The conflation of all illness with psychosis, though, encouraged discomfort around postpartum depression. One article in *Ebony*, a couple years after the case, encouraged Black women to get help for postpartum depression, while noting that "few can forget the case of Andrea Yates, who had a previous history of postpartum depression."[52] Perhaps a mother who saw herself in the article's list of symptoms—sadness, lack of interest in the baby, and being overwhelmed—would get help out of fear of becoming like Yates. Or perhaps she would resist help, refusing to compare herself to Yates.

Yates herself was a complicated figure. White, suburban, and Christian, she received more sympathy than many women with postpartum psychoses. Some media described her not as psychotic, but as someone who "apparently cared too much" about her children. "What could have possibly driven a middle-class suburban mother to drown her five children?" they asked.[53] Articles frequently described the Yates family's neighborhood as middle class and suburban, to emphasize how shocking the murders were—as if the deaths of five young children would have been less shocking for a different family.[54] Some liberal feminists jumped to defend Yates, arguing both that her crime was an extreme manifestation of the pressures of motherhood, and that it illuminated the lack of research on postpartum psychosis.[55] Yates had a history of postpartum depression and psychosis, and had tried to kill herself twice previously. A doctor had warned her not to have more children.[56] While a jury quickly convicted Yates, they refused the death penalty. Yates's conviction was overturned by reason of insanity four years later, and she was transferred from prison to a high-security mental hospital.[57]

Brooke Shields, Tom Cruise, and Sympathetic Stories

Postpartum advocates agreed the Yates case was a turning point for public awareness of postpartum mental illness. They tried to make the most of the hand dealt to them, but the severity of Yates's illness and crimes made her an unfortunate face for postpartum illness.

Four years later, actress Brooke Shields published a memoir on her postpartum depression. Enough time had passed since the Yates case that there was some space for the conversation Shields introduced. Shields revealed that she had had severe depression, but like Marie Osmond, not psychosis. She was not a risk to her baby. Shields was relatable. She was sympathetic. As she revealed her struggles with miscarriage, in vitro fertilization, and a traumatic birth, she became even more sympathetic.

The narrative Shields laid out paralleled many postpartum depression stories. She wanted a baby desperately. Then her emotional response to actually having that baby was nothing like she expected. "At times I even had trouble holding Rowan because of my choking sobs," she explained. "Why was I crying more than my baby?" Her depression seemed to come out of nowhere—she emphasized many times what a positive person she normally is—and left her wrecked, as well as racked with guilt. This was not what motherhood was supposed to be like. "Where," she asked, "was the bliss?"[58]

Shields recounted her struggle to accept professional help, and her discomfort taking psychiatric medication. She was afraid people would find out and "think I was weak or crazy." As soon as she started to improve, she took herself off the medication, not tapering off. This left her sicker than before.[59] She eventually accepted medication and therapy. Shields paired these steps with more social supports, like a baby nurse who left her own children to travel with Shields, and accommodations as she returned to work.

Slowly, Shields improved. She described the causes of her depression as a mix of circumstantial (traumatic birth, the recent death of her father) and biological. Shields's book did not have the conservative take on motherhood that Marie Osmond's book did. Still, it presented a narrative common to postpartum depression. She was a struggling mother, but then recovered into idealized motherhood. While Shields criticized media mythology about good motherhood, she also created a narrative arc that ends with her embracing that version of motherhood.[60] She dedicated her book to her baby, "Who makes life worth living." She described her regret at not appreciating early motherhood, since early postpartum love is "so all-consuming and beautiful it's a shame not to feel it longer."[61] At the end of the book, she weans off her antidepressants. A year later, Shields again proved her restoration by having another child. This time, a profile in *People* magazine emphasized, the star did not have depression or need medication.[62]

When the book first came out, profiles of Shields and her "baby crisis" repeated her narrative.[63] These profiles also typically came with descriptions of or sidebars on postpartum depression. Not only was the book itself awareness raising, but so was the surrounding publicity. "In today's society, where mothers are expected to be supermoms, PPD is often considered a luxury afforded only to whiny, pampered women," said one review. Shields's story illustrated this was not the case, that actually "PPD is biological."[64] As another review put it, Shields offered postpartum depression "an accessible, frank—and, yes, attractive—poster girl."[65] Indeed: she was a sympathetic white actress who demonstrated postpartum depression was real and serious but not the same as psychosis, one who proved psychiatric intervention could lead right back to the maternal ideal.

Still, the publicity for the book in the first couple of weeks was nothing special. There was a big event sponsored by *Good Housekeeping*, and a bunch of newspaper profiles. *People* magazine published an excerpt, illustrated liberally with pictures of Shields holding baby Rowan.[66] It was only when actor Tom Cruise spoke out against Shields that her book got serious attention.

By this point, everyone knew of Cruise's involvement in Scientology, a religion opposed to psychiatry and psychopharmaceuticals. On the *Today Show*, Cruise criticized Shields for using antidepressants. He explained that antidepressants "mask the problem" and that "there is no such thing as a chemical imbalance."[67] His interview became more rambling and confused as he went. Ultimately, though, he proposed that while depression could be a true problem, it was an emotional and not a biochemical problem. They could treat depression with exercise and vitamins, he said.[68]

Shields defended herself with an op-ed in the *New York Times*. Shields joked about Cruise's Scientology, suggesting he "stick to saving the world from aliens and let women who are experiencing postpartum depression decide what treatment options are best for them."[69] She doubted Cruise "ever suffered from postpartum depression," but emphasized that it was very much a medical illness. While her memoir included a balance of social and biological causes for postpartum depression, her op-ed focused only on what Cruise had attacked: imbalances.

Shields flatly stated that hormonal imbalances caused postpartum depression, with none of the standard caveats that scientists don't know the causes exactly.[70] The defense at being told postpartum depression was not a mental illness was to double down on just how much a legitimate (biological) mental illness it was. She described herself as fighting back not just for herself, but also for the "hundreds of thousands of women who suffer from postpartum depression."[71]

Cruise's attack on Shields led the public to rally around her. Cruise's Scientology and other erratic behavior (he had just jumped on Oprah's couch and declared his love for actor Katie Holmes during a widely mocked interview) primed Americans to distrust him. Journalists rushed to cite postpartum depression experts, who countered Cruise's arguments. "Today, doctors overwhelmingly say Cruise, who insists he has read all the research, is misinformed," one news segment explained.[72] The *New York Times* printed five letters in support of Shields. Most agreed postpartum depression was real, and that Cruise put women at risk by suggesting their suffering might not require medical treatment.[73] Women on the internet excoriated Cruise.[74]

The response would have been surprising ten years earlier, and unimaginable twenty years earlier. Growing public comfort with depression and antidepressant use, and especially with this idea of a chemical imbalance, led them to challenge Cruise. Handlers scrapped the actor's upcoming promotional tour. His attack had led to a stunning backlash. It also promoted Shields's narrative of postpartum depression: horrible but common, biological but temporary, afflicting white and middle- to upper-class women striving to be perfect mothers.

The incident provided an extraordinary opportunity for postpartum advocates. They were not explaining an infanticide or suicide. They were on television defending a beautiful white depressed-but-restored mother. Shoshana Bennett, at the time president of Postpartum Support International, described the moment. "Even in his ridiculousness," Cruise has "given us a forum," she told a magazine. "I thank him duly."[75] Jane Honikman said, "There wasn't an American alive that didn't know what was going on," thanks to Tom Cruise. It was a turning point, Honikman said. "Look, if Brooke Shields says it's bad, then this is bad. And she didn't kill her children. She didn't want to kill her children."[76]

If She Can Say It, I Can Say It

Nearly twenty years after Nada Stotland and Nancy Berchtold appeared on *Oprah*, Brooke Shields sat on a tan leather couch next to Oprah and shared her story.[77] Oprah displayed an image of Shields with her baby girl, a picture of "bliss." The picture, Oprah explained, hid a darker reality. "Behind closed doors, Brooke was unraveling," she revealed. It was a "downward spiral of misery and despair." Shields described not having "the angels sing" when she first met her baby. She had a terrifying birthing experience, and was then frightened to be alone with the baby.[78] "I had no desire to even try to pretend to care about her," Shields told Oprah, and she felt like a terrible person. She had suicidal thoughts.

While much of Shields's narrative echoed earlier postpartum depression stories, so much had also changed in twenty years. Oprah asked Shields why she, "an educated woman," did not realize this was some kind of postpartum depression. Shields explained that her image of postpartum depression from the media was so different than what she felt. "Postpartum depression to me was the crazy people that drown their kids, it's the people that drive the cars off into the lakes, it's the people that stab their children." She explained she knew better now, understood the difference between psychosis and depression, understood many nuances.

As therapist Karen Kleiman described it, Shields and Osmond opened the door for the huge number of celebrities who confessed their postpartum depression in the 2010s. "This person, that person, everybody's having babies now and talking about how bad they feel . . . Moms like it. If she can say it, I can say it. If she can go through it, I can go through it." Celebrity stories proved one of the few ways to get postpartum depression in the media when there was not a major tragedy.

So many celebrities have told their depression stories now, noted psychologist Michael O'Hara. These public stories of depression have reshaped the landscape of awareness, understanding, and stigma. "It's hard to overstate how important these women have been," he said, "to acceptance of the field." "I could go out and give 1,000 talks," O'Hara adds, "and wouldn't have the impact of one star coming out and talking about her . . . experience."

But the celebrity confessional, the talk show circuit, the local news segments were all more than simple conduits of information. They did not simply "mainstream" the ideas of postpartum activists and professionals. They also told powerful narratives about what postpartum depression was, who got it, what caused it, and what recovery looked like. As much as mass media raised awareness, it also had serious limits. Part of this lay in who got attention and sympathy.

The narratives that got attention were those of well-off white women, even as research at the time showed Black and Latina women | *185* were at greater risk of postpartum mental illness. The whiteness and social class of celebrities who "came out" about postpartum depression helped craft a sympathetic victimhood. But celebrities did not have the same maternity leave, daycare, health insurance, and financial issues as other women, so these concerns often went undiscussed. Individual diagnosis and recovery, good doctors, and self-care reigned supreme.

For the women who could relate, these narratives were invaluable. In some cases, they were lifesaving. At their best, they directed women to other resources, or put the language of "postpartum depression" in their head. This was the goal. But television news clips and talk shows, and celebrity memoirs, were also a limited venue. The idea of postpartum depression that emerged from this media could be homogeneous and narrow. It would take a new generation of activism to change this.

9. *A New Generation of Activism*

Graeme Seabrook was surprised but excited when she discovered she was pregnant. But the pregnancy was not an easy one. She was exhausted and had preeclampsia. She could barely walk by the end. She cried through every obstetrician's appointment, whether happy or sad. Seabrook had imagined an unmedicated birth but had complications, and the doctor performed an emergency C-section after thirty brutal hours of labor. The situation grew dire; her husband and parents realized she might die. Immediately after the birth, nurses took Seabrook's son to the neonatal intensive care unit (NICU). She did not see her baby until almost twenty-four hours postpartum. The traumatic birth and its aftermath marked her. More than a decade later, she still sometimes has nightmares about it.

Seabrook's traumatic experience compounded other risk factors, like a history of depression. She blamed herself—why had her body failed? Even leaving the hospital she was carrying that guilt and feeling angry that neither rosy natural birth classes nor her obstetrician had warned her how bad things might get. She had no idea how common both cesareans and NICU stays were, something she wished her Lamaze classes or her doctors had explained. Seabrook was also unaware how much greater the risk of maternal complications could be for a Black woman like her.

She spent the next couple of months alternating among panic attacks, fogginess, and rage. She barely remembers the period, and doesn't care to. Neither Seabrook nor her husband understood what was wrong, but they knew something was not okay. Her husband eventually called the obstetrician, who connected them with resources.

Seabrook's story sounds like so many postpartum stories in this book. As she healed, she turned her depression and anger into action. She connected with postpartum advocates. Together they had the information she wished she had been given at birth printed on cards and given out to new parents at her Charleston hospital. But her story is also quite different from the story of a 1980s or 1990s postpartum woman launched from illness into activism. This was the 2010s. It was internet access, social media, and blogs that facilitated Seabrook's recovery and activism.

After her husband called for help, Seabrook was able to adopt a new mental illness framework for what was going on. This helped, but she remained consumed with depressive thoughts that nothing would cure her. She logged on to Facebook in the middle of the night, and happened upon a woman who was years recovered from her own postpartum mental illness. The mere fact that this woman went through something similar to her and survived offered hope. Seabrook messaged the woman, who became her support system. The woman texted Seabrook regularly to check in. That woman's friends, other recovered women, all took turns making sure this internet stranger was okay. "That's what PMAD [perinatal mood and anxiety disorders] moms do," Seabrook says. "They just did not ever let me fall." They messaged her regularly up until Seabrook could get to her first therapy appointment.

As Seabrook recovered, she found a local support group, Postpartum Support Charleston, through a Google search. She became involved in that group, but remained online as well. She connected with other women through the popular blog Postpartum Progress, and became involved in their national activist network.

The 2000s and 2010s were a time of substantial postpartum activism. Some looked familiar: Postpartum Support International (PSI) grew dramatically, and smaller local groups like Postpartum Support Charleston continued work they had been doing since the 1980s. Some looked quite different, though. Depression After Delivery (DAD) folded. Organizations new and old embraced the internet, changing what it meant to find other parents who experienced postpartum illness. They also experienced a racial reckoning, as postpartum activists of color connected and challenged the whiteness of postpartum advocacy.

The End of an Era

In the late 1980s and in the 1990s, Postpartum Support International (PSI) and Depression After Delivery (DAD) dominated postpartum activism. By the mid-1990s, PSI was a little more populated by therapists. DAD saw itself as "more grassroots and women to women," though it too included many postpartum professionals at its national level, especially on its boards.[1] PSI had West Coast headquarters, DAD had East Coast headquarters. The two regularly collaborated, but tensions between the groups and their leadership remained even as it grew harder to remember why. Jane Honikman and Nancy Berchtold, the founders of PSI and DAD, respectively, both stepped back from their leadership roles.

While DAD always had some financial problems, like most non-profits, it struggled especially with balancing its grassroots feel with making enough money to stay afloat. While it charged modest membership fees for years, in the early 2000s some board members pushed for a more inclusive organization that avoided fees. Susan Feingold, a psychologist and DAD executive board member at the time, joked about the problem of a board of "bleeding heart liberals." "I think we all wanted . . . to make a difference, wanted people to be more aware," she says. So the board eliminated membership fees, switching to a donation model.

Could they get enough donations? The question depended on whose donations they would take. One board member at the time was Dr. Zachary Stowe, a researcher at Emory University. He offered to contact drug companies, since he had a close relationship with GlaxoSmithKline. It would turn out that that relationship was a little too close; Stowe got in trouble for taking money from them while conducting federally funded research on how their drugs affected pregnant women.[2] No one at DAD knew anything about this. They had mixed feelings about taking drug company money, though.

The fear, Feingold says, was that "Once we take drug money, then they own us." Nancy Berchtold explained what a hard decision it was for the board. They wanted to continue to help mothers and families, she said, but the only way to survive was by being "very, very medical, very professional." Berchtold always had a psychiatric advisor on board and had no problem with the medicalization of postpartum depression. But she worried about seeing the organization so filled with doctors, especially those who might join the board for professional advancement rather than for their commitment to the cause. That doctors were the ones introducing pharmaceutical money to the mix did not help. "The pharmaceutical company starts filtering into this pure grassroots movement," Berchtold recounted. "They were all happy to give us a donation and put a blurb in our newsletter." While some board members fought it, the fight was a difficult one—a more democratic organization without membership fees, but with pharmaceutical influence, or one that was pharma-free but remained broke and fee based. The board agreed to take $75,000 in fundraising seed money from two pharmaceutical companies.

Unfortunately, this was not the end of DAD's financial woes. It was the start of even worse ones. They hired a Florida-based fundraising firm and gave them $60,000 to invest.[3] The fundraiser either lost or stole the money and went abroad, leaving DAD without the funding they had just compromised over. DAD was both financially broke and broken in spirit. The organization folded. Berchtold reflected on the grim trajectory from 1985 to 2005. It was so hard to think of "the history of a nonprofit like ours that went from that one first phone call . . . and then handing off to a man who took every dime of the organization."

The Rise of Postpartum Progress

Some DAD board members migrated to PSI, and DAD's much-publicized toll-free number (1-800-944-4PPD) became the PSI toll-free number. But there was a hole in the postpartum landscape. PSI was just beginning to coordinate groups around the country, and it did not have support group chapters the way DAD once did. PSI spoke with women and connected women to help, but DAD chapters were the help groups themselves. Now DAD was gone.

Fitting for the early 2000s, it was not a new group exactly, but a blog that filled that chasm. Almost twenty years after Nancy Berchtold placed a tiny newspaper ad about postpartum illness, Katherine Stone made a blog post about her own postpartum anxiety and obsessive-compulsive disorder (OCD). The blog post launched her extremely popular website, Postpartum Progress. In a few years the blog became a movement of sorts, with online groups and an engaged readership with many guest posts. In 2011, Stone incorporated it as a nonprofit. The group held conferences, did political advocacy, and ran fundraisers. "Katherine Stone," another postpartum advocate explained, "was really like the voice of postpartum depression and really made it very real for moms."[4]

Stone started her blog out of an anger common to women with postpartum depression: she wanted to know why no one had warned her about what could happen after having a baby. Following her first child's birth in 2000, she had intrusive thoughts of harming her infant, and extreme anxiety that she might. Since these were not clearly depression symptoms, she did not associate them with postpartum depression. Even as decades of advocacy had made it so she knew what postpartum depression was, Stone, like other women, often had a preconception about what postpartum depression would look like. Other postpartum mental health challenges like anxiety and OCD were not equally visible.

In her inaugural post, Stone outlined her goal for the blog: it would be her contribution to the ongoing need for more support for women with postpartum mental illness. "There are still women who can't get treatment because they either don't have insurance or what they have covers little to no psychiatric care," she wrote. "There are still women killing themselves and/or others. There are still women being undiagnosed or misdiagnosed." While implicitly acknowledging the decades of change up to that point, she made clear how much was left to do. She would fill her blog with women's personal stories and inspiration.[5] Looking back on it eight years later, she described the start as a time when she "wasn't really . . . much of an advocate. I was just reporting."[6]

The blog gained popularity quickly, becoming a safe place for women to ask questions, get peer support, read other women's postpartum stories, and connect with resources.[7] The website housed a "testimonials" section where women detailed what they found in Postpartum Progress. As a woman explained to CNN, reading the blog was like suddenly "reading exactly my symptoms and stories of women who had been through what I had, who had it worse than I had." She continued, "knowing you're not alone has been unbelievable." Half a million women accessed the Postpartum Progress blog annually in 2014.[8]

While Stone initially described herself as not an advocate, this changed about three years in. Her 2009 online Mother's Day Rally for Mom's Mental Health featured twenty-four letters on the importance of maternal mental health, one posted each hour. All of the letters from Warrior Moms, as Stone dubbed Postpartum Progress members, offered an opportunity for awareness raising beyond the blog. Postpartum Progress encouraged women to "Get your Twitter fingers ready" and offered a #momsmentalhealth hashtag for awareness raising.[9] Stone also gained more attention when she began responding to controversies, like Tom Cruise's conflicts with psychiatry.

In 2011, Stone incorporated Postpartum Progress as a nonprofit.[10] Beyond awareness raising, she now also sought to raise money to encourage scientific research. One way was through the Climb Out of Darkness fundraiser, a walkathon. At the first event in 2013, some 177 people raised $40,000. Then, in 2014, a total of 1,600 climbers and walkers raised $165,000.[11] The event continued to grow each year, amid a larger rise in these kind of charity walks and runs.[12]

It was as the blog was becoming a true organization that Graeme Seabrook found it. Seabrook was active in Postpartum Support Charleston, where she participated in an annual 5K fundraiser, despite her hatred of running. It was "me and a bunch of white moms," Seabrook said. When she eventually learned statistics about how common postpartum mental illness was for Black mothers, she was shocked. The self-selection of volunteers probably accounted for its composition. Women needed the time and money to volunteer. The support group meetings themselves were not always fully accessible, and Seabrook pushed to have one meeting easily reached by public transportation. She made sure fliers used both Spanish and English and were hung at laundromats and bus stops, not just Starbucks and gyms. No one opposed any of these measures; they had just never considered them before.

To prepare for helping run support group sessions, Seabrook took an online peer support training put on by Postpartum Support International. Then she found she still wanted to do more, something to prevent postpartum illness rather than just helping already-sick women. Seabrook, who was herself just "coming back to life" through therapy and her volunteer work, encouraged Postpartum Support Charleston to create a trifold brochure for pediatricians and obstetricians. Volunteers then went to obstetricians and offered lists of local therapists they could connect to patients.

For Seabrook, Postpartum Progress was a revelation. The website was populated by women just like her. The Warrior Moms formed tight online friendships driven by their mission. According to Seabrook, they were also driven by fear, a fear of losing moms whom they could possibly save. The atmosphere could be intense.

Postpartum Progress brought bloggers together at several in-person conferences. The first was a small meeting in Boston in 2015, their "Warrior Mom™ Conference." While there were other conferences for postpartum professionals, Katherine Stone wrote in a blog post, "this, my dear Warrior Moms, *is for us!!!*"[13] The conference was meant to bring together volunteers, survivors, and women still in recovery. It nodded at larger divisions in postpartum activism, with Postpartum Progress distinguishing itself from PSI. Seabrook described a pervasive (though not explicit) feeling in Postpartum Progress "that Postpartum Support International was for doctors and that we were here for moms." While she is clear now that this was an unfair distinction, she says the laywomen felt "almost like we were on a mission. They're just doing their job. That we somehow cared more or were more invested or were more important or were more real."

At the conference, about sixty activists shared ideas and resources, explaining what their local organizations were up to that was especially innovative or interesting. They networked and put online names to real-life faces. The conference "felt so good," Seabrook recounted. "None of us had degrees in this. None of us were trained to do any of this, you know, beyond training that we had sought out." It was also the first time Seabrook met other Black postpartum activists in person. The 2015 Postpartum Progress conference, followed by a much larger 2016 conference in Atlanta, brought together this set of highly involved and very online lay postpartum activists. "These people get it!" Seabrook thought.

While attendees were mostly nonprofessionals, the pharmaceutical company Sage Therapeutics sponsored the conference. The company was developing Zulresso, which they hoped would be the first drug specifically aimed at treating severe postpartum depression (which was typically treated with general antidepressants and anti-anxiety medications). Seabrook recalls intense emotion at a presentation on the drug. "I was feeling like an idiot for crying until I looked up and looked around and everybody was crying," because of all the hope they had for the new drug. They could now tell moms it would truly be okay, that "we're going to fix this." It was like a religious experience, she says, all too intense. The relationship with Sage did not seem problematic to Seabrook, who said it was amazing to have this big company come and ask them—regular moms—for input. This, Seabrook says, was especially true for the Black women there. "That is almost antithetical to the idea of being a Black mom," she says, "having somebody ask you what you need? How can we help you?" The camaraderie and excitement of the conference encouraged women to further volunteer their time and energy to the nonprofit.

The Fall of Postpartum Progress

After the Atlanta conference, Seabrook accepted a position working twenty hours a month for Postpartum Progress, while continuing to volunteer substantially more hours. Her main responsibilities were to help with the conference to be held in Denver in 2017. In February 2017, Seabrook got permission from her immediate supervisor to open a Facebook group for the conference. Once she did, though, Katherine Stone posted her annoyance that the group had been opened without consulting her, the CEO. It was a small conflict, but it pushed Seabrook over the edge. The organization centered heavily on Stone and her blog, so slights by Stone felt significant. "She was our mom. She was our savior. She was the person who had saved other moms—who had saved other moms—who had saved us." Seabrook's commitment to Postpartum Progress was emotional and significant, but her list of microaggressions—a literal list she kept—was lengthy. Sarcastic comments, ideas stolen, tokenism.

Seabrook decided to resign, and also to be vocal about why. "I used to volunteer for a wonderful organization dedicated to a cause I care deeply about," Seabrook wrote in a blog post. "It is full of women who have inspired me and helped me heal. I don't work there anymore."[14] She tied the particular microaggression about the Facebook group to a much larger history of racism in the US, from the whiteness of anti-Trump "pussy marches" earlier in the year to her refusal to confront white parents at her child's school lest she be labeled an angry Black woman.

The next morning, she woke up to "a shit storm." Other women of color shared Seabrook's complaints. They sent her direct messages about how their ideas or phrases were used without credit, or how poorly they were treated by Postpartum Progress leadership. While Seabrook would not speak publicly about these women's private communications to her, she says the list of grievances was long and that most were much worse than her experience. "I was just annoyed because there was a sarcastic remark," she says, not mistreated like some of these women. One anonymous white woman described racism as a long-term problem for the organization, that it had a history of serious turnover of women of color in leadership positions.[15] But other women railed against this attack on Stone and Postpartum Progress, framing any division as a threat to the larger goal of helping postpartum women. "Moms are going to die," women emailed her, "and it's going to be your fault." The postpartum activist community buzzed with both support and disdain for Seabrook.

Two days later, Seabrook's friend and fellow Black postpartum activist Jasmine Banks posted a petition demanding that Postpartum Progress make it right. "Postpartum Progress has a history of causing harm toward Black women and women of color. It is time for accountability," she wrote.[16] Banks proposed two options. Either they could remove the CEO and the board and establish a new board that is "intersectional and inclusive." Or they could dissolve "the nonprofit that was built for white women" and use its funds to pay reparations to harmed staff and volunteers and fund Mental Health in Color scholarship.[17]

While the petition gathered signatures, Seabrook and her supporters also worked behind the scenes to apply more pressure to Stone. The only way to put enough pressure on her, they decided, was to go after one of Postpartum Progress's major funding sources: Sage Therapeutics. One of Seabrook's friends drafted a letter to Sage asking them to pressure Stone for an apology. Sage, not wanting to be associated with accusations of racism, agreed. It conditionally pulled its $10,000 sponsorship of the upcoming Denver conference pending a resolution of the problems.

Two days after the petition, and four days after Seabrook's blog post on the microaggressions, Postpartum Progress held a conference call with a major announcement. Seabrook assumed Stone would step down, whether short term or permanently, or that they were instituting some kind of racial sensitivity training. Instead, they announced the end of Postpartum Progress. The group chose to dissolve rather than address the issues at hand.

Postpartum Progress's website remained up, with occasional posts for the next two years. Stone canceled the Denver conference, removed the website donation button, and formally shuttered the nonprofit she had begun six years earlier. The popular Facebook group closed, leaving women unsure where to go. Most who remained with postpartum activism moved to Postpartum Support International. Postpartum Progress gave its money to PSI with the stipulation they create an advisory board that was half women of color.[18]

Seabrook, like most Postpartum Progress members, found the shutdown shocking. People sent comments and messages to her nonstop, some supportive and some threatening. "There's still people who absolutely loathe and despise me," Seabrook says. On the other end, "there's people who believe that I was martyred in some way, which I absolutely was not . . . the whole thing was just really weird, and strange, and like surreal looking back on it. Everyone screwed up."

New Directions for Postpartum Support International

Between the early 2000s and the 2020s, the budget, reach, and profile of Postpartum Support International all grew dramatically. By the mid-2010s, they either absorbed or created chapters in every US state and Puerto Rico. They also developed a system of trainings and certifications that became the only significant certification in maternal mental health in the US. At first the trainings were offered once a year, but by the early 2000s they started having a few a year around the country.[19] Their growth was occasionally controversial—some complained the certification was expensive, elitist, and in the beginning not thoughtful about race—but it represented a profound institutionalization of postpartum activism and postpartum professionals.

Susan Dowd Stone was brought in to chair a conference, and then she was asked to serve as president of PSI in 2008. While Jane Hon-ikman had stepped back from PSI in many ways, it remained her "baby"—she brought Dowd Stone to California beforehand to visit with her and make sure she was a good fit for the presidency.

Dowd Stone had a business background before she became a so-cial worker. The organization had discussed the idea of chapters for years, but shied away from implementation, worrying about liability and whether this diffuse growth was the best way forward. But Dowd Stone accepted the challenge of creating a footprint in every state. She appointed volunteer state coordinator Wendy Davis to the board, since according to Dowd Stone, Davis was already "doing 90 percent of all the work." Between 2008 and 2010, PSI adopted large postpar-tum groups like Postpartum Support Virginia and its counterparts in Washington State, New York, and Ohio.[20] They brought state coordi-nators to their national conferences on scholarships to keep everyone on the same page and better unite the organization.

As PSI expanded its reach and formalized its relationships with other groups, it also took on major awareness-raising projects. The most important of these was probably a series of public service an-nouncements run by CBS Cares. The $2 million campaign included one ad that ran during the Super Bowl, which Dowd Stone was es-pecially proud of. Psychiatrist Margaret Spinelli consulted on the pieces, which used stars from the CBS show *Cold Case* to explain that there were resources for women experiencing postpartum depres-sion.[21] The ads ran in English and in Spanish. In return, PSI awarded CBS Cares their Excellence in Media Outreach Award, and the Na-tional Alliance on Mental Illness also awarded the campaign an Out-standing Media award.[22]

While Dowd Stone made frequent media appearances at the launch of the CBS Cares campaign, she also asserted boundaries that illustrate changing norms among postpartum advocates. Out-lets frequently asked for formerly depressed and psychotic women to appear on their shows, as mass media had done for two decades. Dowd Stone, however, generally refused these requests. She argued that "when women have recovered from PPD, they're so exhilarated that they finally feel better that they're almost willing to do anything. But you don't know how they're gonna feel ten years down the road at having this footage available." Media appearances could be a health hazard to a woman.

In 2010, Wendy Davis became the paid executive director of the organization.[23] Davis was, according to Dowd Stone, "an unsung hero of feet on the ground and holding things together even when all the politics were raging." Davis was already a therapist when she gave birth to her son in Portland, Oregon, in 1994. Severe depression and anxiety followed the birth, but even as a therapist, Davis could not recognize her symptoms. Davis's training had been infused with psychoanalytic mom blaming: any postpartum problems resulted from a dependent personality or a troubled relationship with their mother. While Davis eventually realized something was wrong, she described her problem as a traumatic birth and grief. It took a post-partum doula to tell Davis that she had postpartum depression. The doula, who listened to Davis and visited with her daily, did not have psychological training but had a deep empathy and a sense of what Davis needed.

This experience shaped Davis, who has since valued both expert intervention and lay support, which she sees as complementary. If she had gotten better without the peer support component, Davis says, if it had been purely clinical help, she would still believe she had not been meant to be a mother. Only through peer support could she stop blaming herself.

While Davis was herself still depressed, a former client called to tell her about a community support group for postpartum depression she was starting. The client had no idea Davis was depressed, she just needed someone to serve as a clinical advisor. Davis agreed to this serendipitous request. The client began this group, the Baby Blues Connection, in Portland in 1994. After a couple of months the client moved away, and at ten months postpartum, Davis took the group over. Through it she was introduced to PSI and Jane Honikman. Honikman convinced Davis to volunteer as the PSI state coordinator for both Oregon and Idaho. After that, she recalls, she just did more and more volunteering, until Dowd Stone tapped her to sit on the PSI board. In these years PSI grew, further professionalized, and strengthened its partnership with the Marcé Society.

Then in 2008, country singer Wade Bowen wrote a song about his wife's postpartum depression called "Turn on the Lights." Bowen also hosted an annual charity golf tournament, which he made benefit Postpartum Support International for three years in a row. The first year he donated $66,000. PSI had never received a donation of that magnitude. The next two years, Wade Bowen's fundraiser brought in $100,000 a year. The money allowed the PSI board to hire its first salaried executive director: Wendy Davis.[24]

Davis sold her private therapy practice and joined PSI's one other paid employee, a part-time office manager. Under her leadership, PSI focused on balancing free programming for women and families with pricey trainings for postpartum professionals. Memberships, trainings, and certifications provided the financial scaffolding as the organization worked to meet the needs of professionals and, much more than in decades past, postpartum individuals. The absorption of DAD and the formalization of their state coordinator program abetted this. Sometimes people cannot tell if PSI is a group for families or for professionals, Davis says. Consultants have pushed the organization to pick a side. But, according to Davis, PSI's strength is in its refusal to either be fully for professionals or to be fully peer support. "We provide free support to families," she says. "We train professionals. And we're a bridge to connect the two."

As of 2022, PSI had trained over 40,000 individuals. They have 40 staff members and 4,000 active volunteers. Whereas conferences in the early 2000s might get 90 or 95 attendees, the 2023 conference had 500.[25] Yet its identity remains deeply influenced by its more grassroots origins. One retired PSI trainer, Pec Indman, talked about the organization as a family and recounted dancing to "We Are Family" at a recent conference. "We're really close," Indman explained, "and I don't know that that happens that often in professional organizations." The idea of PSI as family was powerful, and other PSI advocates echoed it. Diana Lynn Barnes, a former PSI president, described how PSI conferences "really feel like I'm coming home to be with my family." Even as the organization grew, she explained, the shared mission and focus, the fact that everyone "gets it," differentiated it from other professional spaces. As close as PSI leadership felt through the 2000s and 2010s, though, the idea that they were all one "family" was not universal. When Postpartum Progress had its reckoning around racism in 2017, PSI also had to address the issue.

The Perinatal Mental Health Alliance for People of Color

Divya Kumar, Jabina Coleman, and Desirée Israel met at a PSI meeting in San Diego in 2016. All women of color, they looked around the room and realized "there's not too many of us Black or brown people here." The content of the conference also included very little about race and ethnicity. "We were tired of being that sidebar slide," Kumar said.[26] You can't just have a couple bullet points on race, culture, and postpartum depression, she says, it is all completely intertwined.

Desirée Israel, a perinatal social worker, could not disentangle systemic racism from her own postpartum. A month after her son's birth in 2012, the murder of seventeen-year-old Trayvon Martin filled the news cycle. Israel had an undiagnosed postpartum depression, compounded by the vicarious trauma of the Martin killing. Psychotherapist Divya Kumar described seeing Black postpartum clients, whose experience of having new babies was shaped by their overall lack of security. "How am I ever gonna feel safe? Like what is safety?" Kumar said women asked her. "And like no white woman was ever gonna CBT [Cognitive Behavioral Therapy] them into feeling safe," she said. In other words, the tools of psychology would not be enough on their own—it mattered who was using those tools. Likewise, Kumar sees many clients who are, like her, the children of immigrants. Popular postpartum discourses like "self-care," she says, fall flat when talking to a population who has grown up with the idea that motherhood is self-sacrifice. Self-care had been one of the great innovations of PSI in the 1990s, but it reflected the organization's composition of the time.

The need for more therapists who understood the needs of postpartum patients of color was great.

Israel went to her first PSI training in 2015, at a golf resort in Michigan. It was "a sea of white women." Israel counted only a handful of BIPOC individuals amid the 300 attendees, but still found the training powerful. It was "very white but interesting," she said, and had both personal and professional meaning to her. The training made her realize the seriousness of what she had been through. It also launched her on a path to a career in postpartum mental illness.

Like Israel, Jabina Coleman found a PSI meeting that changed her personally and professionally. She had undiagnosed and untreated postpartum depression and obsessive-compulsive disorder after the birth of her first child in 2003. Only a decade later, through PSI, did she come to apply that language to her experience. She came to PSI not as a survivor but as a professional, a medical social worker, therapist, and lactation consultant. A pop-up advertisement on her screen one late night alerted her to the existence of the organization, and then she became a hotline volunteer. In 2016, she went to her first training and first PSI conference, in San Diego. There she met Israel and Kumar, and only then realized that she herself had suffered from postpartum depression.

Coleman, Israel, and Kumar remained in touch. When Postpartum Progress dissolved a year later, they were surprised like everyone else and exchanged text messages about the debacle: "Girl, did you see that?" Israel had been on the Postpartum Progress board, but the other two women were not heavily involved in the organization. Realizing that there would be a huge gap in postpartum organizing, they found their spark.[27] They would create their own postpartum organization, run for and by practitioners of color. They knew this was needed before the collapse of Postpartum Progress, said Kumar, but the collapse increased the urgency.

They founded their group, the Perinatal Mental Health Alliance for Women of Color, later changing "Women" to "People." While they began as an independent organization, soon they approached Wendy Davis about the possibility of integrating the Alliance into PSI. They had some hesitations about joining the organization. Kumar described the "emotional exhaustion of being the only one in a room." "How many times have I sat on a board," she explained, "or been at some leadership table as the only person of color? And it is very clear that like—it's like you're a guest at somebody else's lunch table." You might as well have a "token" label on your head, she said, you "are there to be the diversity person." You were not there to have influence, because so often "the people who own that lunch table are not ready to cede power, authority, and control." Simple diversity work, just adding a few token people of color to the table, "is kind of dumb."

They wanted to do more than simple diversity work, and decided access to the resources and infrastructure of PSI was worth the risk. Joining up with PSI was a strategy, Israel explained, and allowed them access to PSI's reputation and connections. PSI leadership was open to diversifying its membership, conferences, and training content. And the heavily white PSI needed them. Davis, who is white, describes their approaching her as one of the happiest days of her life. As the biggest postpartum depression organization in the US, any changes in PSI would be impactful.

The three women met with Davis once a month for years as they built up the organization and developed trust between them. Ultimately, they built a strong relationship through hard conversations about racism and power within PSI. Kumar emphasized the importance of equity in postpartum activist spaces. If you want equity, she says, "that has to come with white women stepping away and . . . ceding power." For the first four and a half years, Israel, Coleman, and Kumar ran the Alliance as volunteers while holding other full-time jobs. In 2021, a grant from the Perigee Fund allowed PSI to hire a paid director for the Alliance. The funding also helped them expand the Alliance's scholarship program, which brought providers of color to PSI trainings and the annual conference. At the 2022 conference they offered seventy-eight scholarships, in addition to the thirty or forty throughout the year for trainings.[28] The money was critical to making this work happen. You can't just say "everybody's welcome here" and expect that to diversify an organization, Kumar explained, they needed to put resources toward that change. The scholarships tapped into a huge unmet need, sometimes netting over ten times as many applications as the program could support.

From Diversity to Justice

The Alliance helped diversify the conference, and each year was more diverse than the previous one. The scholarships contributed to this change. Even the mere existence of the Alliance, with its website and social media presence, seemed to have some impact on the conference's diversity. The first year after the Alliance's creation, at the 2018 conference in Houston, Jabina Coleman says an older Black midwife approached her. The woman had formally been a PSI member for ages but had never considered attending a conference. Then she heard about the Alliance, and for the first time felt like she belonged there.

Beginning the year before, the Alliance hosted a special session for PSI members of color to meet up. Now they were more than one half-filled table, and this remarkably fast change was inspirational. It was "profound and powerful," Divya Kumar explained. There was still work to be done, but the Alliance founders all expressed optimism about the direction of PSI and its increasing integration of race and culture issues into its trainings.

During this time, the long-unspoken problem of whiteness in postpartum activism was increasingly spoken. Women of color stood up to address it, both in Postpartum Progress and in Postpartum Support International. They created their own structures, in and outside of the mainstream organizations, to meet unmet needs.

10. *It Is Not a Political Issue*

In 2001, Melanie Blocker Stokes gave birth to a daughter. She named her Sommer Skyy, after her favorite season. The forty-one-year-old Black mother was a Spelman graduate and a pharmaceutical representative in Chicago for AstraZeneca. She was "beautiful, bubbly, and outgoing."[1] Melanie and her husband, a doctor, had worried they might never conceive and had rejoiced when Melanie became pregnant. Stokes's mother emphasized how desperate Melanie had been to be a mother. "Melanie believed motherhood was her life mission," she said, "and fiercely wanted a daughter of her own."[2]

But after giving birth, nothing went as imagined. Melanie slipped into a psychotic depression. She stopped eating and drinking. She exhibited erratic behavior, like wandering out of the house and over to Lake Michigan in the middle of the night. She was openly suicidal, removing the screen from her mother's high-rise apartment window, hiding a butcher's knife in her bathroom, asking her brother if he could get her a gun. Melanie did not want to hold her daughter, and lamented what a terrible wife and mother she was. "I am not good enough to have a baby," she told her mother. Her family hospitalized Melanie three times in just a couple of months. "The first time I took Melanie to the hospital," her mother recalled, "the nurse met me at

the door and said, 'This is a female thing. Men don't understand it.'
And now I know what she means."[3]

Doctors described Melanie's problem as postpartum depression
and gave her antidepressants and electroconvulsive therapy.[4] One
suggested exercise, some jumping jacks. Nothing worked. While the
doctors also prescribed antipsychotics, no one used the language of
postpartum psychosis. If they had, her mother believes, it might have
helped impart the seriousness of her condition, and the importance
of her remaining somewhere in-patient. Melanie's husband, himself
a doctor, felt overwhelmed and confused. He alternated between taking care of her and telling her to snap out of it.

Newly released from the hospital, about four months postpartum, Melanie got a cab and left home at the first opportunity. The
Chicago news stations covered her disappearance. Her family got
on television to plead with her to come home. But Melanie was too
ill, too far gone. She died by suicide in a local hotel a couple of days
later.

Melanie died just a couple of days before Andrea Yates killed her
children. The women experienced very different versions of postpartum psychosis, but after the Yates tragedy, news stories about Melanie almost always mentioned both women. While there was not as
much sensational coverage of Melanie's suicide, her illness ended up
having national legislative import.

That is because Melanie's mother, Carol Blocker, began campaigning for greater awareness of postpartum mental illness almost immediately after her daughter's death. The lack of understanding she
observed distressed her, especially the medical ignorance about postpartum psychosis. The doctors Melanie encountered seemed to not
know what they were doing, throwing every psychiatric treatment
they could think of at her to see if anything worked. When Blocker
later spoke before Congress about her daughter's illness, she held up
a plastic bag filled with pill bottles, medications prescribed to Melanie over the course of a few months, to punctuate her point. Melanie
also likely had racial barriers to adequate care. Black publications

covering her death noted the much higher rates of Black maternal mortality, often rooted in systemic prejudice.[5]

As Blocker began speaking about Melanie's death, other parents contacted her to relate how their daughters died by suicide following postpartum depression and psychosis, or else were in prison for infanticide. "I started getting phone calls from people all over America," Blocker said. "And then I realized that the reason no one has ever done anything about this illness is because it happens to new moms. If anything happens to a new mom, most people are not that interested."[6] They want to ask light questions and know the sex of the baby. They do not want to think seriously about a mother's well-being. Like postpartum advocates before her, Blocker went on *Oprah*. The phone calls poured in, cementing the importance of this activism.

Carol Blocker founded the Melanie Blocker Stokes Foundation and held Melanie's Walk as a fundraiser and memorial. "I'm not going to let her die in vain," she said.[7] She also reached out to her congressional representative, Bobby Rush, a former civil rights activist and Black Panther. Blocker, a fifth-grade teacher, taught at Rush's grandchildren's school.[8] Rush had only just learned about severe postpartum mental illness by watching the coverage of the search for Melanie on the news. In the months that followed, Blocker and Rush developed a legislative response to postpartum illness. Postpartum advocacy groups joined them.

Advocates for the bill argued that this legislation was bipartisan and politically neutral. As Blocker explained before Congress, "it is not a political issue," it is a matter of public health.[9] They centered arguments on respectable, good motherhood, attacked by hormonal and other biochemical forces. Postpartum depression advocates from Postpartum Support International and Postpartum Progress organized to push the Melanie Blocker Stokes legislation. In the process, they articulated a vision of their political power rooted in their motherhood that echoed a long history of maternalist activism.[10] If postpartum legislation could help the beleaguered American family *and* support women's health, shouldn't Democrats and Republicans alike support it?

State Legislation

The first significant postpartum legislation was not the national Melanie Blocker Stokes Act, but state-level legislation that helped pave the way. Virginia passed a 2003 law requiring parents to receive information on postpartum depression, and Texas passed its "Andrea Yates Bill" requiring the state to establish a website with a resource list on postpartum depression.[11] These were small asks, but they were victories. New Jersey passed some of the first legislation on postpartum screening. The state's first lady, Mary Jo Codey, had herself had severe postpartum depression.

Mary Jo Codey encouraged her husband to also create a State Postpartum Depression Working Group in 2005. The task force included psychiatrists and activists, including Ric Fernandez, the psychiatrist who had consulted with Nancy Berchtold on Depression After Delivery (DAD). The group encouraged legislation, a "first-of-its kind law," that required depression screening and education on postpartum mental illness.[12] The resulting Act Concerning Postpartum Depression led to massive trainings of about 4,500 medical professionals in providing screenings.

Other states passed similar laws. A 2008 Illinois law required the state's departments of Human Services, Healthcare and Family Services, and Public Health to all provide screening and education. West Virginia passed a screening law in 2009. A 2010 law in Minnesota required the Commissioner of Health to develop educational materials on postpartum illnesses.[13]

In California, a woman named Joy Burkhard had been working on a Junior League project on postpartum depression and psychosis. Working with State Representative Pedro Nava, she and her group pushed for a law to create a state task force on postpartum mental illness. While they considered it a small ask compared to something like a screening mandate, it died in committee amid a budgetary crisis. So, the group pushed for a state Maternal Mental Health Awareness Month, hoping they could gain traction on legislation that did not have any price tag attached. The bill passed in 2011 and came with the creation of a volunteer-based, private funder–sponsored task force. Out of this Burkhard created a nonprofit, 2020 Mom, to advocate for maternal mental health policy. It quickly became a national organization, later renamed the Policy Center for Maternal Mental Health. California did ultimately pass a screening mandate in 2018, with legislation spearheaded by a male Republican state representative.

The Melanie Blocker Stokes MOTHERS Act

At the national level, California Representative Lois Capps (a Democrat) and Georgia Representative Jack Kingston (a Republican) had passed House Resolution 163 in 2000. HR 163 was a non-binding resolution that emphasized the importance of recognizing postpartum depression and psychosis.[14] Capps represented Santa Barbara, where Jane Honikman began Postpartum Support International. The resolution encouraged more data collection, more training of healthcare professionals, and screening of new mothers, but did not require anything or allocate any funds.

Representative Bobby Rush's legislation was meant to have funding behind it. In 2003, he introduced the Melanie Blocker Stokes Postpartum Depression Research and Care Act.[15] "It is my hope that through this legislation, we can ensure that the birth of a child is a wonderful time for a new mother and her family," he explained. "Postpartum depression must not steal the joy of a new life from America's families!"[16]

The legislation directed the National Institutes of Health (NIH) and the National Institute of Mental Health (NIMH) to "expand and intensify research . . . with respect to postpartum depression and postpartum psychosis," and promised funding to support that research. It also supported grant-based programs to provide services for postpartum depression and psychosis patients and their families.[17] The legislation used a medical model of postpartum illness, and it encouraged decentralized program building. These projects would still be small, on the spectrum of federal health spending, coming in around $3 million for the first year and "such sums as necessary" for the following two years.

Rush gathered co-sponsors for his bill: three Republicans, one independent, and fifty-eight Democrats. They sent the bill to the House Committee on Energy and Commerce, which referred it to its Subcommittee on Health. Then the bill went untouched for more than a year in the Republican-controlled Congress, until September 2004. When the subcommittee did hold a hearing on it, there was a catch. They would not simply discuss the Blocker Stokes Act. Instead, under the title "Improving Women's Health: Understanding Depression After Pregnancy," the hearing lumped Rush's bill in with another on so-called "post-abortion syndrome."

Anti-abortion activists argued that abortion was counter to women's mental and emotional health. In the 1980s, some of them framed these dangers as an illness akin to postpartum depression or a posttraumatic stress disorder. Conservative activists and psychologists created "post-abortion syndrome" or post-abortion depression. It posited that abortion was so antithetical to a woman's nature that it could make her mentally ill. The language of post-abortion syndrome elevated any guilt, sadness, or doubt after abortion to the level of diagnosable illness. Mainstream psychiatry did not accept this claim, but the idea continued to circulate in anti-abortion circles and influence state laws.[18]

Representative Joseph Pitts, an anti-abortion Republican from Pennsylvania, introduced a bill. HR 4543, the Post-Abortion Depression Research and Care Act, lifted language from the Melanie Blocker Stokes Act.[19] It proposed that the NIH and NIMH "expand and intensify research and related activities . . . with respect to post-abortion depression and post-abortion psychosis." It similarly called for grant programs to provide services to post-abortion women and their families.[20] Pitts gathered thirty-three co-sponsors, all Republicans. Postpartum activists had spent decades building up the legitimacy of postpartum depression as a mental illness. Pitts's legislative cut-and-paste confirmed the extent to which they succeeded. Now, postpartum depression's legitimacy offered a path for the illegitimate disease of post-abortion depression.

The discussions that followed emphasized the construction of postpartum depression as neutral and bipartisan, while abortion was "political" and polarizing. "Unfortunately, my Republican colleagues chose to politicize today's hearing," lamented Representative Sherrod Brown of Ohio.[21] Representative Diana DeGette of Colorado described post-abortion syndrome as "a highly specious topic with almost no scientific basis." Grouping it with postpartum illness was an attempt to "muddy the waters." The subcommittee chair, Republican Representative Joe Barton, acted baffled by the controversy emerging from the combination of these bills. "There's nothing at all where we are trying to be partisan," he explained, "just the opposite." He believed hearings on both bills would be "fair," and would "get two issues that are important, dissimilar in some ways, similar in some ways, on the table for the American people."[22]

For two decades, postpartum activists emphasized the politically neutral, pro-woman *and* pro-family orientation of their activism. The political hijacking of the Rush bill and these hearings hinted at the limits of this. While Pitts insisted he did not oppose the Melanie Blocker Stokes Act, he was not one of its few Republican co-sponsors. The divide in support revealed the partisan split just beneath the idea that postpartum depression was not a partisan political issue. Supporters of the Blocker Stokes Act decried Republican behavior, emphasizing that the "politics of abortion have no place in honoring the memory of Melanie Blocker Stokes."[23] It is unlikely, though, that the subcommittee in this Republican-led Congress would have held any hearings on the Melanie Blocker Stokes Act without the post-abortion bill also up for debate.

Carol Blocker testified about her daughter's postpartum mental illness, but recalls the representatives all chatting and debating their lunch orders during her emotional speech. The brief hearings allowed little other time to discuss postpartum mental illness. Psychiatrist Nada Stotland spoke about postpartum depression, but she was also there to testify against the idea of a post-abortion syndrome.

Her written testimony offered detail on the legitimacy of postpartum depression, but her oral testimony wound up split between the topics. The hearings did not lead to a vote, and the subcommittee tabled the bill for the rest of that congressional session.

Representative Rush again introduced the legislation in the 2005–2006 session but gained no traction. In 2007, though, Democrats had control of Congress and the committee held another hearing on his bill. Again, Republicans introduced the question of abortion and post-abortion syndrome, and reiterated the same specious arguments and false equivalencies. Anti-abortion researcher Patricia Coleman also testified, urging the passing of the Melanie Blocker Stokes Act so long as it included language of depression after pregnancy loss and abortion. Coleman maintained that post-abortion depression was even more common than depression after childbirth, but was overshadowed by talk of postpartum depression. Joseph Pitts explained that "it is sadly evident that post-abortion depression goes widely unrecognized and untreated."[24]

Again, Democrats interjected their frustration at this hijacking, with Representative Diana DeGette and Illinois representative Jan Schakowsky particularly noting the radically unscientific nature of the concept of post-abortion depression. Dr. Nada Stotland again testified, along similar lines. The *DSM-IV*, she noted, does not recognize post-abortion illness.[25] The *DSM* did not fully recognize postpartum depression and psychosis either, but the legitimating claim was clear. Postpartum depression was in the *DSM*, sort of. It was therefore a real mental illness, and it should not get sidetracked by politics.

The bill, supporters argued, was not about abortion and needed to be shielded from such a controversial conversation. This was "a woman's health issue and a children's health issue," one Democratic representative explained.[26] Congressman Rush emphasized that his "non-controversial bill" was bipartisan. Amid creeping abortion talk, they reiterated postpartum depression legislation as neutral pro-family legislation.[27] "PPD isn't a women's illness," testified New Jersey First Lady Mary Jo Codey. "It's a family illness."[28]

Despite these arguments that postpartum depression should

not be discussed anywhere near abortion, the "abortion syndrome" faction succeeded in lightly modifying the bill. After negotiations between Congressman Rush and Congressman Pitts, a new "Sense of Congress" statement was added to the bill. It encouraged the NIH to conduct a longitudinal study of the "mental health consequences for women of resolving a pregnancy (intended and unintended) in various ways, including carrying the pregnancy to term and parenting the child, carrying the pregnancy to term and placing the child for adoption, miscarriage, and having an abortion."[29]

The addition might not sound significant, but post-abortion syndrome advocates had argued for nearly two decades that they needed a large study of at least ten years' duration on post-abortion women and mental health. The advocates were convinced it would prove their point and offer legitimate data that could not be easily dismissed. And that data could then be used as evidence that abortion harmed women and should thus be further restricted. "There is something distinctly offensive about anti-choice politicians thwarting efforts to expand the study of a debilitating, frighteningly common disease" by equating it with the possible effects "of a procedure they already believe is immoral and should be illegal," one columnist reflected.[30]

After the hearings, the House voted on the Melanie Blocker Stokes Act, and it passed. Senator Robert Menendez of New Jersey introduced the legislation in the Senate. Mary Jo Codey, Brooke Shields, and representatives from Postpartum Support International and Postpartum Progress held a Mother's Day 2007 press conference to drum up support, echoing past Mother's Day events.[31] It was no use. The legislation remained in committee in the Senate. The legislation was also permanently changed: when Bobby Rush re-introduced it in 2008 and in 2009, the Sense of Congress statement that included post-abortion research remained in it.

| 213

Taking to the Blogs

Advocates had been involved in the legislation from the start, including testimony from Carol Blocker and Mary Jo Codey, and behind-the-scenes support from Postpartum Support International and Post-partum Progress. As the legislation gained attention, though, these advocates considered how to get the bill more traction. Susan Dowd Stone of PSI, and author and advocate Sylvia Lasalandra-Frodella, went to Congress to advocate for it while it was stuck in commit-tee. "We would drive down with our high heels in the backseat," she recounts, "get dressed in the car, go over to the senators' building there, and just walk door to door sometimes in the days when you could actually do that." While they rarely got meetings this way, they did sometimes get them through Representative Rush and Senator Menendez.

Advocates also sought media attention for the legislation. Carol Blocker had done interviews for years.[32] Katherine Stone of Postpar-tum Progress shared her story in her extremely popular blog, as well as in mainstream print media like *Newsweek*. She told her story so

Figure 10.1 Carol Blocker speaks at a Capitol Hill news conference on May 11, 2007. She is surrounded by other advocates for the Melanie Blocker Stokes Postpartum Depression Research and Care Act. Back row, left to right: Susan Dowd Stone, Brooke Shields, Mary Jo Codey. Front right: Sylvia Lasalandra-Frodella. Photo by Mark Wilson/Getty Images.

often, she said, to raise awareness and also "to ask for even more help for those who suffer." She could not tell women to go to their doctors if the doctors were uninformed, to get treatment if their insurance would not cover it, or to go to support groups if there was none nearby. All these needs, she explained, are "why I've written my congressman and senators and asked them to pass the Melanie Blocker Stokes Act."[33]

As groups focused their energy on the bill, renamed the Melanie Blocker Stokes MOTHERS Act in 2009, they relied heavily on the already-online movement to mobilize women through the internet.[34] Stone tried this first in 2007, when Postpartum Progress launched a special blogging event. "Today is blog for the MOTHERS Act day!!" she announced.[35] More than a hundred bloggers posted their stories of postpartum depression or psychosis, their interviews with survivors, and their arguments for the MOTHERS Act.

Stone encouraged each blogger to emphasize a call to action. Sharing their stories was good, but calling their senators was critical. Stone asked bloggers to "Please tell your readers to keep calling if the lines are busy!! Don't give up!!" Some were postpartum depression–focused blogs, but some were recipe and money-saving "mommy blogs" posting on PPD. Blogs with names like "Missives from Suburbia," "Trenches of Mommyhood," and "Mountain Momma" participated, alongside explicitly political blogs like "Viva La Feminista" and "The Political Voices of Women."[36] A couple of larger websites, like the *Huffington Post*, took part. The women's blog network BlogHer, as well as Postpartum Progress and Postpartum Support International, sponsored this Blog for the MOTHERS Act day. The effect of all this online activism was unclear, Susan Dowd Stone explained. "I don't know what effect it had . . . we did the best we could with the tools we had."

The legislation still stalled. In 2008, backers bundled it into the Advancing America's Priorities Act, a $10 billion package with thirty-five pieces of healthcare and crime-prevention legislation. Senator Harry Reid, a Democrat and the bill's sponsor, emphasized that the legislation was not "partisan or controversial." Still, most Republican senators opposed the spending amid a recession.[37] Despite months of lobbying, the package could not get sixty Senate votes.[38]

In 2009, Senator Menendez and Representative Rush introduced the MOTHERS Act once again. That March it passed the House again, 391 to 8.

But in the Senate, it sat in committee. One roadblock was Republican Senator Tom Coburn of Oklahoma. Sometimes called "Dr. No," Coburn—an obstetrician—blocked all single-disease-based legislation, usually claiming it had nothing to do with the disease itself but was because of his fiscal hawkishness.[39] Still, postpartum depression activists took his hold on the bill personally, noting that Coburn said he had never seen a case of postpartum depression despite delivering over 2,000 babies.[40]

Although Coburn does not appear to have voiced a specific concern about this legislation even as he worked to block a vote on it, others did. A small but vocal group emerged to oppose the bill. The bill's screening mandate violated privacy, opponent Amy Philo argued. And it was a ploy to get women on dangerous antidepressants, she added.[41] The bill did not actually mandate screening, but the argument about antidepressants caught more attention. It also helped anger and mobilize MOTHERS Act supporters.

Philo described herself as a Zoloft survivor; she had an adverse reaction to the antidepressant during her own postpartum illness. She created a website to tell her story and oppose the legislation, where she accused its proponents of taking money from pharmaceutical companies. As the 2009 push for a Senate vote intensified, the opposition grew vocal. An article in *Time* gave equal weight to the opinion of opponents, including Philo, who said the act would force drugs on postpartum women.[42] Then actor (and Scientologist) Kirstie Alley took to Twitter to rant against the bill. It would force antidepressants on mothers *and newborns*, she warned. As Tom Cruise had done four years earlier, Alley's attack on postpartum antidepressant use offered a familiar, visible, and clear enemy. It encouraged postpartum advocates to rally, especially in the blogosphere. "If I could, I would thank

Kirstie Alley personally," Katherine Stone wrote on *Postpartum Progress*. "Hug her, even."[43]

Vocal MOTHERS Act supporters spread their rebuttals and personal postpartum stories online. Susan Dowd Stone emphasized the Scientology roots of the opposition on her personal blog. The bill does not push medication, she explained, and each woman's needs must be assessed individually.[44] Dowd Stone argued that she never took a dime of money for her advocacy. In a snarky post, Katherine Stone rallied women: "You can sit by on the sidelines and watch them win . . . You can let them convince the rest of the world that the MOTHERS Act is a conspiracy to drug the mothers of the world." Or, she encouraged, you can call and write your senators, add your name to a petition, and spread the word.[45] After the *Time* article, popular postpartum blogger Ivy Shih Leung posted her own letter to *Time*, describing the opposition's agenda and misrepresentation of the law.[46]

Postpartum Progress tried to counter the dual roadblocks of Senator Coburn and the vocal anti-psychopharmaceutical crowd. Postpartum Progress and PSI launched a blog week, an extended version of the blog day of 2007.[47] In a press release, Senator Menendez described the need for "an intense dose of public pressure." The blog week "helps reinforce the type of grassroots movement that will create the pressure that is needed."[48]

The bill remained in committee, so advocates put together another carefully constructed Mother's Day event to push for it. The use of Mother's Day could be read as subversive, an acknowledgment that motherhood was not as peaceful as popular culture might suggest. It also could be read as a doubling down on postpartum depression as an anomaly. Motherhood *should* be like the holiday suggests, and would be, were it not for disease. Senator Menendez emphasized the dual tenets of postpartum advocacy in his speech, the importance of "protecting women's health and maintaining strong families." Susan Dowd Stone of PSI made a similar point, about how the MOTHERS Act could help "better protect our nation's most critical social dyad of mother and child."[49]

Then, unexpectedly, the seemingly doomed MOTHERS Act was folded into President Barack Obama's Affordable Care Act (ACA) in late 2009. It is unclear exactly what kind of backroom negotiation led to its inclusion in the sprawling legislative package. Most advocates were surprised by the news. Only in this format did it pass through the Senate that Christmas Eve. Then, in March 2010, the House passed the ACA. The legislation dropped Melanie Blocker Stokes's name, and simply became Section 2952: "Support, education and research for postpartum depression."[50] The language of the section mirrored the MOTHERS Act, right down to the Sense of Congress statement on researching post-birth and post-abortion mental health.

As part of Obama's ACA, it was hard to deny the partisanship of the legislation. Yes, it included the abortion concession, and yes, its proponents kept their support filled with language of natural motherhood and the family. But postpartum advocates had to tread cautiously. "No matter how you feel about healthcare reform," wrote Katherine Stone on the Postpartum Progress blog, "it would be a blessing to women around the country if the MBSMA becomes law."[51] This Act, she reiterated, still referring to it as the Melanie Blocker Stokes MOTHERS Act, was for *all* mothers.

Advocates again used Mother's Day, this time for a celebratory press conference. "Today we celebrate this gift for women," said Senator Menendez.[52] Similar language permeated the event, alongside talk of the importance of women's health issues. Menendez repeated the familiar refrain that had this been a men's issue, it would have been addressed long ago. He also repeated the explanation seemingly required after any political talk of postpartum depression as a women's issue, talk of motherhood and the family. "I've always said, that while our focus is on mothers, this is about families at the end of the day," he said. "It's about the child that was just born and the relationship with their mother who are suffering from postpartum depression, it's about the husband, it's about the grandparents, it's about everybody in the family coming together to help meet this challenge."[53]

Postpartum activists praised Menendez and Rush for their efforts. "You are not just the Senator from New Jersey, you are the Senator of America's mothers," Susan Dowd Stone told Menendez.[54] "I've always said most men aren't interested in women's illnesses, but they were," Carol Blocker said.[55] Activists also praised their own work, and all the labor involved in finally making the bill a reality. "To every person who signed the petition, know that your signature was seen; that it carried weight," Dowd Stone blogged. "You fearlessly listed your names, dared to make your stand known . . . You have won."[56] She emphasized the importance of this virtual activism, like online petitions, alongside letters and calls to Congress. The specifics of getting the MOTHERS Act into the ACA remained obscure in both congressional and activist tellings of the passage. All insisted this brand of women's activism mattered.

Menendez described the legislation as an entering wedge, the beginning of federal attention to postpartum depression. The victory established not only the legitimacy of postpartum depression but also "tells every American that postpartum depression is a national problem that deserves and demands a national response."[57]

This sudden passage is not a simple story of postpartum depression activism's victory, or even a story of compromised victory alongside abortion and family values politics. The language of the Melanie Blocker Stokes MOTHERS Act passed within the ACA, but the appropriations never came. Katherine Stone described where postpartum depression was, even a couple years after the ACA's passage: "We're still not a priority . . . Perhaps we're not even somewhere in the middle of the priority list."[58] What has been accomplished by the Act? a reporter asked Carol Blocker in 2013. "Absolutely nothing," Blocker told her.[59] Their experience mirrored the prior two decades of postpartum activists' experiences, the feeling they were marginalized as both a women's health issue and a mental health issue.

Out of the Shadows

Six years after what turned out to be a symbolic victory in the ACA, activists had another federal-level victory with the "Shadows Act" introduced in 2015.

The Bringing Postpartum Depression Out of the Shadows Act used a state-based intervention model. It built on New Jersey's postpartum legislation, as well as a new Massachusetts program, the Massachusetts Child Psychiatry Access Program (MCPAP) for Moms. MCPAP for Moms offered consultations and a support line to obstetricians unsure what to do with postpartum mental health issues. The Shadows Act proposed grants to states to build their own programs like these.

Psychiatrist Nancy Byatt spearheaded the MCPAP for Moms program, which was modeled after a program that offered a psychiatric consult for pediatricians. Byatt observed obstetricians who did not know what to do about postpartum mental illness, which she says meant they also were not even bringing it up with patients. Postpartum advocates' longstanding complaint that obstetricians did not screen, or even ask about emotions and mental health, seemed as true to Byatt in the 2010s as it had to activists fifteen years prior. In focus groups, patients told Byatt that the OBs don't know what they are doing, and that they were afraid to bring up depression and anxiety with their doctors. The OBs also rarely brought it up. Perinatal mental illness is twice as common as gestational diabetes, Byatt said. While "it would be considered probably malpractice to not screen for—address diabetes . . . we have this illness that impacts birth outcomes, it impacts families, and no one even asks."

Byatt wanted to connect obstetricians with psychiatrists knowledgeable in postpartum illness. Maybe then obstetricians would feel more comfortable screening, prescribing, or referring women. She won a grant to develop a pilot program in 2013. Serendipitously, the state of Massachusetts started a postpartum depression commission, the Ellen Story Commission, at the same time. The commission met resistance from the American College of Obstetrics and Gynecology when it proposed mandatory screening. The commission needed some other intervention to propose, something that would be effective but not attract the controversy of a screening mandate. Byatt presented her psychiatry-obstetrics bridge program to the commission, which formed a workgroup and pushed for making Byatt's program a statewide reality. MCPAP for Moms was born. In 2015, with substantial grassroots advocacy, supporters got the program funded as a line item in the state budget.

With the program established through the pilot program, Byatt says, it was much easier to get the support for continued funding. Instead of abstractly funding an idea, what they had was a program that doctors and medical professional organizations said they could not afford to lose. The program benefited from the fact that it was a voluntary call-in line, rather than a mandate like universal screening. The family values argument also helped. "The baby is the hook," Byatt said. "[A] lot of people don't care frankly about pregnant and postpartum individuals ... They're often reduced to a vessel." "But," she explained, "everybody cares about babies." It was emotion more than data that drove policy making, and the stories women at advocacy days at the State House told about their families' experiences brought more support than the statistics could.

MCPAP for Moms offered an important model for new federal legislation. Massachusetts Democrat Katherine Clark led the charge for the Shadows Act, using her state-based knowledge. The Shadows Act would direct the Secretary of Health and Human Services to establish, expand, and maintain postpartum mental health programs focused on either screening or treatment. It prioritized care in primary care settings, rather than creating separate avenues of maternal mental healthcare.[60] MCPAP for Moms did exactly this, without raising the concerns about mandates that screening legislation did.

Like so much postpartum legislation, the Shadows Act and its supporters often used family- and child-centered language. A press release of Clark's focused on the risks to children of depressed women, who might have "difficulties eating and sleeping, and often experience delays in language development." They also could "develop passivity, withdrawal, and self-regulatory behavior as a response to maternal disengagement." The law itself included the language of maternal risk too: "The consequences of maternal depression include poor bonding between mother and infant, which may have negative effects on cognitive development, social-emotional development, and behavior of the child."[61] The advocates for the bill did not actually conceptualize it as all about infant wellness; they believed in maternal mental health for the mother's sake as well. When it came to public framing, though, this portrayal of an untreated mother as a threat built on decades of postpartum political craft. Yet even with the most sympathetic framing, passing it at the federal level would not be easy.

Massachusetts State Representative Jamie Zahlaway Belsito became a fierce advocate for the federal bill. She survived two rounds of postpartum mental illness herself. She mobilized nationwide advocates for the Shadows Act, introduced by Congresswoman Katherine Clark, through her computer, she says, "with a toddler on my knee and a baby on my breast from my red kitchen table." Advocates from postpartum groups like PSI and Postpartum Progress helped, as did figures like Carol Blocker. Belsito also found individuals in Congress who supported the legislation, and then worked to get more people to support it. There was some good fortune too, with the moment of introduction. In 2015, Belsito explained, "for the first time ever there were several congressional representatives that were pregnant and had babies." This led to the creation of a bipartisan Congressional Maternity Care Caucus headed up by former members Congresswomen Lucille Roybal Allard and Jaime Herrera Beutler. In 2018, the Black Maternity Health Caucus was created by Representatives Lauren Underwood and Alma Adams. More and more people on the Hill started talking about maternal health. Representation matters, Belsito says.

The legislation, Belsito emphasized, received bipartisan support.
She describes Republicans who might not support other women's health legislation, but who could get on board with the Shadows Act. Pennsylvania Republican Congressman Ryan Costello, for instance, was a new dad and so he got it, Belsito says. He served as a co-sponsor. Other congressional aides and representatives told Belsito their own stories of their miscarriages, of family members' depression, and of other personal ties that made them sympathetic to the bill. Belsito says, "It was those stories that we started to find, someone's mother had gone away for a few months when they were young . . . it was these sort of putting the pieces together." One Republican politician

from Utah acknowledged the extent of the unspoken problem among LDS women. When speaking with Republicans especially, she says, it has been important to emphasize that postpartum health is "a pro-family issue, not just a women's issue." Personal experience seemed to trump political division and helped Congressmembers conceive of the legislation as outside partisan politics.

There were some Republicans skeptical of the legislation, but it came from what advocates saw as a misunderstanding. These politicians worried the bill somehow supported abortion, and they could not be associated with any bill that even implicitly supported abortion. Wait, "you mean it doesn't have to do with abortion?" Belsito recalls representatives asking. Talking about "women's health at the legislative level has always been abortion, abortion, abortion, abortion. It's never been focused on anything else," she says. It was critical to distance themselves from those politics. The abortion concerns "had nothing to do with reality," she says, and when she helped them understand it as pro-family legislation, they often changed their minds. It was also a modest ask of $5 million, "scraps," Belsito says, but an important entering wedge. With this framing, even with a Republican-held House and Senate, the Shadows Act advocates won bipartisan support. Advocate Adrienne Griffen described the hunt for bipartisan support not as a strategy but as a necessity. "Having bipartisan support is the only way that any bill gets passed," she said. Joy Burkhard of the advocacy organization 2020 Mom emphasized that their organization will only put forward legislation with bipartisan support and works with a lobbying organization that specializes in bipartisan legislation on women and children's issues.

Bipartisan support was one thing, but as the MOTHERS Act saga had shown, getting signatures was not the same as getting a bill passed or funded. Belsito organized an Advocacy Day in 2016, with ninety-one visits to the Senate. Joy Burkhard helped prepare the talking points and leave-behinds. Katherine Clark and Ryan Costello held a congressional briefing. The Shadows Act ultimately passed as part of a larger medical research funding package, similar to how the MOTHERS Act finally passed. It became part of the 21st Century

Cures Act, and President Obama signed it into law December 2016. The bill requested $5 million per year for postpartum mental health programming between 2018 and 2022.

The next summer, Representatives Clark and Beutler secured appropriations for the act. They did not want another unfunded bill, like the MOTHERS Act. They succeeded in part, Belsito explains, because advocates "put sneakers on and ran around Capitol Hill and made sure that we got the monies appropriated." In 2018, states applied for access to the funding. Thirty states and territories applied, but the relatively small budget resulted in only seven grants of around $3.2 million each being awarded.[62] Yet the program inspired others. As of 2022, some twenty-five states had MCPAP-style psychiatry programs. Only seven are federally funded, and the others are funded by either states or philanthropy.[63]

Into the Light

Carol Blocker has continued to advocate for women with postpartum psychosis, particularly women imprisoned for infanticide. For years she gathered signatures on petitions, made scrapbooks to bring to court, and testified in hopes of getting women released. She recalled one instance in the mid-2000s where she got petitions signed that asked for a new hearing for a woman convicted of infanticide. She took them to Illinois governor Rod Blagojevich's office. "I took it down with a photographer and a lawyer," she explained, but they were stopped at the gate. "I said I had this and I want . . . to make sure that it gets into the governor's hands." The man at the gate told her she had wasted her time, and that Blagojevich only worked from home and never came into the office. The failed gesture spoke volumes to Blocker, who was getting all too used to that kind of discouragement.

Occasionally she succeeded. She convinced family members of ill women to take their sickness seriously. Women with depression and psychosis from around the country reached out to Blocker, and she would talk with them, encourage them, and offer advice about how they might find better medical care than Melanie had. Despite these contributions, Blocker felt defeated. Too many people "just don't care."

Problems of indifference continued to plague advocates, but their advocacy groups grew more organized and professional. By 2018, Postpartum Support International, 2020 Mom, and the Maternal Mental Health Leadership Alliance made advocacy days an annual affair. Advocates pushed legislation more generally on maternal mortality, especially focused on maternal mortality rates among Black women. Among the most ambitious legislative projects of maternal health activists in recent years was Representative Lauren Underwood's Black Maternal Health Momnibus Act of 2021. Designed to address the larger crisis of Black maternal mortality, it combined nine bills on maternal health. These included maternity care for incarcerated women and funding for Black maternal community organizations. It also included the mental health–focused Moms Matter Act, which would have provided community-based support for mothers with either mental health or substance abuse problems.[64]

The Momnibus Act stalled, in part because some bills it contained had only Democratic support. The bills included support for incarcerated mothers and an expansion of the Special Supplemental Nutrition Program for Women, Infants, and Children (WIC). Postpartum Support International and other advocacy groups supported the Momnibus Act, but also understood the uphill battle such legislation faced. They only had so much time and energy, and had learned to use it strategically. As advocate Adrienne Griffen explained, it did not make sense to exert tons of energy on federally mandated maternity leave, no matter how necessary it is for maternal mental health. "That's never going to go through. Right? So I'm not even going to try that." Instead, she argued, it was important to focus on what they can actually change.

Advocates have found major success with their more modest and bipartisan asks. "It's happened in such a short time," Jamie Belsito says. "It's unheard of for any new policy to move this fast on Capitol Hill." Decades of postpartum depression awareness and advocacy have coalesced, making for a mainstream women's health issue. In part the legislation seemed to succeed because advocates convinced politicians that postpartum problems were relatable and family oriented, and reminded them of their personal experiences. Belsito emphasized the "need to get more women and more moms elected," since they would be among the most likely to understand the ask.

Postpartum depression advocates also benefited from the changing national conversation on mental health and substance abuse, which they could plug into the 21st Century Cures Act. "I think if that particular legislative session didn't have a mental health bill moving," Belsito says, "this wouldn't have gone anywhere . . . No, not at all." The issue was not resistance so much as apathy, and a belief that the issue is obscure or small. Resistance to their lobbying is pretty limited, and usually reflects either disinterest, misunderstanding, or an unwillingness to spend public funds, not a specific rejection of the postpartum depression programs proposed.

Other policy fixes remain targets for postpartum advocates. Psychiatrist Margaret Spinelli has spent years campaigning to the American Psychiatric Association for the addition of postpartum psychosis to the *DSM-5*. Psychologist Susan Feingold fights for changes to infanticide law with a state-by-state strategy. Adrienne Griffen's Maternal Mental Health Leadership Alliance champions legislation to study military mothers' mental health and to increase the funding for the Out of the Shadows Act with an "Into the Light" bill.[65] The bill increased funding for psychiatry access programs, and also supported the creation of a federally funded maternal mental health hotline. The National Maternal Mental Health Hotline was launched on Mother's Day of 2022. It featured a paid staff and was administered by Postpartum Support International.

Before 2000, few postpartum advocates saw a future in legislative solutions. There had long been policy and legal fights, pushes for professional organizations to better train doctors and nurses, for the American Psychiatric Association to recognize postpartum illness in the *DSM*, and for a consideration of postpartum context in infanticide crimes. They sought other reforms through support groups, awareness raising and media, and medical research. Postpartum issues

were always ruled by debate over family values and women's responsibilities, but mostly stayed out of the realm of partisan politics.

By the 2000s, advocates changed this, pushing for state and national legislation. It was a slow-moving process, shaped by the aim
of bipartisanship, and by avoiding divisive women's health politics
whenever possible. While some advocates wrote about the relevance
of more partisan issues like parental leave, postpartum Medicaid expansion, gun control, and universal healthcare, the asks advocates
made in terms of legislation were usually more moderate, medically
oriented, and plausibly bipartisan.[66] Sometimes they strategically
used an emphasis on babies, but they separated themselves from
more conservative arguments by centering the mother alongside the
baby. Adrienne Griffen attributed recent success to the fact that "everybody loves mothers and babies." In conversations with advocates
they frequently jumped between describing the risks of untreated
mothers to babies, and emphasizing that the woman was "more than
a vessel" and needed support and services. Joy Burkhard described
how bipartisan legislation did not mean everyone agreed on motherhood, just that they agreed motherhood was important. Democrats
and Republicans agree that "mothers are critical to society . . . Republicans may think that mothers should stay at home and take care of
their kids, but they should be happy and healthy." They also did not
agree on how much money should be spent on projects to keep mothers happy and healthy, she agreed, which has meant advocates' legislative asks have been as "fiscally responsible" as possible. This does
not mean advocates have given up on paid family leave or childcare, | 227
issues they frequently say are important. But it does mean they do
not prioritize passing federal legislation to address the issues in the
near term. Postpartum advocates instead emphasized a pragmatic
politics that was at once pro-woman and pro-family, that sought both
to challenge the status quo and to preserve it.

Conclusion

Depression After Delivery founder Nancy Berchtold experienced psychosis after the 1983 birth of her daughter. Her suffering launched her into postpartum advocacy. Decades later, Berchtold's daughter had her own child. Now, hospital staff handed her a postpartum depression screener as standard protocol. For Berchtold this was a revelation: all her activism had mattered.

But a screener so soon after birth could do only so much, as most symptoms of postpartum mood disorders come later. When Berchtold's daughter did later experience postpartum anxiety, there were limited resources available. There was a moms support group, but it was not a postpartum depression group. Berchtold was grateful to find it for her daughter, but it also echoed her own struggles so many years earlier, sitting in "which diapers are the best diapers" groups while not telling anyone about her bout of psychosis. But so much *was* different. Her daughter found support through online groups. As of 2023, Postpartum Support International runs more than twenty-five online support groups, including those organized specifically for queer and trans parents, South Asian parents, and Black parents, trying to address past gaps. This was in some ways more than Berchtold could have ever imagined for the next generation. But also so much remained undone, she realized. Her daughter's suffering had been seen and treated, but it had not been prevented.

About a year after my interview with Berchtold, she sent me an email. Lindsay Clancy, a thirty-eight-year-old mother in Massachusetts, took the lives of her three young children and tried to end her own life. Clancy was charged with three counts of murder, and the sensational story was everywhere. If Clancy had been in the UK or Canada, with their infanticide laws, she would not be charged with murder. Activists and professionals in Illinois had successfully passed a 2018 law requiring postpartum illness to be considered as a mitigating factor in a case like this. Massachusetts did not have a similar law; recent attempts to get it on the books failed.[1]

As she processed this tragedy, Berchtold reflected again on what had changed and what had not. She was grateful that Boston had a number of postpartum mental illness experts. The state is a hotspot for postpartum advocacy, from a commission in the 2010s to psychiatric telehealth advocacy programs through the MCPAP for Moms program. There was immediate advocate outcry about the murder charges. While the prosecution portrayed Clancy as a calculating killer, numerous op-eds and interviews with advocates and psychiatrists argued for the likelihood of postpartum psychosis.

To Berchtold, the importance of women's networking and social support was immediately clear. She reached out to a friend from her Depression After Delivery days, Jeanne Watson Driscoll, to process the tragedy. Driscoll lamented the villainization of Clancy in the media but was optimistic about all the postpartum advocacy she was seeing around the case. Berchtold, Driscoll, and so many other advocates would support Clancy however they could. Berchtold also reached out to another advocate from those days, Angela Burling. Burling had taken her infant son's life during a 1983 psychotic incident. Berchtold hoped that when the time was right Burling could reach out to the Clancy family. "PPP [Postpartum Psychosis] is a monster and Lindsay needs to know she didn't take her children's lives," Berchtold explained. "PPP did."[2] Who better than another survivor to help her understand this?

A few days later, Postpartum Support International circulated a short essay by support coordinator Hajara Kutty. The Clancy case was a tragedy, Kutty said. And it has sparked important conversations. Clancy was not the only mother with postpartum psychosis to take her children's lives recently, though. Kutty pointed to three other cases, from the prior six months. The cases of Erin Merdy, Dimone Fleming, and Paulesha Green-Pulliam all involved Black mothers who allegedly killed their young children.

Those cases did not get major media attention, and the limited attention they did get was largely unsympathetic to the women. While some articles included family members' beliefs that the women might have had postpartum depression (none I found used the language of psychosis), there was no flood of advocate interviews, op-eds, and sound bites. "As a postpartum community," Kutty wrote, "we need to do a better job of stepping up to bat when tragedies involve racialized mothers."[3]

When advocates jumped to address the Lindsay Clancy case in 2023, postpartum advocates faced a familiar scenario. It echoed a much longer history of postpartum illness advocates scrambling to defend women accused of crimes while also raising awareness without scaring women further. They sought to make strategic use of the sudden interest in postpartum mental illness. Adrienne Griffen, executive director of the Maternal Mental Health Leadership Alliance, went on NPR to explain postpartum psychosis and also to discuss other kinds of postpartum mental illness. Postpartum psychosis is very rare but very serious, she said. Other postpartum illness is extremely common, affecting one in five women.

Griffen described her own postpartum depression and the anxieties it produced, like a deep fear she would fall down the stairs holding her infant son. "Who would find us? How long would we lie there? Would we be injured?" Griffen described going down the stairs on her backside while her baby was young, illustrating the lengths most women with postpartum illnesses go to avoid harming their children.[4] Advocates like Griffen tried to use the public appetite for one story as a means of educating and encouraging screening and care. They encouraged new parents to call the new National Maternal Mental Health Hotline, hosted by the federal Health Resources and Services Administration, the result of substantial lobbying work. They worried about how to make such a stigmatizing case into one that would not frighten parents, but might empower them to seek help.

This book tells the story of how much has changed in postpartum mental health activism in a matter of decades of work and advocacy, even as many of the underlying stressors on mothers and new parents have not. In early 2023, I attended a Postpartum Support International two-day virtual training session. The trainings are meant to fill a gap in perinatal training, to make sure healthcare providers who deal with pregnant and postpartum patients understand possible mood disorders in the way that PSI does. They are also a critical moneymaker for the organization. The trainings are primarily aimed at therapists, but also include lactation consultants, doulas, nurses, and other professionals.

The wide-ranging coverage of the training, in terms of both audience and content, says a lot about where the postpartum movement is today. A morning session on the role of social support, an afternoon on the role of psychopharmaceuticals. It was simultaneously a training in clinical experience and in advocacy. Hundreds of professionals of different sorts gathered. They learned about different diagnoses, not just postpartum depression and psychosis like they would have focused on even fifteen years earlier, but also postpartum versions of anxiety, obsessive-compulsive disorder, bipolar I and II, and post-traumatic stress disorder. The array of postpartum diagnoses illustrated how specialized the subfield of perinatal mental health had become, and how important the language of diagnosis was to them. Yet the embrace of a psychiatric language and medicalization always came alongside a commitment to understanding postpartum distress holistically.

Even though the organization is careful to be bipartisan, it uses a public health lens to frame a number of "progressive" issues as being outside politics. Following an overhaul of their curriculum a

few years ago to improve inclusivity and representation, the training moved from having a little section on "culture" to bringing up issues of diversity and equity through the sessions. Attendees learned
about the importance of cultural humility, the problem of Black maternal mortality, and systemic racism in medicine. They watched a
video about trans and queer parents navigating pregnancy and the
postpartum. There is often a comment or two from participants complaining about these "liberal" choices on the post-training evalua-
tions, trainer Birdie Meyer told me, but they are outliers. Meyer explains that "we always say PSI is not Democrat. It's not Republican.
It's not Christian. It's not Jewish. It's made up of all those people . . .
We don't make statements about things that are politically volatile.
Right? But we are very clear about anti-racism. We are absolutely
anti-racism, anti-racist."

The trainings have now become part of the formal postpartum
mental health certification that PSI originated in the 2010s. For a
professional to earn the letters "PMH-C" (Perinatal Mental Health
certified) after their name, they must complete an approved fourteen-
hour perinatal training like PSI's, an advanced training in their specialty, and show two years of experience with perinatal populations.
Then they take a standardized test. Once they pass, they must sub-
mit continuing education credits every two years to maintain their
certification.

The certification program was expensive. PSI founder Jane Honikman reflected on the importance of certifications to the organization today, lamenting the way certification programs recognized formal training over lived experience. Some women, Honikman noted,
who have been in this field for decades refuse to take the expensive
tests. But, she adds, "it was brilliant of PSI to do it, in terms of financial gain."[5]

While the financial health of PSI is tied to its trainings and to the
certification, the development of the PMH-C is also a fulfillment of
the decades-long pursuit of legitimacy. Whereas some general therapists will say they can see postpartum patients despite not having
one minute of specialized training, said Birdie Meyer, the certification

program "legitimized our field." She explains proudly that "when you see PMH-C after someone's name that means they are legitimately trained in this field." Perhaps it would also help insurance companies take it more seriously, she added. Women's health advocates who had once wondered how to find anyone who would take their situation seriously have transformed into a professional body that defines a specialization.

Postpartum advocates have worked to balance a fight for the health of pregnant people, mainly women, with the reality that women's health politics in the US are a volatile landscape. Activists and advocates have sought to maintain as non-divisive a politics as possible. They have done this by centering children and families, and by often defining postpartum depression as a biologically based medical problem. This rarely actually meant advocates discounted social and structural issues like parental leave and affordable childcare, but more often they did not see them as the most addressable components of postpartum health. Postpartum depression is not a liberal or a conservative issue, they reiterate, it is an everyone issue. It is a women's health issue *and* a family issue. Society should change, ideally, but it is not always easy to agree on exactly *how* those changes would look. Easier is the certainty that psychiatry and psychology must change in ways that prioritize postpartum illness.

This constant runs through decades of postpartum mental health activism and advocacy: a demand that women's pain be taken seriously. Sometimes advocates had different stances on the best way to take it seriously, on balancing demands for medicalization and social change, on whether it was best to emphasize the health of the infant or the family or the mother. But what has remained consistent is this belief that mothers, and all parents, must have their stresses and suffering made legible and treated as legitimate.

234 |

Acknowledgments

When I first set out to write this book, I imagined writing a history based on medical journals. It took me ages to realize that was not the story I cared about, that I was more interested in the story of the advocates and activists who made postpartum mental illness visible. It took me even longer to accept this would mean calling these men and women up and asking them to talk to me. Much to my amazement, many agreed. While conducting oral history was a learning experience for me, the interviews were the best decision I made in writing this book; I cannot imagine it without them. Over thirty-five individuals who made important contributions to postpartum activism, advocacy, psychology, and psychiatry enthusiastically shared their stories and reflections with me. I owe an extraordinary thanks to those whose stories I use extensively and to those who provided me with background knowledge and context. When other researchers use the transcripts of these interviews someday, I am optimistic they will be able to do justice to some of the amazing life stories that had to be reduced to a quote or short paragraph in my final text.

Most of these transcripts are now part of the University of North Texas Oral History Program's collections, where they will be available for future researchers. It was incredibly fortuitous to have the Oral History Program and its infrastructure for permissions, editing, binding, cataloging, and storing oral histories just minutes from my office. Many thanks to Todd Moye for helping me navigate the basics of oral history, and to Sara Wilson for her patience with me as I worked through the logistics. Robin Reeder provided fantastic transcriptions.

Some of these interviewees also shared letters, photographs, and other documents with me. Jane and Terry Honikman welcomed me into their home so I could go through cassette recordings of meetings, conference programs, scrapbooks, and news clippings. Jane's archive is now housed in special collections at the University of Santa Barbara. Nancy Berchtold and Laurence Kruckman also kindly shared materials. Like so much women's activism, and so much mental health history, traditional archives are often limited. Access to the materials they saved proved invaluable.

I did use traditional archives when they were available and incurred many debts in the process. I want to thank Beth DeFrancis Sun at the American College of Obstetricians and Gynecologists, Stephen Greenberg at the National Library of Medicine, and Elisa Stroh at the Barbara Bates Center for the Study of the History of Nursing at the University of Pennsylvania. Thanks also to archivists and staff at the University of Pennsylvania, Syracuse University, the National Archives at College Park, the Schlesinger Library, and the Countway Library. At many of these sites, archivists not only helped me find postpartum documents but also went above and beyond to help me find spaces where I could pump breast milk.

This book was made possible through financial support from a few sources. Above all, a National Science Foundation Scholars Award (Award 1849533) from the Science, Technology and Society Program funded travel, transcription, and writing. I also would like to acknowledge support from the American College of Obstetricians and Gynecologists, the Barbara Bates Center for the Study of the History of Nursing, and the University of North Texas.

I owe many debts to the University of North Texas and my incredible colleagues here. Staff members Jami Thomas, Megan Bryan, and Miranda Leddy managed my grant monies on top of all their other responsibilities. Jennifer Wallach and Sandra Mendiola García served as both mentors and friends. Terra Rowe and Clark Pomerleau commented on very early drafts. I am thankful for all my colleagues but want to mention a handful by name: Jenn Aglio, Katy Beebe, Arunima Datta, Suzanne Enck, Jacqueline Foertsch, Megan Morrissey, Chad Pearson, Wes Phelps, Nancy Stockdale, Harold Tanner, ToniAnn Treviño, and Mike Wise. Leah Walsh helped me brainstorm titles. UNT librarians Doug Campbell and Julie Leuzinger helped me immensely, as did our amazing interlibrary loan team.

I tested much of this book's content out at conferences over the years and want to thank the co-panelists and audience members who helped me think through the project. Generous scholars at the Dallas Area Social History Workshop (DASH), including Stephanie Cole, Kara Dixon Vuic, Sarah Rose, and Rebecca Sharpless, helped me work through my earliest ideas. Chloe Silverman invited me to give a talk at Drexel, and then introduced me to Joyce Kelly, who gave me great advice about applying to NSF grants. I have benefited enormously from feedback at talks and conferences from so many. Those whose comments and questions left a mark on the project include Agatha Beins, Lara Freidenfelds, Alexandra Rutherford, Emily Seitz, Courtney Thompson, and Whitney Wood. Discussion with the Consortium for the History of Science, Technology and Medicine's working group in New Histories of Psychology helped shape my approach. Finally, I am grateful to Rebecca Godderis and Benjamin Breen for helping me think through the enigma that is James Hamilton, and to Hilary Marland for sharing archival finds.

I am also grateful for the continued insights and mentorship of individuals from my PhD program, who at this point have been mentoring me for well over a decade. Thanks to Gary Cross, Greg Eghigian, Lori Ginzberg, and Jennifer Mittelstadt.

Writing the second book was much more of a solo endeavor than writing the first, so I am indebted to the writing community I built up along the way. Kat Aoyama, Teresa Golden, Andreana Prichard, Adam Schwartz, and Annette Totten all helped keep me accountable for those daily writing minutes.

| 237

My editor at the University of Chicago, Tim Mennel, has been wonderful. He supported the book from our first meeting and has pushed me throughout to think about how to write for a broader audience. I am also appreciative of the insights of the anonymous manuscript readers for the press, and to Andrea Blatz for all her work with the final manuscript.

I also owe much to the support of my family, including my mother and father, Marilyn and Tom Moran, and my wonderful in-laws, Lisa and Rick Gregg and Julie and Tom Hlavacik. Thanks as well to my brother Mike, nephew Kian, and niece Salma.

My spouse, Mark Hlavacik, deserves more than the sentences of thanks I can give here. He cared for our children while I was in archives and talked through so many half-baked ideas with me. Mark was there when I first found letters about postpartum illness at the National Archives, and he watched the kids while I submitted the final manuscript. This book would not exist without his support and love.

In truth my children have made writing a book much harder, but also have given it purpose. Just today I set out to write acknowledgments and was interrupted to make cupcakes, paint pumpkins, and be pelted with stuffed animals. In the difficulty of the postpartum, I could not have imagined all the joy and beauty ahead. Thank you, Brendon, Oskar, and Ruth.

Notes

Introduction

1.   This book relies on oral histories conducted by the author. The transcripts for many of these interviews are housed by the University of North Texas's Oral History Project, in the University of North Texas Special Collections. Unless otherwise indicated, quotes from the following people come from their interviews (date of interview in parentheses): Diana Lynn Barnes (7/25/23); Cheryl Beck (11/4/19); Shoshana Bennett (2/13/20); Nancy Berchtold (3/2/21); Carol Blocker (10/14/22); Joy Burkhard (10/6/22); Nancy Byatt (9/16/22); Jabina Coleman (11/3/22); Wendy Davis (10/7/22); Carol Dix (3/29/21); Paula Doress-Worters (2/10/20); Susan Dowd Stone (9/23/22); Jeanne Watson Driscoll (1/30/23); Ann Dunnewold (4/21/21); Susan Feingold (4/14/21); Adrienne Griffen (8/12/22); Jane Honikman (11/13/19); Pec Indman (1/6/23); Karen Kleiman (3/30/21); Laurence Kruckman (1/10/23); Divya Kumar (10/7/22); Barry Lewis (4/13/21); Birdie Gunyun Meyer (1/17/23); Michael O'Hara (9/19/19); Barbara Parry (12/10/19); Margaret Spinelli (1/24/20); Nada Stotland (8/29/19); Katherine Wisner (1/14/20); Dennie Wolf (9/9/19). Interviews that are not part of the UNT collection have transcripts in possession of the author. These interviews include: Jamie Belsito (9/14/22); Desirée Israel (10/21/22); Graeme Seabrook (8/8/22).

2.   Lisa Held and Alexandra Rutherford, "Can't a Mother Sing the Blues? Postpartum Depression and the Construction of Motherhood in Late 20th-Century America," *History of Psychology* 15, no. 2 (May 2012): 107–23, https://doi.org/10.1037/a0026219.

3. A note of clarification on language. Most of this book is about cis-gendered women. In places I directly discuss postpartum illness today, like the introduction and conclusion, I opt for more inclusive language. Pregnancy and postpartum depression are not wholly the domain of women. Historically, though, that was not the language used or the conception of pregnancy held by most professionals or advocates. When I speak historically, then, I usually rely on the language of womanhood and motherhood. The story my sources tell is about a particular construction of "women's health" and women's mental health.

4. Michael W. O'Hara and Jennifer E. McCabe, "Postpartum Depression: Current Status and Future Directions," *Annual Review of Clinical Psychology* 9, no. 1 (March 28, 2013): 379–407, https://doi.org/10.1146/annurev-clinpsy-050212-185612.

5. O'Hara and McCabe, "Postpartum Depression," 379–407.

6. Joseph Dumit, "Illnesses You Have to Fight to Get: Facts as Forces in Uncertain, Emergent Illnesses," *Social Science & Medicine* 62, no. 3 (February 2006): 577–90, 580, https://doi.org/10.1016/j.socscimed.2005.06.018.

7. Dana Becker, *The Myth of Empowerment: Women and the Therapeutic Culture in America* (New York: New York University Press, 2005).

8. Laura D. Hirshbein, *American Melancholy: Constructions of Depression in the Twentieth Century* (New Brunswick, NJ: Rutgers University Press, 2009).

9. Michelle N. Lafrance and Janet M. Stoppard, "Constructing a Non-Depressed Self: Women's Accounts of Recovery from Depression," *Feminism & Psychology* 16, no. 3 (August 2006): 307–25, https://doi.org/10.1177/0959353506067849.

10. Verta A. Taylor, *Rock-a-by Baby: Feminism, Self Help, and Postpartum Depression* (New York: Routledge, 1996), 157.

11. Sandra Morgen, *Into Our Own Hands: The Women's Health Movement in the United States, 1969–1990* (New Brunswick, NJ: Rutgers University Press, 2002); Wendy Kline, *Bodies of Knowledge: Sexuality, Reproduction, and Women's Health in the Second Wave* (Chicago: University of Chicago Press, 2010).

12. Kirsten Swinth, *Feminism's Forgotten Fight: The Unfinished Struggle for Work and Family* (Cambridge, MA: Harvard University Press, 2018).

13. Judith Houck, *Hot and Bothered Women, Medicine, and Menopause in Modern America* (Cambridge, MA: Harvard University Press, 2008), 13.

14. Amy Koerber, *From Hysteria to Hormones: A Rhetorical History* (University Park: Pennsylvania State University Press, 2018).

15. Johanna Schoen, *Abortion after Roe: Abortion after Legalization* (Chapel

Hill: University of North Carolina Press, 2015); Susan Markens, "The Problematic of 'Experience': A Political and Cultural Critique of PMS," *Gender & Society* 10, no. 1 (February 1996): 42–58; Jenifer Dodd, "'The Name Game': Feminist Protests of the *DSM* and Diagnostic Labels in the 1980s," *History of Psychology* 18, no. 3 (August 2015): 312–23.

16. Tasha N. Dubriwny, *The Vulnerable Empowered Woman: Feminism, Post-feminism, and Women's Health* (New Brunswick, NJ: Rutgers University Press, 2013), 71.

17. Seth Dowland, *Family Values and the Rise of the Christian Right* (Philadelphia: University of Pennsylvania Press, 2015); Robert O. Self, *All in the Family: The Realignment of American Democracy Since the 1960s* (New York: Hill and Wang, 2013).

18. For a critique of the politics of "happiness," see Sara Ahmed, "Killing Joy: Feminism and the History of Happiness," *Signs: Journal of Women in Culture and Society* 35, no. 3 (March 2010): 571–94, https://doi.org/10.1086/648513.

19. Nancy Fraser, *Fortunes of Feminism: From State-Managed Capitalism to Neoliberal Crisis* (New York: Verso Books, 2013).

20. Melinda Cooper, *Family Values: Between Neoliberalism and the New Social Conservatism* (New York: Zone Books, 2017).

21. Brent Cebul, "Frugal Governance, Family Values, and the Intimate Roots of Neoliberalism," in *Intimate States: Gender, Sexuality, and Governance in Modern US History*, ed. Margot Canaday, Nancy F. Cott, and Robert O. Self (Chicago: University of Chicago Press, 2021).

22. Sharon Batt, *Health Advocacy, Inc.: How Pharmaceutical Funding Changed the Breast Cancer Movement* (Vancouver: University of British Columbia Press, 2019); Jessica L. Martucci, *Back to the Breast: Natural Motherhood and Breastfeeding in America* (Chicago: University of Chicago Press, 2015).

23. Samantha King, *Pink Ribbons, Inc.: Breast Cancer and the Politics of Philanthropy* (Minneapolis: University of Minnesota Press, 2008); Jessica Polzer, "The Personal Is Political: Breast Cancer Risk, Genetic(optim)ization, and the Proactive Subject as Neoliberal Biological Citizen," in Elaine M. Power and Jessica Polzer, *Neoliberal Governance and Health: Duties, Risks, and Vulnerabilities* (Montreal: McGill-Queen's University Press, 2016), 133.

24. Alexandra Rutherford, "Feminism, Psychology, and the Gendering of Neoliberal Subjectivity: From Critique to Disruption," *Theory & Psychology* 28, no. 5 (October 2018): 619–44, https://doi.org/10.1177/0959354318797194.

25. Lisa Levenstein, *They Didn't See Us Coming: The Hidden History of Feminism in the Nineties* (New York: Basic Books, 2020); Myrl Beam, *Gay, Inc.:*

The Nonratification of Queer Politics (Minneapolis: University of Minnesota Press, 2018).

Chapter 1

1.   Charles Carner, "Don't Be Surprised by After-Baby Blues," *Today's Health*, December 1967, 33, 34.

2.   Margaret B. McFarland and John B. Reinhart, "The Development of Motherliness," *Children* (April 1959): 50.

3.   Lisa Held and Alexandra Rutherford, "Can't a Mother Sing the Blues? Postpartum Depression and the Construction of Motherhood in Late 20th-Century America," *History of Psychology* 15, no. 2 (May 2012): 107–23.

4.   Hippocrates of Cos, "Epidemics 1, 3," trans. W. H. S. Jones (Cambridge, MA: Harvard University Press, 1923), https://doi.org/10.4159/DLCL .hippocrates_cos-epidemics_i_iii.1923, p. 281. Several prominent postpartum researchers question the Hippocrates origin story, most notably Ian F. Brockington, *Motherhood and Mental Health* (Oxford: Oxford University Press, 1996), 200–201; Lauren M. Osborne, "Recognizing and Managing Postpartum Psychosis: A Clinical Guide for Obstetric Providers," *Obstetrics and Gynecology Clinics of North America* 45, no. 3 (September 2018): 455–68, https://doi.org/10.1016/j.ogc.2018.04.005; Veerle Bergink, Natalie Rasgon, and Katherine L. Wisner, "Postpartum Psychosis: Madness, Mania, and Melancholia in Motherhood," *American Journal of Psychiatry* 173, no. 12 (December 2016): 1179–88, https://doi .org/10.1176/appi.ajp.2016.16040454.

5.   Ian Brockington and Abram Coen, "Esquirol et Marcé: contributions à la Psychiatrie de la grossesse," *Le Carnet PSY* 179, no. 3 (2014): 22–29.

6.   F. W. Mackenzie, "On the Pathology and Treatment of Puerperal Insanity: Especially in Reference to Its Relation to Anemia," *London Journal of Medicine* 3, no. 30 (June 1851): 504–21; T. Salter, "Case of Puerperal Mania: Occurring at an Early Period of Utero-Gestation, and Relieved by Induced Abortion," *BMJ* s1-11, no. 13 (June 30, 1847): 346–48; Rebecca Godderis, "Managing Mad Mothers: Postpartum Depression and the Psychiatric Gaze" (PhD diss., University of Calgary, 2009), 64; Joseph Silverman, "Louis-Victor Marcé, 1828–1864: Anorexia Nervosa's Forgotten Man," *Psychological Medicine* 19, no. 4 (November 1989): 833–35; Jean-Pierre Luauté, Thérèse Lempérière, and Pascal Arnaud, "Death of an Alienist: Louis-Victor Marcé's Final Year," *History of Psychiatry* 25, no. 3 (September 2014): 265–82, https://doi.org/10.1177 /0957154X14529219.

7.   Puerperal insanity is not actually mentioned in the text, but much analysis of the story emphasizes the postpartum context of her suffering and of the "rest cure." Charlotte Perkins Gilman, *"The Yellow Wallpaper" and Other Stories*, Dover Thrift Editions (Mineola, NY: Dover Publications, 1997); Nancy Theriot, "Diagnosing Unnatural Motherhood: Nineteenth-Century Physicians and 'Puerperal Insanity,'" *American Studies* 30, no. 2 (Fall 1989): 69–88, 70.

8.   Udodiri Okwandu, conference paper, "Madness and Mothering: Race, Citizenship, and Maternal Insanity in Late 19th and Early 20th Century American Medicine, Science, and Law," presented at the American Association for the History of Medicine, May 14, 2021; Felicity M. Turner, *Proving Pregnancy Gender, Law, and Medical Knowledge in Nineteenth-Century America* (Chapel Hill: University of North Carolina Press, 2022).

9.   Theriot, "Diagnosing Unnatural Motherhood," 83; Hilary Marland, *Dangerous Motherhood: Insanity and Childbirth in Victorian Britain* (Basingstoke: Palgrave Macmillan, 2004), 201.

10.   Emil Kraepelin, *Lectures on Clinical Psychiatry*, trans. Thomas Johnstone (London: Baillière, Tindall and Cox, 1904), 129; Marland, 203.

11.   Edward Strecker and Franklin Ebaugh, "Psychoses Occurring During the Puerperium," *Archives of Neurology & Psychiatry* 15, no. 2 (1926): 242, 243.

12.   American Psychiatric Association, Diagnostic and Statistical Manual of Mental Disorders, 1st ed. (Washington, DC: American Psychiatric Association, 1952), xii.

13.   Allan V. Horwitz, *DSM: A History of Psychiatry's Bible* (Baltimore: Johns Hopkins University Press, 2021), 30–31; James Alexander Hamilton, *Postpartum Psychiatric Problems* (St. Louis: C. V. Mosby Company, 1962), 200.

14.   James Alexander Hamilton, *Research Opportunities Avoided Since 1962 in the Areas Related to Postpartum Psychiatric Illness*, circulated but unpublished manuscript, 1996, Honikman Archive, pp. iii, 1.

15.   James Hamilton, "Prophylactic Measures," speech to the Second Annual Conference on Postpartum Depression, Medical Center at Princeton, June 24–26, 1988, pp. 18–19, Honikman Archive, Hamilton letters Jan. 9, 1984–Oct. 7, 1988.

16.   Gregory Zilboorg, "Malignant Psychoses Related to Childbirth," *American Journal of Obstetrics and Gynecology* 15, no. 2 (February 1928): 145–58, https://doi.org/10.1016/S0002-9378(28)90462-7; Gregory Zilboorg, "The Dynamics of Schizophrenic Reactions Related to Pregnancy and Childbirth," *American Journal of Psychiatry* 85, no. 4 (January 1929): 733–67, https://doi.org/10.1176/ajp.85.4.733.

| 243

17. Helene Deutsch, *The Psychology of Women: A Psychoanalytic Interpretation*, vol. 2: Motherhood (New York: Grune & Stratton, 1945), 269.

18. Edward Shorter, *From Paralysis to Fatigue: A History of Psychosomatic Illness in the Modern Era* (New York: Free Press, 1992).

19. Conference programs, Box 4/B/9/b, "Annual Programs and Exhibit Guides," J. Bay Jacobs Library for the History of Obstetrics and Gynecology in America, American College of Obstetricians and Gynecologists, Washington, DC.

20. Special Interest Course #6, Psychosomatic Obstetrics and Gynecology, Cassette 1: Psychological Considerations in Pregnancy, 1974, J. Bay Jacobs Library for the History of Obstetrics and Gynecology in America, American College of Obstetricians and Gynecologists, Washington, DC.

21. Mrs. Dave Becker to Prenatal Care (Dept. Health), U.S. Government, February 15, 1943, National Archives, College Park, MD, RG 102: Children's Bureau, Central File 1941–1944, Entry A1 E3A, Box 134, Folder 4-12-4-7 Adult Life.

22. Katherine Bain to Mrs. Dave Becker, February 20, 1943, National Archives, College Park, Maryland, RG 102: Children's Bureau, Central File 1941–1944, Entry A1 E3A, Box 134, Folder 4-12-4-7 Adult Life.

23. Children's Bureau, US Department of Labor, *Prenatal Care*, 1942, 17.

24. Children's Bureau, US Department of Health, Education, and Welfare, *Prenatal Care*, 1962, 80.

25. Julia Grant, *Raising Baby by the Book: The Education of American Mothers* (New Haven, CT: Yale University Press, 1998), 202.

26. Peter N. Stearns, *Anxious Parents: A History of Modern Child-Rearing in America* (New York: New York University Press, 2004), 48.

27. Elaine Tyler May, *Homeward Bound: American Families in the Cold War Era*, rev. ed. (New York: Basic Books, 2017), 16; Laura McEnaney, *Civil Defense Begins at Home: Militarization Meets Everyday Life in the Fifties* (Princeton, NJ: Princeton University Press, 2000); Lynn Spigel, *Make Room for TV: Television and the Family Ideal in Postwar America* (Chicago: University of Chicago Press, 1992); Michael S. Sherry, *In the Shadow of War: The United States since the 1930s* (New Haven, CT: Yale University Press, 1995).

28. Ellen Herman, *The Romance of American Psychology: Political Culture in the Age of Experts* (Berkeley: University of California Press, 1995), 279; Rebecca Jo Plant, *Mom: The Transformation of Motherhood in Modern America* (Chicago: University of Chicago Press, 2010); Anne Harrington, "Mother Love and Mental Illness: An Emotional History," *Osiris* 31 (1) 2016: 94–115; Chloe Silverman, *Understanding Autism: Parents, Doctors, and the History of a Disorder* (Princeton, NJ: Princeton University Press, 2012), 38; Roel Van Den Oever, *Mama's Boy: Momism and Homophobia in Postwar American Culture* (Basingstoke: Palgrave Macmillan, 2012).

29. Benjamin Spock, *Problems of Parents* (Boston: Houghton Mifflin Company, 1962), 101–2.

30. Edward Strecker, *Their Mothers' Sons: A Psychiatrist Examines an American Problem* (Philadelphia: J. B. Lippincott Company, 1946), 13–22; Harrington, "Mother Love and Mental Illness," 94–115.

31. Premilla Nadasen, *Welfare Warriors: The Welfare Rights Movement in the United States* (New York: Routledge, 2005).

32. Ruth Feldstein, *Motherhood in Black and White: Race and Sex in American Liberalism, 1930–1965* (Ithaca, NY: Cornell University Press, 2000), 148–49.

33. Daniel Patrick Moynihan, *The Negro Family: The Case for National Action* (US Government Printing Office, 1965).

34. Rebecca Ann Wanzo, *The Suffering Will Not Be Televised: African American Women and Sentimental Political Storytelling* (Albany: State University of New York Press, 2009).

35. Hyman Spotnitz and Lucy Freeman, *How to Be Happy Though Pregnant: A Guide to Understanding and Solving the Normal Emotional Problems of Pregnancy and Postpartum Blues* (New York: Coward-McCann, 1969), 145.

36. Spotnitz and Freeman, *How to Be Happy Though Pregnant*, 145.

37. Phyllis Ehrlich, "Parental Problem: First-Baby Blues," *New York Times*, August 14, 1960, sec. Sunday Magazine, p. 68.

38. Judith Kruger, *My Fight for Sanity* (Philadelphia: Chilton Company, 1959), 2, 64.

39. Herman N. Bundensen, "Third-Day Blues," *Ladies Home Journal*, December 1952, 87.

40. Helen Puner, "Those After-Baby Blues," *Parents* 33 (December 1958): 90.

41. Wendy Kline, *Coming Home: How Midwives Changed Birth* (New York: Oxford University Press, 2021), 15.

42. Leo Doyle, MS, MD, *Handbook of Obstetrics and Diagnostic Gynecology*, 1st ed. (Palo Alto, CA: University Medical Publishers, 1950), 31.

43. Carner, "Don't Be Surprised by After-Baby Blues," 33.

44. George C. Thosteson, "Post-Maternity Blues Common," *Eugene Register-Guard* (June 2, 1975).

45. Spotnitz and Freeman, *How to Be Happy Though Pregnant*, 140.

46. Terra Ziporyn, "'Rip van Winkle Period' Ends for Puerperal Psychiatric Problems," *Journal of the American Medical Association* 251, no. 16 (April 27, 1984).

47. James H. Winchester, "What to Do About 'After-Baby Blues,'" *Gadsden Times* (July 20, 1969), sec. Family Weekly insert, p. 6.

48. Lara Freidenfelds, *The Myth of the Perfect Pregnancy: A History of Miscarriage in America* (Oxford: Oxford University Press, 2020), 63–64.

49. John Bowlby, "Maternal Care and Mental Health," *Bulletin of the World Health Organization* 3 (1951): 355–533; Inge Bretherton, "The Origins of Attachment Theory: John Bowlby and Mary Ainsworth," *Developmental Psychology* 28, no. 5 (1992): 759–75; Marga Vicedo, "The Social Nature of the Mother's Tie to Her Child: John Bowlby's Theory of Attachment in Post-War America," *British Journal for the History of Science* 44, no. 3 (September 2011): 401–26.

50. Ruth Brecher and Edward Brecher, "Why Some Mothers Reject Their Babies," *Redbook* (May 1968): 145.

51. Carner, "Don't Be Surprised by After-Baby Blues," 33.

52. Yanna Kroyt Brandt, "What Doctors Now Know About Depressed Young Mothers," *Redbook*, March 1968, 162. Note: The woman is named Joanna, not Anna, but I shortened her name to differentiate her from Joanne at the start of the chapter.

53. Brandt, "What Doctors Now Know About Depressed Young Mothers," 69; Phyllis Ehrlich, "Parental Problem: First-Baby Blues," *New York Times*, August 14, 1960, sec. Sunday Magazine, 68.

54. Benjamin Spock, *Problems of Parents* (Boston: Houghton Mifflin Company, 1962), 33–34.

55. Brandt, "What Doctors Now Know About Depressed Young Mothers," 69; "The Doctor Talks about Postnatal Blues," *McCall's*, June 1957, 143.

56. Ehrlich, "Parental Problem: First-Baby Blues," 68.

57. Joan Troan, "If Mama Gets 'Baby Blues'—It's Not the Infant's Fault," *Pittsburgh Press*, May 15, 1955.

58. Lisa Held and Alexandra Rutherford, "Can't a Mother Sing the Blues? Postpartum Depression and the Construction of Motherhood in Late 20th-Century America," *History of Psychology* 15, no. 2 (May 2012): 107–23.

59. Benjamin Spock, *The Common Sense Book of Baby and Child Care* (New York: Duell, Sloan and Pearce, 1946).

60. Lizabeth Cohen, *A Consumers' Republic: The Politics of Mass Consumption in Postwar America* (New York: Knopf, 2003); Gary S. Cross, *An All-Consuming Century: Why Commercialism Won in Modern America* (New York: Columbia University Press, 2000).

61. Benjamin Spock, *Problems of Parents* (Boston: Houghton Mifflin Company, 1962), 34.

62. Ehrlich, "Parental Problem: First-Baby Blues," 68.

63. Myrtle Eldred, "'Blues' Come Naturally to New Mothers," *Pittsburgh Press*, February 3, 1953, 20.

64. George C. Thosteson, "Post-Maternity Blues Common," *Eugene Register-Guard*, June 2, 1975, 5B.

65. "The Doctor Talks about Postnatal Blues," *McCall's*, June 1957, 143.

66. Eldred, "'Blues' Come Naturally to New Mothers," 20.
67. Benjamin Spock, *A Baby's First Year* (New York: Duell, Sloan and Pearce, 1950), 9.
68. Winchester, "What to Do About 'After-Baby Blues,'" 6.
69. Hamilton, *Postpartum Psychiatric Problems*.
70. Carner, "Don't Be Surprised by After-Baby Blues," 34-35.
71. George E. Judd, "After the Baby Is Born (Column: The Expectant Mother)," *Redbook*, May 1964, 44.
72. Spotnitz and Freeman, *How to Be Happy Though Pregnant*, 148.
73. "The Doctor Talks about Postnatal Blues," *McCall's*, June 1957, 4.
74. Andrea Tone, *The Age of Anxiety: A History of America's Turbulent Affair with Tranquilizers* (Basic Books, 2012); Jonathan Metzl, *Prozac on the Couch: Prescribing Gender in the Era of Wonder Drugs* (Durham, NC: Duke University Press, 2003).
75. David Herzberg, *Happy Pills in America: From Miltown to Prozac* (Baltimore: Johns Hopkins University Press, 2010).
76. Gay Pauley, "Drugs Help Mothers Shed Their Blues," *Windsor Daily Star*, Sep. 2, 1959, p. 3L.
77. "Personality Spotlight," *The Chicago Defender (National Edition) (1921-1967)*, Nov. 28, 1959, p. 6.
78. Pauley, "Drugs Help Mothers Shed Their Blues," p. 3L.
79. Edward Shorter, *Before Prozac: The Troubled History of Mood Disorders in Psychiatry* (Oxford: Oxford University Press, 2009), 137, 223.
80. Betty Friedan, *The Feminine Mystique* (New York: Norton, 2001), 376, 378.
81. Betty Friedan, 1957 *[84 questionnaires completed by married women—Smith College class of 1942, 15th reunion]*. Gender: Identity and Social Change collection, available through Adam Matthew, Marlborough, http://www.genderidentityandsocialchange.amdigital.co.uk/Documents/Details/sch00059c00354 [accessed January 29, 2021], Schlesinger MC 575, T-97, T-125, Vt-1, Phon-7.
82. Plant, *Mom*, 154.
83. Stephanie Coontz, *That Strange Stirring: The Feminine Mystique and American Women at the Dawn of the 1960s* (New York: Basic Books, 2011), 83, 84.
84. Carner, "Don't Be Surprised by After-Baby Blues," 34.
85. Plant, *Mom*, 16.

Chapter 2

1. Kathy Davis, *The Making of Our Bodies, Ourselves: How Feminism Crosses Borders* (Durham, NC: Duke University Press, 2007), 21.

2. Stephenson Heather and Kiki Zeldes, "'Write a Chapter and Change the World': How the Boston Women's Health Book Collective Transformed Women's Health Then—and Now," *American Journal of Public Health* 98, no. 10 (October 2008): 1741–45, https://doi.org/10.2105/AJPH.2007 .132159.

3. Marci Coleman, "Woman to Doctor to Woman," *Women: A Journal of Liberation* 7, no. 3 (1981): 10.

4. Barbara Ehrenreich and Deirdre English, *Complaints and Disorders: The Sexual Politics of Sickness*, 2nd ed., Contemporary Classics (New York: Feminist Press, 2011).

5. Carol Downer, address to 1972 American Psychological Association meeting, "Covert Sex Discrimination Against Women as Medical Patients," September 5, 1972, Duke University Libraries, Atlanta Lesbian Feminist Alliance Archives, Box 12 Folder 6, accessed at https:// dukelibraries.contentdm.oclc.org/digital/collection/p15957coll6/id/775 /rec/3.

6. Ellen Herman, *The Romance of American Psychiatry*, 288–89.

7. Belita Cowen, *Women's Health Care: Resources, Writings, Bibliographies*, 2nd printing (Ann Arbor, MI: Anshen Publishing, 1978), p. 34.

8. Marilyn Becker and Alice Krakauer, "Politics of Therapy for Women," *Women: A Journal of Liberation* 3, no. 3 (1972): 3, 5.

9. Report draft, "Recommendations of the Women's Health Concerns Committee to the Health Systems Agency Regarding Mental Health Services," December 15, 1977, Box 13, Folder 163, Ms. Coll. 588, Women's Health Concerns Committee records, Kislak Center for Special Collections, Rare Books and Manuscripts, University of Pennsylvania.

10. Ruth Darmstadter et al., "Childbirth and Madness," *Women: A Journal of Liberation* 3, no. 3 (1972): 16.

11. Judith Walzer Leavitt, *Brought to Bed: Childbearing in America, 1750 to 1950*, 30th anniversary ed. (New York: Oxford University Press, 2016); Wendy Kline, *Coming Home: How Midwives Changed Birth* (New York: Oxford University Press, 2021); Sandra Morgen, *Into Our Own Hands: The Women's Health Movement in the United States, 1969–1990* (New Brunswick, NJ: Rutgers University Press, 2002); Hannah Dudley-Shotwell, *Revolutionizing Women's Healthcare: The Feminist Self-Help Movement in America* (New Brunswick, NJ: Rutgers University Press, 2020).

12. Sarah Crook, "The Women's Liberation Movement, Activism and Therapy at the Grassroots, 1968–1985," *Women's History Review* 27, no. 7 (November 10, 2018): 1152–68, https://doi.org/10.1080/09612025.2018 .1450611; Judith A. Houck, *Hot and Bothered Women, Medicine, and Menopause in Modern America* (Cambridge, MA: Harvard University Press, 2008), 211.

13. Joan Ditzion et al., Panel, "A Revolutionary Moment: Women's Liberation in the late 1960s and early 1970s," Formative Years: The Birth of *Our Bodies Ourselves* conference, Boston University, March 27-29, 2014, transcript accessed at https://www.bu.edu/wgs/files/2013/10/Ditzion -Formative-Years-The-Birth-of-Our-Bodies-Ourselves.pdf.

14. Transcript of Kathy Davis interviewing Paula Doress-Worters, Dec. 2, 1998, Box 1, Folder 5: "Doress," MC 902: Oral history interviews, 1998-1999, Schlesinger Library, Cambridge, MA, p. 6.

15. Transcript of Kathy Davis interviewing Paula Doress-Worters, Schlesinger Library, pp. 6-7.

16. Boston Women's Health Book Collective, *Women and Their Bodies: A Course* (self-published, 1970), 163, 167.

17. It notably included the work of Dr. James Alexander Hamilton, who became central to postpartum support group activism of the 1980s, and who centered the thyroid in his explanations of postpartum illness.

18. Lucas Richert, *Break on Through: Radical Psychiatry and the American Counterculture* (Cambridge, MA: MIT Press, 2019).

19. Boston Women's Health Book Collective, *Women and Their Bodies*, 167.

20. Boston Women's Health Book Collective, *Women and Their Bodies*, 170, 171.

21. Joan Ditzion et al., Panel, "A Revolutionary Moment."

22. Boston Women's Health Book Collective, *Women and Their Bodies*, 171-72.

23. Boston Women's Health Book Collective, *Our Bodies, Ourselves: A Book by and for Women* (New York: Simon and Schuster, 1973), 209, 214.

24. R. E. Gordon, E. E. Kapostins, and K. K. Gordon, "Factors in Postpartum Emotional Adjustment," *Obstetrics and Gynecology* 25 (February 1965): 158-66.

25. Lucas Richert, "'Therapy Means Political Change, Not Peanut Butter': American Radical Psychiatry, 1968-1975," *Social History of Medicine* 27, no. 1 (February 1, 2014): 104-21, https://doi.org/10.1093/shm/hkt072.

26. Boston Women's Health Book Collective, *Our Bodies, Ourselves*, 209, 216, 218.

27. Boston Women's Health Book Collective, *Our Bodies, Ourselves*, 299, 309.

28. Boston Women's Health Book Collective, "Postpartum Blues: As Natural as Childbirth," *Ms.* (March 1976), 110-17, quote on 117.

29. Correspondence from Minneapolis to *Ms.*, n.d., Box 7, Folder 76: "Girl Scouts; Postpartum Blues, March 1976," MC 331: Letters to Ms., 1970-1998, Schlesinger Library, Cambridge, MA.

30. Correspondence from Minneapolis to *Ms.*

31. Correspondence from Massachusetts to *Ms.*

32. Correspondence from Maryland to *Ms.*

33. Correspondence from Paris, France, to *Ms.*, July 20, 1976, Box 7, Folder 76: "Girl Scouts; Postpartum Blues, March 1976," MC 331: Letters to *Ms.*, 1970–1998, Schlesinger Library, Cambridge, MA.

34. Correspondence from Nashville to *Ms.*, March 16, 1976, Box 7, Folder 76: "Girl Scouts; Postpartum Blues, March 1976," MC 331: Letters to *Ms.*, 1970–1998, Schlesinger Library, Cambridge, MA.

35. Boston Women's Health Book Collective, *Our Bodies, Ourselves*, 308.

36. Kline, *Coming Home.*

37. Jessica L. Martucci gives a comprehensive critique of the problems with maternal claims to the "natural" in *Back to the Breast: Natural Motherhood and Breastfeeding in America* (Chicago: University of Chicago Press, 2015).

38. Carol Lease, "Prepared, Educated Childbirth Shows the Joy of Birth," *Big Mama Rag* 3, no. 5 (November 1974): 6.

39. "A Question of Biology," *A Forum for Changing Men*, no. 58 (March 1980): 9, Gender: Identity and Social Change collection, available through Adam Matthew, Marlborough, http://www.genderidentityandsocialchange .amdigital.co.uk/Documents/Details/MSU_HQ1090_L53.

40. Kline, *Coming Home*, 79.

41. Raven Lang, *Birth Book* (Palo Alto, CA: Genesis Press, 1972).

42. "Home-Grown Babies," *Country Women* 13 (1974): 37.

43. Ina May and the Farm Midwives, *Spiritual Midwifery* (Summertown, TN: The Book Publishing Company, 1975), 303.

44. Deborah Tanzer, *Why Natural Childbirth?* (New York: Schocken Books, 1976), 136–37.

45. Janet Isaacs Ashford, *The Whole Birth Catalog: A Sourcebook for Choices in Childbirth* (Trumansburg, NY: Crossing Press, 1983), 198.

46. Ina May Gaskin, *Babies, Breastfeeding, and Bonding* (South Hadley, MA: Bergin & Garvey, 1987), 112, 119.

47. May Gaskin, *Babies, Breastfeeding, and Bonding*, 121.

48. "the pregnant glow?," *off our backs* 1, no. 24 (Summer 1971): 15.

49. "the pregnant glow?," 15.

50. Ti-Grace Atkinson, "The Institution of Sexual Intercourse," *Notes from the Second Year* (New York: New York Radical Women, 1970).

51. Adrienne Rich, *Of Woman Born* (New York: W. W. Norton, 1976), 267.

52. Rich, *Of Woman Born*, 282–83.

53. "Fuck Motherhood," *Burning River* 1, no. 8 (June 18, 1970): 4.

54. "the pregnant glow?"

55. "To Be Done with Motherhood Forever," *Ain't I a Woman* 4, no. 2 (May 1974).

56. Ruth Darmstadter et al., "Childbirth and Madness," *Women: A Journal of Liberation* 3, no. 3 (1972): 16.

57. "the pregnant glow?"

58. t.d., "childbirth: not so simple," *off our backs* 3, no. 9 (July/August 1973): 7.

59. Downer, "Covert Sex Discrimination Against Women as Medical Patients."

60. t.d., "childbirth: not so simple," 7.

61. Coalition for the Medical Rights of Women, *The Rock Will Wear Away: Handbook for Women's Health Advocates* (San Francisco: self-published, 1980), 11.

62. "Proceedings of the 1975 Conference on Women and Health," April 4–7, 1975, Boston, accessed online at https://www.ourbodiesourselves.org /wp-content/uploads/2014/04/Harvard-Conference-on-Women-and -Health-Part-1.pdf.

63. C. T. Beck, "Predictors of Postpartum Depression: An Update," *Nursing Research* 50, no. 5 (October 2001): 275–85, https://doi.org/10.1097 /00006199-200109000-00004; Keira Williams, "Defending Depression: Intersectionality and American Infanticide," *Journal of the Motherhood Initiative for Research and Community Involvement* 5, no. 2 (2015): 115, https://jarm.journals.yorku.ca/index.php/jarm/article/view/39763. See also Benita Roth, *Separate Roads to Feminism: Black, Chicana, and White Feminist Movements in America's Second Wave* (New York: Cambridge University Press, 2004).

64. Deirdre Cooper Owens and Sharla M. Fett, "Black Maternal and Infant Health: Historical Legacies of Slavery," *American Journal of Public Health* 109, no. 10 (October 2019): 1342–45, https://doi.org/10.2105/AJPH.2019 .305243.

65. Byllye Avery and Susan Reverby, "Ask a Feminist: Byllye Avery Discusses the Past and Future of Reproductive Justice," *Signs: Journal of Women in Culture and Society* 46, no. 3 (March 1, 2021): 765, https://doi .org/10.1086/712068.

66. Gwendolyn Osborne, "Motherhood in the Black Community," *The Crisis* 84 (December 1977): 479–86.

67. Joanna Clark, "Motherhood," in Toni Cade Bambara, ed., *The Black Woman: An Anthology* (New York: Washington Square Press, 2005), 76, 85.

68. Clark, "Motherhood," 81.

69. Clark, "Motherhood," 81–82.

70. J. H. Howard, "How to End Colonial Domination in Black America," *Negro Digest* 19 (January 1970): 4–10.

71. Jennifer Nelson, *More Than Medicine: A History of the Feminist Women's Health Movement* (New York: NYU Press, 2015), 116–17.

72. Evan Hart, "Building a More Inclusive Women's Health Movement: Byllye Avery and the Development of the National Black Women's Health Project, 1981–1990" (PhD diss., University of Cincinnati, 2012).

73. Byllye Y. Avery, "Breathing Life into Ourselves: The Evolution of the National Black Women's Health Project," in *Black Women's Health Book*, ed. Evelyn White (Seattle: Seal Press, 1990), 5.
74. Avery, "Breathing Life into Ourselves," 6.
75. Evelyn Barbee, "African American Women and Depression: A Review and Critique of the Literature," *Archives of Psychiatric Nursing* 6 (1992): 257–65; Jonathan Metzl, *The Protest Psychosis: How Schizophrenia Became a Black Disease* (Boston: Beacon Press, 2009); "Black and White Depression," *Human Behavior* (August 1973), 38–39; Jonathan Sadowsky, *The Empire of Depression: A New History* (Medford, MA: Polity Press, 2021); Kylie M. Smith, "No Medical Justification: Segregation and Civil Rights in Alabama's Psychiatric Hospitals, 1952–1972," *Journal of Southern History* 87 (November 2021): 645–72.
76. Francis J. Kane Jr. et al., "Post-Partum Depression in Southern Black Women," *Diseases of the Nervous System* (July 1971): 486, 488, 489.
77. Avery, "Breathing Life into Ourselves," 128.
78. Susan D. Greenbaum, *Blaming the Poor: The Long Shadow of the Moynihan Report on Cruel Images about Poverty* (New Brunswick, NJ: Rutgers University Press, 2015), p. 54.
79. Kelly Ann Joyce, Jennifer E. James, and Melanie Jeske, "Regimes of Patienthood: Developing an Intersectional Concept to Theorize Illness Experiences," *Engaging Science, Technology, and Society* 6 (March 14, 2020): 185–92, https://doi.org/10.17351/ests2020.389.
80. Lena Wright Myers, *Black Women: Do They Cope Better?* (Englewood Cliffs, NJ: Prentice Hall, 1980).
81. Christine H. Carrington, "Depression in Black Women: A Theoretical Appraisal," in *The Black Woman*, ed. La Frances Rodgers-Rose (Beverly Hills, CA: Sage Publications, 1980), 265–71, 267.
82. Delores P. Aldridge, "Black Female Suicides: Is the Excitement Justified?," in *The Black Woman*, ed. La Frances Rodgers-Rose (Beverly Hills, CA: Sage Publications, 1980), 273–84.
83. Opal Palmer Adisa, "Rocking in the Sun Light: Stress and Black Women," *Black Women's Health Book*, ed. Evelyn White (Seattle: Seal Press, 1990), 11–14, 13.
84. Kelly O'Donnell, "Our Doctors, Ourselves: Barbara Seaman and Popular Health Feminism in the 1970s," *Bulletin of the History of Medicine* 93, no. 4 (2019): 550–76, https://doi.org/10.1353/bhm.2019.0072.
85. Amy Koerber, *From Hysteria to Hormones: A Rhetorical History* (University Park: Pennsylvania State University Press, 2018).
86. Mary Lou Rozdilsky and Barbara Banet, "What Now? A Handbook for Couples (Especially Women) Postpartum," 1972, Box 18, Folder 1, Boston

Association for Childbirth Education, Schlesinger Library, Cambridge, MA, p. 15.

87. Ruth Darmstadter et al., "Childbirth and Madness," *Women: A Journal of Liberation* 3, no. 3 (1972): 11–13.

88. Darmstadter et al., "Childbirth and Madness," 11–13.

89. Darmstadter et al., "Childbirth and Madness," 13.

90. Darmstadter et al., "Childbirth and Madness," 14, 12.

91. Sharon Wallace, *The Amazon* 3, no. 3 (July 1974): 12–14.

92. Darmstadter et al., "Childbirth and Madness," 11.

93. Naomi Weisstein, "Psychology and Mental Health Counselling," Gender: Identity and Social Change collection, available through Adam Matthew, Marlborough, http://www.genderidentityandsocialchange .amdigital.co.uk.

94. Memo from Elaine Dittmer and Marianne Lambert to Postpartum Pilot Program and Nursing Mothers' Council, May 31, 1973, Box 6, Folder 13: Nursing Mothers Council: Postpartum Project, 1973-1974, MC 515: Boston Association for Childbirth Education, Schlesinger Library, Cambridge, MA.

95. Laurence Kruckman, interview by Rachel Moran, January 10, 2023, transcript, University of North Texas Oral History Program, UNT Special Collections, Denton, TX.

Chapter 3

1. James Hamilton to Ralph Paffenbarger, November 23, 1984, Honikman Archive, Folder Carol Dix Letters; Carol Dix to Jane Honikman, Letter, May 20, 1984, Honikman Archive, Folder Carol Dix Letters.

2. Phone interview with Jane Honikman by author, transcript in possession of author, June 19, 2020.

3. Carol Dix, memo for Joan Silvern, Family Resource Coalition, "The New Mother Syndrome: Why You Should Know What PPD Means" (1986), Honikman Archive, Folder: Family Resource Coalition, p. 5.

4. Ancestry.com, California, US, Death Index, 1940–1997 [database online] (Provo, UT: Ancestry.com Operations Inc., 2000).

5. 1920; Census Place: Long Beach, Los Angeles, CA; Roll: T625_104; Page: 1B; Enumeration District: 87.

6. James Alexander Hamilton, *Toward Proficient Reading* (Claremont, CA: Saunders Press, 1939).

7. "University Coeds Announce Weddings and Engagements," *The Daily Californian*, June 17, 1936, 2.

8. James A. Hamilton, M.D., to Martha M. Eliot, M.D., US Children's Bureau, letter, October 2, 1958, National Archives II, College Park, MD, RG 102 Record of the Children's Bureau, Entry A1 3B Central File, 1958–62, Box 815 Folder 4-2-2-2 1958–1962 Maternal Mortality Statistic; James Hamilton, *Postpartum Psychiatric Problems* (St. Louis, MO: C. V. Mosby Company, 1962).

9. John Clancy, "Postpartum Psychiatric Problems," *Archives of Internal Medicine* 110, no. 2 (August 1, 1962): 275; Peter Barglow, "Postpartum Psychiatric Problems," *Archives of General Psychiatry* 7, no. 3 (September 1, 1962): 231–32.

10. John M. Credson, "Abuses in Testing of Drugs by C.I.A. to Be Panel Focus," *New York Times*, September 20, 1977, 1.

11. "Ex-CIA Aide Asks Immunity to Testify," *New York Times*, September 7, 1977, 11.

12. Advisory Committee on Human Radiation Experiments, *Final Report: Advisory Committee on Human Radiation Experiments*, Supplemental Volume 2: Sources and Documentation (Washington, DC: US Government Printing Office, 1995), 53; Advisory Committee on Human Radiation Experiments, *Final Report: Advisory Committee on Human Radiation Experiments*, Supplemental Volume 2A: Sources and Documentation (Washington, DC: US Government Printing Office, 1995), B109.

13. Benjamin Breen, personal communication, July 27, 2021.

14. Carol Dix, *The New Mother Syndrome: Coping with Postpartum Stress and Depression* (New York: Pocket Books, 1985 [1988 rev. ed.]), 39.

15. Ian Brockington, "Obituary for James A. Hamilton," *Archives of Women's Mental Health* 1, no. 2 (1998): 1.

16. Terra Ziporyn, "'Rip van Winkle Period' Ends for Puerperal Psychiatric Problems," *Journal of the American Medical Association* 251, no. 16 (April 27, 1984).

17. James Hamilton to Jane Honikman, letter, June 29, 1988, Honikman Archive, Folder Hamilton letters Jan. 9, 1984–Oct. 7, 1988.

18. John Cox and Kathy Wisner, "Recollections on the Early Days of the Marcé Society for Perinatal Mental Health from Professor John Cox," *Archives of Women's Mental Health* 19 (2016): 197–200; "History of the Marcé Society," 2013, http://marcesociety.com/wp-content/uploads/2013/11/HistoryofMarce.pdf; Channi Kumar, "Editorial," *Bulletin of the Marcé Society* (Spring 1983): 11, Wendy Savage Archives, Wellcome Collection, PP/WDS/B.7/1 Marcé Society: bulletins and conferences, 1982–1988.

19. Ian Brockington, "Obituary Dr. James Hamilton," *Archives of Women's Mental Health* 1, no. 2 (1998): 1.

20. Ziporyn, "'Rip van Winkle Period' Ends."

21. Kumar, "Editorial," 11.

22. Kumar, "Editorial," 11.
23. Hannah S. Decker, *The Making of DSM-III: A Diagnostic Manual's Conquest of American Psychiatry* (Oxford: Oxford University Press, 2013), 53.
24. Barbara Parry to James Alexander Hamilton, July 3, 1984, Parry-Hamilton Correspondence, Honikman Archive.
25. David Danforth, ed., *Obstetrics and Gynecology* (New York: Harper & Row, 1977), 449-50, quoted in Dix, *The New Mother Syndrome*, 221.
26. Decker, *The Making of DSM-III*, 53-77.
27. American Psychiatric Association, *DSM-III* (Washington, DC: APA Press, 1980), 373.
28. Brockington, "Obituary Dr. James Hamilton," 1.
29. James Hamilton to Marlene E. Haffner, letter, January 30, 1987, Honikman Archive, Folder Parry-Hamilton correspondence.
30. Rebecca Godderis, "Managing Mad Mothers: Postpartum Depression and the Psychiatric Gaze" (PhD diss., University of Calgary, 2009), 90.
31. James Hamilton to Jane Honikman, letter, February 18, 1991, Honikman Archive, Folder Hamilton letters Nov. 21, 1998-Oct. 25, 1992; Dix, *The New Mother Syndrome*, 39.
32. Allan V. Horwitz, "Creating an Age of Depression: The Social Construction and Consequences of the Major Depression Diagnosis," *Society and Mental Health* 1, no. 1 (March 2011): 41-54.
33. Joseph E. Davis, *Chemically Imbalanced: Everyday Suffering, Medication, and Our Troubled Quest for Self-Mastery* (Chicago: University of Chicago Press, 2020), 61.
34. Horwitz, "Creating an Age of Depression," 41-54.
35. Jonathan Sadowsky, *The Empire of Depression: A New History* (Medford, MA: Polity Press, 2021), 97-99.
36. Laura D. Hirshbein, "Science, Gender, and the Emergence of Depression in American Psychiatry, 1952–1980," *Journal of the History of Medicine and Allied Sciences* 61, no. 2 (April 1, 2006): 187–216; Edward Shorter, *How Everyone Became Depressed: The Rise and Fall of the Nervous Breakdown* (Oxford: Oxford University Press, 2013).
37. Janet M. Stoppard and Linda M. McMullen, "Introduction," in Janet M. Stoppard and Linda M. McMullen, eds., *Situating Sadness: Women and Depression in Social Context* (New York: New York University Press, 2003), 6-7.
38. Laura D. Hirshbein, *American Melancholy: Constructions of Depression in the Twentieth Century* (New Brunswick, NJ: Rutgers University Press, 2009), 101.
39. Hirshbein, *American Melancholy*, 95.
40. Jonathan Metzl, *Prozac on the Couch: Prescribing Gender in the Era of Wonder Drugs* (Durham, NC: Duke University Press Books, 2005); Verta

Taylor, "Self-Labeling and Women's Mental Health: Postpartum Illness and the Reconstruction of Motherhood," *Sociological Focus* 28, no. 1 (February 1995): 23–47.

41. Ian Brockington, "Future Directions, A Review by the Outgoing President," *Marcé Society Bulletin* (Winter 1985): 15, Honikman Archive, Folder Marcé Bulletins.

42. Ziporyn, "'Rip van Winkle Period' Ends."

43. Ian F. Brockington, *Motherhood and Mental Health* (Oxford: Oxford University Press, 1982), 136.

44. Katharina Dalton, *Depression after Childbirth: How to Recognize and Treat Postnatal Illness* (Oxford: Oxford University Press, 1980), 125.

45. Ziporyn, "'Rip van Winkle Period' Ends."

46. Metzl, *Prozac on the Couch*, 4.

47. Boston Women's Health Book Collective, ed., *The New Our Bodies, Ourselves: A Book by and for Women* (New York: Simon & Schuster, 1984), 406.

48. Boston Women's Health Book Collective, *The New Our Bodies, Ourselves*, 406–7, 404.

49. Boston Women's Health Book Collective, *The New Our Bodies, Ourselves*, 404, 408.

50. Sumitra Devi Shrestha et al., "Reliability and Validity of the Edinburgh Postnatal Depression Scale (EPDS) for Detecting Perinatal Common Mental Disorders (PCMDs) among Women in Low- and Lower-Middle-Income Countries: A Systematic Review," *BMC Pregnancy and Childbirth* 16, no. 1 (December 2016): 72.

51. A.C.O.G. Committee Opinion No 757, "Summary: Screening for Perinatal Depression," *Obstetrics & Gynecology* 132 (2018): 1314–16.

52. Zoom interview with John L. Cox, February 11, 2022, notes in possession of author.

53. Aaron T. Beck, "An Inventory for Measuring Depression," *Archives of General Psychiatry* 4, no. 6 (June 1, 1961): 561, https://doi.org/10.1001/archpsyc.1961.01710120031004.

54. Brian Harris et al., "The Use of Rating Scales to Identify Post-Natal Depression," *British Journal of Psychiatry* 154, no. 6 (June 1989): 813–17, https://doi.org/10.1192/bjp.154.6.813.

55. John Cox and Jeni Holden, *Perinatal Mental Health: A Guide to the Edinburgh Postnatal Depression Scale (EPDS)* (London: Gaskell, 2003), 16.

56. Michael W. O'Hara, L. P. Rehm, and S. B. Campbell, "Postpartum Depression. A Role for Social Network and Life Stress Variables," *Journal of Nervous and Mental Disease* 171, no. 6 (June 1983): 336–41.

57. John L. Cox, Jeni M. Holden, and Ruth Sagovsky, "Detection of Postnatal Depression: Development of the 10-Item Edinburgh Postnatal Depression Scale," *British Journal of Psychiatry* 150, no. 6 (June 1987):

782-86; John Cox, "Personal Reflections on the Early Development of the EPDS," in *Perinatal Psychiatry: The Legacy of Channi Kumar*, ed. Carmine M. Pariante et al. (Oxford: Oxford University Press, 2014), 21.

58.　John Cox, "Use and Misuse of the Edinburgh Postnatal Depression Scale (EPDS): A Ten Point 'Survival Analysis,'" *Archives of Women's Mental Health* 20, no. 6 (December 2017): 789-90, https://doi.org/10.1007/s00737-017-0789-7.

59.　Ellie Lee, *Abortion, Motherhood, and Mental Health: Medicalizing Reproduction in the United States and Great Britain* (Hawthorne, NY: Aldine de Gruyter, 2003), 204-5.

60.　Cheryl Tatano Beck and Robert Gable, "Postpartum Depression Screening Scale: Development and Psychometric Testing," *Nursing Research* 48, no. 5 (September-October 2000): 272-82, doi: 10.1097/00006199-200009000-00006.

61.　"Minutes of BGM, San Francisco," *Marcé Society Bulletin* (Winter 1985): 5, Honikman Archive, Folder Marcé Bulletins.

62.　Nine Glangeaud, "History of the Marcé Society (1980-2016)," https://marcesociety.com/wp-content/uploads/2013/11/Marce-Society-History-1980-2016_nine_1September2016.pdf.

63.　James Hamilton, "Introduction," in Dix, *The New Mothers Syndrome*, 14-15.

64.　Ziporyn, "'Rip van Winkle Period' Ends."

65.　Dix, *The New Mother Syndrome*, 41-42.

66.　Jane Honikman to Beth Alder, letter, January 21, 1991, Honikman Archive, Folder Marcé.

67.　Ian Brockington, email correspondence with author, January 23, 2022.

68.　Ian F. Brockington, "Apologia," accessed February 14, 2022, https://ianbrockington.wordpress.com/career/.

69.　"CME Courses: American Psychiatric Association, 142nd Annual Meeting, May 6-11, 1989," p. 39, from personal papers of Laurence Kruckman.

Chapter 4

1.　Jane Honikman, "Parents Helping Parents," *American Baby*, April 1979, Honikman Archive.

2.　Jane Honikman, "PEP Volunteers Assist Parents in Santa Barbara," *Family Resource Coalition Newsletter*, October 1982, 2, Honikman Archive.

3.　Follow-up interview with Jane Honikman, by Rachel Moran, June 19, 2020, transcript in possession of author.

4.　Honikman, "PEP Volunteers Assist Parents in Santa Barbara," 1.

5. Jane I. Honikman, *My Diary: A Postpartum Journey from Pain to Purpose* (self-published, 2015), 22.
6. "Postpartum Education for Parents," pp. 1–2, enclosure in letter, Jane Honikman to *Ladies' Home Journal*, January 2, 1984, Honikman Archive, PEP folder.
7. Honikman, "PEP Volunteers Assist Parents in Santa Barbara," 1; Julie Armstrong, Judy Edmondson, Jane Honikman, and Judy Mrstik, *A Guide for Establishing a Parent Support Group in Your Community* (Santa Barbara, CA: self-published, 1979), Honikman Archive, 89.
8. [Redacted], letter to Jane Honikman, March 28, 1979, Honikman Archive, Folder Letters 1979 After Articles; [Redacted] to Jane Honikman, April 2, 1979, Honikman Archive, Folder Letters 1979 After Articles; [Redacted] to Jane Honikman, Feb. 9, 1980, Honikman Archive, Folder Letters 1979 After Articles; Jane Honikman, "Parenting in the '80s—A National Movement," speech, April 1986, draft in Honikman Archive, Folder Family Resource Coalition papers.
9. Armstrong et al., *A Guide for Establishing a Parent Support Group in Your Community*.
10. Charlene Marmer Solomon, "Dial Help," May 1978, publication unknown, 27–28, Honikman Archive; Jessica L. Martucci, *Back to the Breast: Natural Motherhood and Breastfeeding in America* (Chicago: University of Chicago Press, 2015), 192–93; [Redacted] to Jane Honikman, letter, March 30, 1979, Honikman Archive, Folder Letters 1979 After Articles; [Redacted] to Honikman, letter, April 2, 1979; Elayne Rapping, *The Culture of Recovery: Making Sense of the Self-Help Movement in Women's Lives* (Boston: Beacon Press, 1996); Hannah Dudley-Shotwell, *Revolutionizing Women's Healthcare: The Feminist Self-Help Movement in America* (New Brunswick, NJ: Rutgers University Press, 2020); Carol Dix to Jane Honikman, letter, October 20, 1983, Honikman Archive, Folder Carol Dix Letters; Honikman, "Parenting in the '80s."
11. [Redacted], letter to Jane Honikman, September 15, 1978, Honikman Archive, Letters 1979 After Articles; Jane Honikman, recording on audio cassette, 1987, Honikman Archive, audio collection.
12. Andrew Hartman, *A War for the Soul of America: A History of the Culture Wars*, 2nd ed. (Chicago: University of Chicago Press, 2019); Premilla Nadasen, *Welfare Warriors: The Welfare Rights Movement in the United States* (New York: Routledge, 2005), 238; Patricia Strach, *All in the Family: The Private Roots of American Publican Policy* (Stanford, CA: Stanford University Press, 2007); Seth Dowland, *Family Values and the Rise of the Christian Right* (Philadelphia: University of Pennsylvania Press, 2015). Rachel Louise Moran, "Fears of a Nanny State: Centering Gender in the Political History of Regulation," in Brent Cebul, Lily Geismer,

and Mason B. Williams, eds., *Shaped by the State: Toward a New Political History of the Twentieth Century* (Chicago: University of Chicago Press, 2019).

13. John K. Rosemond, *Parent Power: A Common Sense Approach to Raising Your Children in the Eighties* (Charlotte, NC: East Woods Press, 1981), 24; Melinda Cooper, *Family Values: Between Neoliberalism and the New Social Conservatism* (New York: Zone Books, 2017), 9; Deborah Weinstein, *The Pathological Family: Postwar America and the Rise of Family Therapy* (Ithaca, NY: Cornell University Press, 2013).

14. Bruce J. Schulman, *The Seventies: The Great Shift in American Culture, Society, and Politics* (New York: Da Capo Press, 2002), 187.

15. News clipping, "Textbook Is Trash," *Albuquerque Tribune*, April 28, 1981, A6, Box 9, Folder 16: FF: ER: Odds & Ends, 1975-1979, MC 667: Boston Women's Health Book Collective papers, Schlesinger Library, Cambridge, MA.

16. Paul M. Renfro, *Stranger Danger: Family Values, Childhood, and the American Carceral State* (New York: Oxford University Press, 2020).

17. Carol Dix, "Our Bodies," *Guardian*, August 9, 1973, sec. Woman's Guardian, 9.

18. Carol Dix, *The New Mother Syndrome: Coping with Postpartum Stress and Depression* (Garden City, NY: Doubleday, 1985), 3.

19. Dix, *The New Mother Syndrome*, 6.

20. Carol Dix, "Carol Dix talk to PaNDa," speech transcript, Feb. 1987 talk, Ormond, Victoria, Australia, 4-6, Honikman Archive, Carol Dix letters.

21. Dix, *The New Mother Syndrome*, 213-14.

22. Carol Dix to Jane Honikman, letter, March 6, 1984, Honikman Archive, Carol Dix Letters.

23. Dix, *The New Mother Syndrome*, 39.

24. Dix, *The New Mother Syndrome*, 44.

25. Dix to Honikman, letter, March 6, 1984.

26. Nancy Berchtold, interview with Rachel Moran.

27. Dix, *The New Mother Syndrome*, ix; Betty Friedan, *The Feminine Mystique* (New York: W. W. Norton, 1963).

28. Carol Dix, *The New Mother Syndrome: Coping with Postpartum Stress and Depression* (New York: Pocket Books, 1985 [1988 rev. ed.]), 16.

29. Anne Harrington, *Mind Fixers: Psychiatry's Troubled Search for the Biology of Mental Illness* (New York: W. W. Norton & Company, 2019); David Herzberg, *Happy Pills in America: From Miltown to Prozac* (Baltimore: Johns Hopkins University Press, 2010).

30. Carol Dix, memo for Joan Silvern, Family Resource Coalition, "The New Mother Syndrome: Why You Should Know What PPD Means," 1986, Honikman Archive, Family Resource Coalition papers, 6-7.

31. Dowland, *Family Values and the Rise of the Christian Right*; Samuel L. Blumenfeld, *The Retreat from Motherhood* (New Rochelle, NY: Arlington House, 1975), 172, 43.

32. Allyson Sherman Grossman, "Special Labor Force Reports— Summaries—Working Mothers and Their Children," *Monthly Labor Review* (May 1981): 49–50; Beth L. Bailey, "She 'Can Bring Home the Bacon: Negotiating Gender in the 1970s," in Beth L. Bailey and David R. Farber, eds., *America in the Seventies* (Lawrence: University Press of Kansas, 2004), 107–28; Arlie Russell Hochschild and Anne Machung, *The Second Shift: Working Parents and the Revolution at Home* (New York: Viking, 1989); Gwendolyn Mink, *The Wages of Motherhood: Inequality in the Welfare State, 1917–1942* (Ithaca, NY: Cornell University Press, 1996); Annelise Orleck, *Storming Caesars Palace: How Black Mothers Fought Their Own War on Poverty* (New York: Beacon Press, 2006).

33. Kirsten Swinth, "Post–Family Wage, Postindustrial Society: Reframing the Gender and Family Order through Working Mothers in Reagan's America," *Journal of American History* 105, no. 2 (September 2018): 311–35; Helen McCarthy, *Double Lives: A History of Working Motherhood in Modern Britain* (London: Bloomsbury, 2020).

34. Claudia Tate, "Should We Expect Black Women to Be Supermothers?," *Ebony*, September 1984, 84.

35. Barbara J. Berg, *The Crisis of the Working Mother: Resolving the Conflict between Family and Work* (New York: Summit Books, 1986), 46.

36. Virginia Woods, "Supermom Heads into Holiday Stress," *Lewiston Morning Tribune*, December 9, 1981, 1E.

37. Woods, "Supermom Heads into Holiday Stress," 1E.

38. Kimberly J. Morgan, *Working Mothers and the Welfare State: Religion and the Politics of Work-Family Policies in Western Europe and the United States* (Stanford, CA: Stanford University Press, 2006), 136–37; Swinth, "Post–Family Wage, Postindustrial Society," 311–35.

39. Tate, "Should We Expect Black Women to Be Supermothers?," 84, 88.

40. "Status of Women in America (Part IV)," ABC Evening News for Thursday, May 17, 1984, clip #89972, Vanderbilt Television News Archive, Nashville.

41. Kirsten Swinth, *Feminism's Forgotten Fight: The Unfinished Struggle for Work and Family* (Cambridge, MA: Harvard University Press, 2018).

42. Glenn Collins, "Lack of 'Commitment' Worries Doctor," Countway Library of Medicine, Center for the History of Medicine, Brazelton, T. Berry, 1918, Papers, 1949–2007 (inclusive), 1971–2004 (bulk), H MS c244 Box 67, folder 126.

43. Judith Warner, *Perfect Madness: Motherhood in the Age of Anxiety* (New York: Riverhead Books, 2005), 99.

44. Rebecca Godderis, "Motherhood Gone Mad? The Rise of Postpartum Depression in the United States during the 1980s," in *Body Subjects: Essays on Gender and Health 1800-2000*, ed. Tracy Penny Light et al. (Montreal: McGill Queens University Press, 2014), 303-18.

45. Dix, *The New Mother Syndrome*, 8.

46. Dix, *The New Mother Syndrome*, 284-86.

47. Ziporyn, "'Rip van Winkle Period' Ends."

48. Dowland, *Family Values and the Rise of the Christian Right*.

49. Abigail Van Buren, "Housewife Angered by Super Mom Phrase," *The Item* (Sumter, SC), September 16, 1988, 4A.

50. Carol Felsenthal, *Phyllis Schlafly: The Sweetheart of the Silent Majority* (Chicago: Regnery Gateway, 1982), 124-25.

51. Phyllis Schlafly, interview by Mark DePue, January 5, 2011, transcript ISE-A-L-2011-001.01, ERA Oral History Project, Abraham Lincoln Presidential Library, accessed at https://presidentlincoln.illinois.gov.

52. Phyllis Schlafly, *The Power of the Positive Woman* (New Rochelle, NY: Arlington House Publishers, 1977), 47.

53. Schlafly, *The Power of the Positive Woman*, 51.

54. Michelle M. Nickerson, *Mothers of Conservatism: Women and the Postwar Right* (Princeton, NJ: Princeton University Press, 2014); Marjorie J. Spruill, *Divided We Stand: The Battle over Women's Rights and Family Values That Polarized American Politics* (New York: Bloomsbury, 2018); Schlafly, *The Power of the Positive Woman*, 17, 57-58.

55. Carol Rischer, *Insights for Young Mothers* (Irvine, CA: Harvest House Publishers, 1986), 75.

56. Karissa Haugeberg, *Women Against Abortion: Inside the Largest Moral Reform Movement of the Twentieth Century* (Urbana and Chicago: University of Illinois Press, 2017); Rachel Louise Moran, "A Women's Health Issue? Framing Post-Abortion Syndrome in the 1980s," *Gender & History* 33, no. 3 (October 2021): 790-804.

57. Ruth Alig and Stephanie Wright, *The New Mothers Guide* (Colorado Springs: Navpress, 1988), 69-70.

58. Gary Ezzo and Robert Bucknam, *On Becoming Baby Wise: Giving Your Infant the Gift of Nighttime Sleep* (Simi Valley, CA: Growing Families International, 1993), 24.

59. Karen Hall, *The Mommy Book: Advice for New Mothers from Women Who Have Been There* (Grand Rapids, MI: Zondervan Publishing House, 1986), 26.

60. Karen Hall, *The Mommy Book*, 8-29.

61. Alig and Wright, *The New Mothers Guide*, 34, 35; Hall, *The Mommy Book*, 27.

62. Bonnie Washuk, "Breaking the 'Supermom' Fallacy," *Lewiston Journal* (Lewiston-Auburn, ME), vol. 125, May 11, 1985, 1.

63. Anne Lorimer, "A Friendship Network for New Mothers," *Christian Science Monitor*, October 18, 1982, Honikman Archive.

64. Armstrong et al., *A Guide for Establishing a Parent Support Group in Your Community*, 4.

65. Armstrong et al., *A Guide for Establishing a Parent Support Group in Your Community*, 81.

66. Enclosure, Jane Honikman to *Ladies Home Journal*, January 2, 1984, Honikman Archive.

67. Armstrong et al., *A Guide for Establishing a Parent Support Group in Your Community*, 111.

Chapter 5

1. Carol Dix, *The New Mother Syndrome: Coping with Postpartum Stress and Depression*, 2nd ed. (New York: Pocket Books, 1988), 65–68.

2. Verta A. Taylor, *Rock-a-by Baby: Feminism, Self Help, and Postpartum Depression* (New York: Routledge, 1996).

3. Wendy Kline, *Bodies of Knowledge: Sexuality, Reproduction, and Women's Health in the Second Wave* (Chicago: University of Chicago Press, 2010), 85–86; Robert O. Self, *All in the Family: The Realignment of American Democracy Since the 1960s*, reprint ed. (New York: Hill and Wang, 2013); R. Marie Griffith, *Moral Combat: How Sex Divided American Christians and Fractured American Politics* (New York: Basic Books, 2017).

4. Athena Helen McLean, "From Ex-Patient Alternatives to Consumer Options: Consequences of Consumerism for Psychiatric Consumers and the Ex-Patient Movement," *International Journal of Health Services* 30, no. 4 (October 2000): 821–47, https://doi.org/10.2190/3TYX-VRRK-XKHA-VB1Q.

5. "About Us," Pacific Post Partum Support Society, https://postpartum.org/about-us/#/history, accessed December 1, 2021.

6. Audio recording of 1987 postpartum depression meeting, tape 3, Santa Barbara, CA, June 27, 1987, Honikman Archive, cassette collection.

7. Carol Dix, memo for Joan Silvern, Family Resource Coalition, "The New Mother Syndrome: Why You Should Know What PPD Means," 1986, Honikman Archive, Family Resource Coalition papers, 8.

8. Elaine Jarvik, "Victim Breaks Silence on 'Depression After Delivery,'" *Deseret News*, July 7, 1989.

9. Diana Letkmann, "A Cry for Help," *Heart Strings* 5, no. 3 (Winter/Spring 1995): 1, Nancy Berchtold's personal papers.

10. Verta Taylor, "Emotions and Identity in Women's Self-Help Movements," in *Self, Identity, and Social Movements*, ed. Sheldon Stryker, Timothy J. Owens, and Robert W. White (Minneapolis: University of Minnesota Press, 2000), 277.

11. Taylor, *Rock-a-by Baby*, 75.
12. Rich Strack, "Not Just the 'Baby Blues,'" *Times News* (Lehighton, PA), March 7, 2014, https://www.tnonline.com/20140327/not-just-the-baby-blues/; Nancy Berchtold, email, March 2021.
13. Sarah Strohmeyer, "Post-Partum Depression Behind Her, Woman Fights 'A Conspiracy of Silence,'" *The Central New Jersey Home News* (New Brunswick, NJ), August 25, 1985, 13.
14. Peggy O'Crowley, "When Birth Brings the Blues: Postpartum Depression Triggered Suicide," *The Record* (Hackensack, NJ), November 19, 1989, 15.
15. Sue MacDonald, "Beating the Baby Blues: Depression Befalls Many New Mothers," October 4, 1987, *Cincinnati Inquirer*, E1, E9.
16. Taylor, *Rock-A-By Baby*, 83.
17. Jarvik, "Victim Breaks Silence on 'Depression After Delivery.'"
18. James Hamilton to Nancy Berchtold, letter, January 16, 1987, Honikman Archive, Hamilton papers Jan. 8, 1984–Oct. 7, 1988.
19. James Hamilton to Nancy Berchtold, letter, January 16, 1987, Honikman Archive, Hamilton papers Jan. 8, 1984–Oct. 7, 1988.
20. Dix, "The New Mother Syndrome," 6.
21. Carol Dix to Jane Honikman, letter, September 21, 1984, Honikman Archive, Carol Dix Letters.
22. Jane Honikman, "A System of Action: One Community's Response to Postpartum Stress and Depression in Santa Barbara, California, USA," *Marcé Society Bulletin* (Summer 1986): 12–13, Honikman Archive, Marcé Bulletins.
23. Carol Dix to Jane Honikman, letter, March 3, 1986, Honikman Archive, Carol Dix Letters.
24. Carol Dix to Jane Honikman, letter, November 21, 1986, Honikman Archive, Carol Dix Letters.
25. Audio recording of 1987 postpartum depression meeting, Santa Barbara, CA, June 27, 1987, Honikman Archive, cassette collection.
26. James Hamilton to Jane Honikman, letter, March 1, 1984, Honikman Archive, Hamilton letters Jan. 8, 1984–Oct. 7, 1988.
27. "Pacific Postpartum Support Society," pamphlet, n.d., Honikman Archive, brochure collection.
28. Taylor, *Rock-a-By-Baby*, 77.
29. Audio recording of 1987 postpartum depression meeting, tape 1.
30. "Help When You Really Need It: Postpartum Support International," *Preemie Magazine*, in Honikman Archive, PSI, scrapbook, Summer 2005, 20.
31. Carol Dix to Jane Honikman, letter, September 24, 1986, Honikman Archive, Carol Dix letters.
32. Audio recording of 1987 postpartum depression meeting, tape 1.

33. Audio recording of 1987 postpartum depression meeting, tape 2.
34. Audio recording of 1987 postpartum depression meeting.
35. Audio recording of 1987 postpartum depression meeting.
36. Jeanne Watson Driscoll, interview with Rachel Moran.
37. James Hamilton to Jane Honikman, letter, June 30, 1987, Honikman Archive, Hamilton letters Jan. 9, 1984–Oct. 7, 1988.
38. Jane Honikman to James Hamilton, letter, June 9, 1988, Honikman Archive, Hamilton letters Jan. 8, 1984–Oct. 7, 1988.
39. James Hamilton to Jane Honikman, letter, June 30, 1987, Honikman Archive, Hamilton letters Jan. 9, 1984–Oct. 7, 1988.
40. Phone interview with Jane Honikman by author, transcript in possession of author, June 19, 2020.
41. 4th annual conference—PSI audio tapes Honikman collection.
42. "Role of the Volunteer and the Professional," Honikman Archive, PEP papers.
43. Phone interview with Honikman by author, June 19, 2020.
44. James Hamilton to Jane Honikman, letter, November 3, 1990, Honikman Archive, Hamilton letters Nov. 21, 1988–Oct. 25, 1992.
45. Patricia Neel Harberger, Nancy Gleason Berchtold, and Jane Israel Honikman, "Cries for Help," in *Postpartum Psychiatric Illness: A Picture Puzzle* (Philadelphia: University of Pennsylvania Press, 1992), 41–60.
46. Audio recording of 1987 postpartum depression meeting, tape 3.
47. Audio recording of 1987 postpartum depression meeting, tape 3.
48. Linda M. Blum and Nena F. Stracuzzi, "Gender in the Prozac Nation: Popular Discourse and Productive Femininity," *Gender & Society* 18, no. 3 (June 2004): 269–86, https://doi.org/10.1177/0891243204263108.
49. [Redacted No. 12] to Jane Honikman, November 7, 1988, Honikman Archive, Letters 1979 After Articles.
50. [Redacted No. 12] to Jane Honikman, October 29, 1988, Honikman Archive, Letters 1979 After Articles.
51. [Redacted No. 12] to Jane Honikman, November 7, 1988, Honikman Archive, Letters 1979 After Articles.
52. Nancy Berchtold and Melanie Burrough, "Reaching Out: Depression After Delivery Support Group Network," *Clinical Issue in Perinatal and Women's Health Nursing* (NAACOG) 1, no. 3 (December 1990): 385–94, 387.
53. Phone interview with Honikman by author, June 19, 2020.

Chapter 6

1. Verta A. Taylor, *Rock-a-by Baby: Feminism, Self Help, and Postpartum Depression* (New York: Routledge, 1996), 4–5.

2. Carol Dix, speech draft, "Motherhood Blues: Psychiatric Illness after Childbirth," p. 2, 1984, Honikman Archive, Carol Dix letters.

3. Jane Honikman to James Hamilton, letter, February 9, 1988, Honikman Archive, Hamilton Letters Jan. 8, 1984–Oct. 7, 1988.

4. Audio recording of 1987 postpartum depression meeting, tape 1, Santa Barbara, CA, June 27, 1987, Honikman Archive, cassette collection.

5. James Hamilton to John L. Cox, letter, June 3, 1987, Honikman Archive, Parry-Hamilton correspondence.

6. Hamilton to Cox, letter, June 3, 1987.

7. James Hamilton to Jane Honikman, letter, June 3, 1988, Honikman Archive, Hamilton letters Jan. 8, 1984–Oct. 7, 1988.

8. "1986 BGM Meeting Minutes," *Marcé Society Bulletin* (Summer 1987): 50, Honikman Archive, Marcé Bulletins.

9. James Hamilton to Carol Dix, letter, October 2, 1986, Honikman Archive, Hamilton letters.

10. James Hamilton, "Prophylactic Measures," speech to the Second Annual Conference on Postpartum Depression, Medical Center at Princeton, June 24–26, 1988, p. 19, Honikman Archive, Hamilton letters Jan. 9, 1984–Oct. 7, 1988.

11. James Hamilton to Désirée Zamorano, letter, July 10, 1987, Honikman Archive, Hamilton letters Jan. 9, 1984–Oct. 7, 1988.

12. Carol Dix, press release, "Motherhood Blues: Psychiatric Illness after Childbirth," 1984, p. 3, Honikman Archive, Carol Dix letters.

13. Audio recording of 1987 postpartum depression meeting, tape 1.

14. Carol Dix, "Motherhood Blues: Psychiatric Illness after Childbirth," p. 9.

15. James Hamilton to Jane Honikman and Anne Simpson, letter, March 29, 1984, Honikman Archive, Hamilton letters Jan. 8, 1984–Oct. 7, 1988.

16. Hamilton to Honikman and Simpson, letter, March 29, 1984.

17. Jane Honikman, "Abstract [for 1984 Marcé Society meeting]," Summer 1984, Honikman Archive, Hamilton letters.

18. James Hamilton to Jane Honikman, letter, November 28, 1984, Honikman Archive, Hamilton letters.

19. James Hamilton to John L. Cox, letter, June 3, 1987, Parry-Hamilton correspondence, Honikman archive.

20. Jane Honikman, talk, recording on audio cassette, 1987, Honikman Archive, audio collection.

21. K. J. Mapes, "Comitz Sentenced to 8 to 20 Years for Killing Son," *Daily Collegian* (State College, PA), Oct. 28, 1985.

22. Gay Elwell, "Parole Urged for Mother of Baby Found in Stream Her Defense was Post-Partum Depression," *The Morning Call* (December 21, 1988), https://www.mcall.com/news/mc-xpm-1988-12-22-2658776-story.html.

63. Quoted in Linfield, "A Bundle of Sadness," 104.

64. Taylor, *Rock-a-by Baby*, 207n159.

65. Katherine Wisner, speaking at the 1991 Postpartum Support International conference, cassette recording, Honikman Archive.

66. Michael O'Hara, Zoom conversation with Rachel Moran, August 4, 2021, notes in possession of the author.

Chapter 7

1. Wendy Kline, *Bodies of Knowledge: Sexuality, Reproduction, and Women's Health in the Second Wave* (Chicago: University of Chicago Press, 2010), 4-5.

2. Alexandra Rutherford, Kelli Vaughn-Blount, and Laura C. Ball, "Responsible Opposition, Disruptive Voices: Science, Social Change, and the History of Feminist Psychology," *Psychology of Women Quarterly* 34, no. 4 (December 2010): 460-73, https://doi.org/10.1111/j.1471-6402.2010.01596.x; Catrina Brown, "Speaking of Women's Depression and the Politics of Emotion," *Affilia* 34, no. 2 (May 2019): 151-69, https://doi.org/10.1177/0886109919836825.

3. Karen R. Kleiman and Valerie D. Raskin, *This Isn't What I Expected: Recognizing and Recovering from Depression and Anxiety after Childbirth* (New York: Bantam Books, 1994), 43, 57.

4. Shoshana Bennett, "Thank God I Had Postpartum Depression," in John Castagnini. *Thank God I—: Stories of Inspiration for Every Situation*, vol. 2 (Las Vegas: Inspired Authors, 2009), 294-300, 299.

5. Shoshana Bennett, email to author, March 29, 2022.

6. Jason Schnittker, Jeremy Freese, and Brian Powell, "Who Are Feminists and What Do They Believe? The Role of Generations," *American Sociological Review* 68, no. 4 (August 2003): 607, https://doi.org/10.2307/1519741.

7. Janet Currie and Jonathan Gruber, "Saving Babies: The Efficacy and Cost of Recent Changes in the Medicaid Eligibility of Pregnant Women," *Journal of Political Economy* 104, no. 6 (December 1996): 1263-96, https://doi.org/10.1086/262059.

8. Vikki Wachino, CMCS Informational Bulletin, "Maternal Depression Screening and Treatment: A Critical Role for Medicaid in the Care of Mothers and Children," Department of Health and Human Services, May 11, 2016, https://www.medicaid.gov/federal-policy-guidance/downloads/cib051116.pdf.

9. Verta A. Taylor, *Rock-a-by Baby: Feminism, Self Help, and Postpartum Depression* (New York: Routledge, 1996), 77.

10.   Sarah Pattee, "Maternal Instinct Gone Awry: A Mother Who Kills Her Child Deserves Help, Not Prison, Psychologist Says," *Los Angeles Times*, September 30, 1989, https://www.latimes.com/archives/la-xpm-1989-09 -30-vw-132-story.html.

11.   Taylor, *Rock-a-by Baby*, 77.

12.   Shoshana S. Bennett, *Pregnant on Prozac: The Essential Guide to Making the Best Decision for You and Your Baby* (Guilford, CT: GPP Life, 2009), 65.

13.   Karen Kleiman, email to author, March 29, 2022.

14.   Teresa Mariani, "Supermom a Mythical Character," *The Telegram-Tribune* (San Luis Obispo, CA), May 21, 1998, B1.

15.   Audre Lorde, *A Burst of Light: And Other Essays* (Mineola, NY: Ixia Press, 2017).

16.   Catherine Rottenberg, "The Rise of Neoliberal Feminism," *Cultural Studies* 28, no. 3 (May 4, 2014): 418–37, https://doi.org/10.1080/09502386 .2013.857361; Jina B. Kim and Sami Schalk, "Reclaiming the Radical Politics of Self-Care," *South Atlantic Quarterly* 120, no. 2 (April 1, 2021): 325–42, https://doi.org/10.1215/00382876-8916074; Alyson K. Spurgas and Zoë C. Meleo-Erwin, *Decolonize Self-Care* (New York: OR Books, 2023).

17.   Susan Feingold, *Happy Endings, New Beginnings: Navigating Postpartum Disorders* (Far Hills, NJ: New Horizon Press, 2013), xvii–xviii.

18.   Eric Zorn, "Quinn Brave Where Blago Was Cowardly—Announces He Will Release Debra Gindorf," May 1, 2009, https://blogs.chicagotribune .com/news_columnists_ezorn/2009/05/quinn-to-release-debra-gindorf .html.

19.   Susan Benjamin Feingold and Barry M. Lewis, *Advocating for Women with Postpartum Mental Illness: A Guide to Changing the Law and the National Climate* (Lanham, MD: Rowman & Littlefield, 2020).

Chapter 8

1.   Verta A. Taylor, *Rock-a-by Baby: Feminism, Self Help, and Postpartum Depression* (New York: Routledge, 1996), 115. | 269

2.   Tasha N. Dubriwny, "Television News Coverage of Postpartum Disorders and the Politics of Medicalization," *Feminist Media Studies* 10, no. 3 (September 2010): 285–303, https://doi.org/10.1080/14680777 .2010.493647.

3.   Samantha King, *Pink Ribbons, Inc.: Breast Cancer and the Politics of Philanthropy* (Minneapolis: University of Minnesota Press, 2008), 77.

4.   Eva S. Moskowitz, *In Therapy We Trust: America's Obsession with Self-Fulfillment* (Baltimore: Johns Hopkins University Press, 2001), 255–56, 267.

5. Moskowitz, *In Therapy We Trust*, 267.
6. Carol Dix to Lorri Benson, January 9, 1986, in Honikman Archive, Carol Dix Letters.
7. Sarah Banet-Weiser, "Postfeminism and Popular Feminism," *Feminist Media Histories* 4, no. 2 (April 1, 2018): 152–56, 153, https://doi.org/10.1525/fmh.2018.4.2.152.
8. Dix to Benson, January 9, 1986.
9. Carol Dix, *The New Mothers Syndrome: Coping with Postpartum Stress and Depression* (New York: Pocket Books, 1985 [1988 edition]), 236.
10. Nancy Berchtold to author, email, March 1, 2021.
11. Carol Dix to Jane Honikman, letter, February 6, 1987, Honikman Archive, Carol Dix letters.
12. Jane Honikman to Donahue to Lillian Smith, April 28, 1988, Honikman Archive, Honikman Scrapbook.
13. Jane Honikman to James Hamilton, letter, July 7, 1988, Honikman Archive, Hamilton letters Jan. 9, 1984–Oct. 7, 1988.
14. Honikman to Hamilton, letter, July 7, 1988.
15. *The Joan Rivers Show*, 1989, http://www.visual-icon.com/detail.php?id=70323.
16. "Inside Sunday: Woman of the '80s: Women in Trouble, Women at Risk, Women at Work," *CBS Evening News*, May 8, 1988, Vanderbilt Television News Archive, Nashville.
17. "The Latest Excuse," *The Liberator* 15, no. 2 (February 1989): 10; Washington, DC, United States; Forest Lake, Minnesota, United States; Men's Rights Association; American Coalition for Fathers and Children; Gender: Identity and Social Change collection, available through Adam Matthew, Marlborough, http://www.genderidentityandsocialchange.amdigital.co.uk/Documents/Details/MSU_HQ1090_L53 [accessed January 28, 2021].
18. "Postpartum Recovery," America Up Close, *NBC Evening News*, May 14, 1993, #592828, Vanderbilt Television News Archive, Nashville.
19. "Postpartum Depression," Eye on America, *CBS Evening News*, June 9, 1993, #351450, Vanderbilt Television News Archive, Nashville.
20. *Oprah Show*, 1996, clip from https://postpartumstress.com/karen-kleiman-msw-lcsw/media/.
21. Betty Holcomb, *Not Guilty! The Good News about Working Mothers* (New York: Scribner, 1998), 40.
22. Dennis Brown and Pamela Toussaint, *Mama's Little Baby: The Black Woman's Guide to Pregnancy, Childbirth, and Baby's First Year* (New York: Dutton, 1997), 340; Hilda Hutcherson and Margaret Williams, *Having Your Baby: A Guide for African American Women* (New York: Ballantine Books, 1997), 381.

23. "How to Beat Depression: Experts Say You Can," *Ebony*, August 1995, 102-6, 102.

24. "Black Women and the Blues," *Ebony*, May 1999, 140-44, 143.

25. Meri Nana-Ama Danquah, *Willow Weep for Me: A Black Woman's Journey through Depression, a Memoir* (New York: Norton, 1998), 20.

26. Edward Shorter, *A History of Psychiatry: From the Era of the Asylum to the Age of Prozac* (New York Weinheim: Wiley, 1997), 320.

27. David Herzberg, *Happy Pills in America: From Miltown to Prozac* (Baltimore: Johns Hopkins University Press, 2010).

28. Sandi Gubin, "Prozac: The Miracle Drug?," *Sojourner: The Women's Forum*, March 1993, 5H.

29. Zachary Stowe, "Depression After Childbirth: Is It the 'Baby Blues' or Something More?," brochure (Pfizer, 1998), Honikman Archive.

30. Susan J. Douglas and Meredith W. Michaels, *The Mommy Myth: The Idealization of Motherhood and How It Has Undermined All Women* (New York: Free Press, 2005), 122; "The New Sexy Moms," *People*, May 26, 1997.

31. Nancy Collins, "Demi's Big Moment," *Vanity Fair*, August 1991.

32. Raka Shome, *Diana and Beyond: White Femininity, National Identity, and Contemporary Media Culture* (Chicago: University of Illinois Press, 2014), 56.

33. "15 Million Brits Hear Diana Tell of Despair, Love Affair," *Wilmington Morning Star*, November 21, 1995, 10A.

34. Transcript of BBC1 *Panorama* interview with the Princess of Wales, broadcast in November 1995, https://www.pbs.org/wgbh/pages/frontline/shows/royals/interviews/bbc.html.

35. Transcript of the BBC1 *Panorama* interview with the Princess of Wales.

36. Ellie Lee, *Abortion, Motherhood, and Mental Health: Medicalizing Reproduction in the United States and Great Britain* (Hawthorne, NY: Aldine de Gruyter, 2003), 198.

37. "Marie Osmond on Her Struggles with Depression in Motherhood," *The Oprah Winfrey Show*, https://www.youtube.com/watch?v=SehwEstKzs8, accessed August 2, 2023.

38. Dennis Lythgoe, "Behind the Smile of Marie Osmond," *Deseret News*, May 2, 2001, D1.

39. Deborah Starr Seibel, "Out of the Darkness," *McCall's Magazine*, February 2000, 34-38.

40. "Marie Osmond Discusses Depression in Her New Book," *Lewiston Morning Tribune*, May 7, 2001, 10A.

41. Seibel, "Out of the Darkness," 38.

42. Marie Osmond and Marcia Wilkie, *Behind the Smile: My Journey out of Postpartum Depression* (New York: Warner Books, 2001), 5.

43. "Osmond Writes Book on Depression," *The Hour* (Norwalk, CT), January 23, 2001, A2.
44. "Marie Osmond Fights Depression," *Deseret News*, October 18-19, 1999, A2.
45. Dennis Lythgoe, "Behind the Smile of Marie Osmond," *Deseret News*, May 2, 2001, D1.
46. Jim Yardley, "Death Penalty Sought for Mother in Drownings of Children," *New York Times*, August 9, 2001.
47. Rebecca Hyman, "Medea of Suburbia: Andrea Yates, Maternal Infanticide, and the Insanity Defense," *Women's Studies Quarterly* 32, no. 3/4 (2004): 192-210, 193.
48. "Domain Name Gift from Larry Kruckman and Carolyn White," *PSI News*, p. 6, from Laurence Kruckman's personal papers.
49. "A Closer Look (Depressed Condition)," *ABC Evening News*, June 21, 2001, clip #197651, Vanderbilt Television News Archive, Nashville.
50. "Postpartum Depression," Sunday Cover, *CBS Evening News*, August 1, 2004, clip #761346, Vanderbilt Television News Archive, Nashville.
51. Larry Kruckman to author, email, January 11, 2023.
52. Lynette R. Holloway, "What Every Woman Should Know About Mental Health Ailments," *Ebony*, October 2005, 154-58, 158.
53. Bob Herbert, "Empathy for a Killer," *New York Times*, July 5, 2001, A17.
54. "Mother Who Drowned 5 'Not Herself,' Husband Says," *Toldeo Blade*, June 22, 2001, A1.
55. Hyman, "Medea of Suburbia," 195.
56. Jim Yardley, "Texas Jury Convicts Mother Who Drowned Her Children: Verdict of Capital Murder Came Quickly," *New York Times*, March 13, 2002.
57. "Woman Not Guilty in Retrial in the Deaths of Her 5 Children," *New York Times*, July 27, 2006.
58. Brooke Shields, *Down Came the Rain* (New York: Hyperion, 2005), 69.
59. Shields, *Down Came the Rain*, 90, 127.
60. Hilary Clark, "Confessions of a Celebrity Mom: Brooke Shields's *Down Came the Rain: My Journey through Postpartum Depression*," *Canadian Review of American Studies* 38, no. 3 (2008): 449-61, 456.
61. Jennifer Mendelsohn, "Brooke Shields: The Truth about New Moms and Depression," *USA Weekend*, September 16-18, 2005, 18.
62. Clark, "Confessions of a Celebrity Mom," 450-51.
63. "Brooke's Baby Crisis," *People* 63, no 18 (May 2005): 203-6.
64. Beth Levine, "Brooke Shields: 'I Felt Worthless,'" *The Blade* (Toledo, OH), June 5, 2005, E3.
65. Ronnie Polaneczky, "Model-Actress Describes Her Struggle With Illness," *Reading Eagle* (*Knight Ridder* article), June 7, 2005, A12.

66. "Brooke's Baby Crisis," 203–6.
67. Sharon Ginn, "Postpartum Debate," *St. Petersburg Times*, June 28, 2005, 3E.
68. Jocelyn Fenton Stitt, "Tom vs. Brooke, or Postpartum Depression as Bad Mothering in Popular Culture," in *Mediating Moms: Mothers in Popular Culture*, ed. Elizabeth Podnieks (Montreal: McGill-Queen's University Press, 2012), 339–57, 339.
69. Brooke Shields, "War of Words," *New York Times*, July 1, 2005, A17.
70. Shields, "War of Words," A17.
71. "Cruise-Shields Debate," *ABC Evening News*, July 1, 2005, clip #795073, Vanderbilt Television News Archive, Nashville.
72. "Cruise-Shields Debate."
73. "A Serious Look at Her Depression (6 Letters)," *New York Times*, July 5, 2005, https://www.nytimes.com/2005/07/05/opinion/a-serious-look-at -her-depression-6-letters.html.
74. Stitt, "Tom vs. Brooke," 340.
75. "Jennifer, Mendelsohn, Brooke Shields: The Truth about New Moms and Depression," *USA Weekend*, September 16–18, 2005, 18.
76. Follow-up phone interview with Jane Honikman, by Rachel Moran, June 19, 2020, transcript in possession of author.
77. "Postpartum Depression," *Oprah.com*, https://www.oprah.com /oprahshow/postpartum-depression/all, accessed August 2, 2023.
78. "Brooke Shields' Struggle for Sanity," *The Oprah Winfrey Show: The Podcast*, podcast audio, May 18, 2021, https://www.oprah.com/own-podcasts /brooke-shields-struggle-for-sanity.

Chapter 9

1. Jeanne Watson Driscoll, interview by Rachel Moran, January 30, 2023, transcript, University of North Texas Oral History Program, Special Collections, Denton, TX.
2. David Armstrong, "Emory Psychiatrist Cited in Conflicts of Interest," *Wall Street Journal*, June 10, 2009, https://www.wsj.com/articles /SB124460466072501139.
3. "The Organization Known as D.A.D. Is Asking for Help," *Depression Info* (blog), July 7, 2004, accessed October 3, 2022, http://infoaboutdepression .blogspot.com/2007/08/depression-after-delivery-dad-is.html.
4. Adrienne Griffen, interview by Rachel Moran, August 12, 2022, transcript, University of North Texas Oral History Program, Special Collections, Denton, TX.

12. "Law Encourages Screening for Postpartum Depression," Associated Press, *The Union Democrat* (Sonora, CA), May 1, 2006, 8A; Findings, Declarations Relative to Postpartum Depression (2006) NJ. Stat. Ann. Title 26—Health and Vital Statistics Sec 26:2-175.
13. Rhodes and Segre, "Perinatal Depression."
14. "Sense of Congress with respect to Postpartum Depression," 146 Cong Rec H 9524, October 10, 2010, Congressional Record Daily Edition—House, v. 146 no. 125, p. H9524.
15. Rhodes and Segre, "Perinatal Depression," 263.
16. "Chicago Woman's Suicide Prompts Rep. Bobby Rush to Push for Postpartum Bill," *Jet*, July 23, 2001, 26.
17. Congress.gov, "Text—H.R.846—108th Congress (2003-2004): Melanie Blocker Stokes Postpartum Depression Research and Care Act," February 26, 2003, http://www.congress.gov/.
18. Rachel Louise Moran, "A Women's Health Issue? Framing Post-Abortion Syndrome in the 1980s," *Gender & History* 33, no. 3 (October 2021): 790-804, https://doi.org/10.1111/1468-0424.12554.
19. Joe Pitts R-PA press release, September 28, 2004, "House Subcommittee Examines Post-Abortion Stress."
20. Congress.gov, "Text—H.R.4543—108th Congress."
21. "Improving Women's Health: Understanding Depression After Pregnancy," hearings, Subcommittee on Health, Committee on Energy and Commerce, 108th Congress, 2nd sess., September 29, 2004, 2.
22. "Improving Women's Health: Understanding Depression After Pregnancy," 3.
23. Jane Eisner, "An Issue of Education, Not Politics," *The Spokesman-Review*, February 5, 2005, B4.
24. "H.R. 20: The Melanie Blocker Stokes Postpartum Depression and Care Act," hearings, 5.
25. "H.R. 20: The Melanie Blocker Stokes Postpartum Depression and Care Act," 59.
26. "H.R. 20: The Melanie Blocker Stokes Postpartum Depression and Care Act," 7.
27. Ellie Lee, *Abortion, Motherhood, and Mental Health: Medicalizing Reproduction in the United States and Great Britain* (Hawthorne, NY: Aldine de Gruyter, 2003), 207.
28. "H.R. 20: The Melanie Blocker Stokes Postpartum Depression and Care Act," 36.
29. "Pallone Statement at Health Subcommittee Markup," Press Release, July 19, 2007, https://pallone.house.gov/press-release/pallone-statement-health-subcommittee-markup; report on public bill, 110 H Rpt 375 Mel-

anie Blocker Stokes Postpartum Depression Research and Care Act, Oct. 15, 2007.

30. Julia Dahl, "The Politics of Postpartum Depression," *Salon.com*, July 30, 2007.

31. Robert Menendez, Press Release, "A Mother's Day Message on Postpartum Depression," May 11, 2007.

32. "Mom Tells Daughter's Tale of Fatal Postpartum," March 12, 2003, *Chicago Daily Herald*.

33. Katherine Stone, "I Was Scared That I Might Hurt My Baby," *Newsweek*, June 7, 2004, 22.

34. MOTHERS = Mom's Opportunity To access Health, Education, Research, and Support for Postpartum Depression.

35. Katherine Stone, "Today Is Blog for the MOTHERS Act Day!!," *Postpartum Progress*, Oct. 24, 2007, https://postpartumprogress.com/today-is-blog-f.

36. Katherine Stone, "Today Is Blog for the MOTHERS Act Day!!"

37. David Stout, "Democrats Fail to Overcome Senator's Grip on Bill," *New York Times*, July 28, 2008, https://www.nytimes.com/2008/07/28/washington/28cnd-cong.html.

38. Kimberlee Evert, "Congress Fails Families Affected by Postpartum Depression," *Pittsburgh Post-Gazette*, August 19, 2008.

39. Robert D. McFadden, "Tom Coburn, the 'Dr. No' of Congress, Is Dead at 72," *New York Times* (March 29, 2020), A24.

40. Katherine Stone, "Senator Blocking MOTHERS Act Is Obstetrician (Seriously)," April 20, 2009, https://postpartumprogress.com/senator-blocking-mothers-act-is-obstetrician-seriously.

41. Rachel Zimmerman, "Birth Trauma: Stress Disorder Afflicts Moms," *Wall Street Journal*, August 5, 2008.

42. Catherine Elton, "Postpartum Depression: Do All Moms Need Screening?," *Time*, July 12, 2009, https://content.time.com/time/subscriber/article/0,33009,1909628-1,00.html.

43. Katherine Stone, "Actress Kirstie Alley Brings Attention to Lies About MOTHERS Act," *Postpartum Progress*, May 22, 2009, https://postpartumprogress.com/postpartum-depression-actress-kirstie-alley-mothers-act.

44. Susan Dowd Stone, "The Melanie Blocker Stokes MOTHERS Act Becomes a Shaky Platform for Frustrated Anti-Pharma Faction," *Perinatal Pro*, April 7, 2009, https://web.archive.org/web/20220524174105/http://perinatalpro.com/blog/?p=291.

45. Katherine Stone, "MOTHERS Act to Drug America's Moms for Fake Postpartum Depression," *Postpartum Progress*, April 7, 2009, https://

postpartumprogress.com/postpartum-depression-mothers-act-dont
-let-the-women-children-families-suffer.

46. Ivy Shih Leung, "Time Article Off the Mark . . . But What Else Is New?,"
     Ivy's PPD Blog, July 12, 2009, https://ivysppdblog.wordpress.com/2009
     /07/12/time-article-off-the-mark/.

47. Katherine Stone, "Blog Week for the Melanie Blocker Stokes MOTHERS
     Act Kicks Off Today," April 20, 2009, *Postpartum Progress*, https://
     postpartumprogress.com/postpartum-depression-blog-week-for-the
     -melanie-blocker-stokes-mothers-act-kicks-off-today.

48. Senator Robert Menendez, Press Release, "Menendez, Author of Legis-
     lation to Combat Postpartum Depression, Applauds Grassroots Show
     of Force on Blog Day," April 20, 2009.

49. Robert Menendez, Press Release, "Menendez, Mary Jo Codey, Advocates
     Join in A Mother's Day Push for Legislation to Combat Postpartum De-
     pression," May 11, 2009.

50. "The Patient Protection and Affordable Care Act," Public Law 111-148,
     March 23, 2010.

51. Katherine Stone, "MOTHERS Act Passes in Senate Version of
     Healthcare Reform Bill," *Postpartum Progress*, January 2010, https://
     postpartumprogress.com/mothers-act-passes-in-senate-version-of
     -healthcare-reform-bill.

52. "Rep. Rush, Sen. Menendez and Mrs. Carol Blocker Salute Mothers,
     Praise Passage of the Melanie Blocker Stokes MOTHERS Act," Rep.
     Bobby L. Rush (D-IL) News Release, LexisNexis (May 6, 2010).

53. Robert Menendez, press conference celebrating the enactment of the
     MOTHERS Act, May 6, 2010, https://www.youtube.com/watch?v
     =_00sq2oQuzA&t=334s.

54. Press Release, Robert Menendez, "Major Initiative to Combat Postpar-
     tum Depression to be Signed into Law as Part of Health Insurance Re-
     form," March 22, 2010.

55. Carol Blocker, press conference celebrating the enactment of the
     MOTHERS Act, May 6, 2010, https://www.youtube.com/watch?v
     =_00sq2oQuzA&t=334s.

56. Susan Dowd Stone, "Postpartum Depression Legislation Becomes
     the Law of the Land!!," *Perinatal Pro*, March 21, 2010, https://web
     .archive.org/web/20230208224014/http://perinatalpro.com/blog/?p
     =788.

57. Robert Menendez, press conference celebrating the enactment of the
     MOTHERS Act, May 6, 2010.

58. Katherine Stone, "No Action on Melanie Blocker Stokes MOTHERS
     Act," January 14, 2013, https://postpartumprogress.com/no-action-on
     -melanie-blocker-stokes-mothers-act.

59. Lisa Black, "Mom Voices Frustration That Postpartum Depression Fight Has Moved So Slowly," *Chicago Tribune*, January 9, 2013.
60. H.R.3235—114th Congress (2015-2016), Bringing Postpartum Depression Out of the Shadows Act of 2015, House—Energy and Commerce, https://www.congress.gov/bill/114th-congress/house-bill/3235.
61. H.R.3235—114th Congress (2015-2016), "Bringing Postpartum Depression Out of the Shadows Act of 2015."
62. Adrienne Griffen et al., "Perinatal Mental Health Care in the United States: An Overview of Policies and Programs: Study Examines Perinatal Mental Health Care Policies and Programs in the United States," *Health Affairs* 40, no. 10 (October 1, 2021): 1543-50, https://doi.org/10.1377/hlthaff.2021.00796 p. 1545.
63. Adrienne Griffen, interview by Rachel Moran.
64. Kay Matthews et al., "Pathways to Equitable and Antiracist Maternal Mental Health Care: Insights from Black Women Stakeholders: Study Examines Pathways to Equitable and Antiracist Maternal Mental Health Care," *Health Affairs* 40, no. 10 (October 1, 2021): 1597-604.
65. Maternal Mental Health Leadership Alliance, "Resources," accessed Sept. 28, 2022, https://www.mmhla.org/mmhresources/.
66. Vu-An Foster et al., "Reimagining Perinatal Mental Health: An Expansive Vision for Structural Change: Commentary Describes Changes Needed to Improve Perinatal Mental Health Care," *Health Affairs* 40, no. 10 (October 1, 2021): 1592-96; Maeve E. Wallace et al., "Firearm Relinquishment Laws Associated with Substantial Reduction in Homicide of Pregnant and Postpartum Women: Study Examines the Association of Firearm Relinquishment Laws with Homicide of Pregnant and Postpartum Women," *Health Affairs* 40, no. 10 (October 1, 2021): 1654-62.

Conclusion

1. Shelley Murphy, John R. Ellement, and Sonel Cutler, "Prosecuting the Unthinkable: Experts Question Handling of Cases Where Mothers Are Accused of Killing their Children," *Boston Globe*, January 31, 2023, https://www.bostonglobe.com/2023/01/31/metro/when-postpartum-psychosis-turns-mother-into-killer-advocates-call-alternatives-prosecuting-unthinkable/, accessed February 6, 2023.
2. Nancy Berchtold to Rachel Moran, email in possession of the author, January 2, 2023.
3. Hajara Kutty, "PMADS Don't Discriminate and Neither Should We," *Postpartum Support International Blog*, February 3, 2023, https://www.postpartum.net/pmads-dont-discriminate-and-neither-should-we/.

4.   Robin Young and Karyn Miller-Medzon, "Massachusetts Children's Deaths Spotlight Postpartum Psychosis," *WBUR Here & Now*, January 31, 2023.

5.   Follow-up phone interview with Jane Honikman, by Rachel Moran, transcript in possession of author, June 19, 2020.

Index

family (*continued*)
98, 211–12, 223; and postpartum
depression, 223–24, 234; responsibility, 84; and social change,
126; threats to, 82, 90, 93, 171, 218;
white, 87
family histories, 21
family structures, 24, 27
family values, 9, 11–13, 69, 81, 84, 211,
219, 221, 227; conservative, 9, 94
fatigue, 68, 97
federal health spending, 210
Feingold, Susan, 147, 158–63, 189–90,
226
feminism, 12, 104, 180; and activism, 59, 79, 117, 134, 163, 169, 171;
and Ti-Grace Atkinson, 49, 51;
backlash to, 84, 95, 173; Black,
39, 52, 55, 156; and community,
57; and depression, 89; and Depression After Delivery (DAD),
103; and Carol Dix, 85; and the
family, 70; and gender roles, 39;
and health centers, 54; and Jane
Honikman, 171; and magazines,
44, 46, 48, 85; and medicalization, 70, 175; and medical sexism,
56–57, 69; and mental health, 38;
and motherhood, 79, 94, 96, 98,
174; and natural birth, 45, 48;
and network-building, 40; and
postpartum depression, 7, 56–58,
90, 119, 148, 168, 171; and psychiatry, 89; radical, 48–49, 51, 55, 58,
92, 156; reception of, 154, 171; and
Phyllis Schlafly, 95; second-wave,
12; and self-help, 57–59; and sexism, 69, 95; and spaces, 43; and
therapy, 38, 58, 154; white, 39;
and women's health advocacy, 11,
36, 39–40, 45, 89, 117; and writers,
38, 50

Frank, Ellen, 134–41
Frazier, E. Franklin, 24
Friedan, Betty, 34–36, 39, 49, 86–87, 98

Gindorf, Debra, 160–61
Good Housekeeping, 35, 182
Griffen, Adrienne, 223, 225, 226, 227,
231
gut health, 8

Hamilton, James A., 61–63; and
American Psychiatric Association, 130–32; and Nancy
Berchtold, 108, 116; and Ian
Brockington, 64; and consumer
movement, 164; and the *DSM*,
67–68, 131–37, 140; and Jane Honikman, 114, 127; and International
Postpartum Social Support
Network, 113; and Marcé Society, 75–76, 124–25, 130, 134; and
postpartum activists, 110, 126;
and postpartum depression, 62,
64–65, 87, 123–24, 129, 135–37; and
Postpartum Education for Parents (PEP), 77; and postpartum
professionals, 164; and postpartum research, 65–66, 75–76; and
Postpartum Support International (PSI), 114–15, 145; and
Deborah Sharp, 111; and Edward
Strecker, 20–21
health insurance, 68, 75–76, 104, 116,
124, 133, 140, 149–51, 185, 192, 215,
234
health magazines, 15
Health Resources and Services Administration, 232
Honikman, Jane, 79, 171; and
Shoshana Bennett, 148; and
Nancy Berchtold, 113, 116, 119, 128,
146, 189; and Carol Dix, 109–10,